Machine Learning Methods for Engineering Application Development

Edited by

Prasad Lokulwar

Associate Professor Department of Computer Science and Engineering, G H Raisoni College of Engineering, Nagpur, India

Basant Verma

Professor in Emerging Technology (AI/ML, Data Science, Cyber Security) Panipat Institute of Engineering and Technology, India

N. Thillaiarasu

Associate Professor School of Computing and Information technology REVA University, Banglore, India

Kailash Kumar

Assistant Professor College of Computing and Informatics Saudi Electronic University, Riyadh, Kingdom of Saudi Arabia

Mahip Bartere

Department of Computer Science and Engineering, P. R. Pote Patil College of Engineering and Management, India

&

Dharam Singh

Senior Developer, Machine Learning and BI, Wallmart, USA

Machine Learning Methods for Engineering Application Development

Editors: Prasad Lokulwar, Basant Verma, N. Thillaiarasu, Kailash Kumar, Mahip Bartere and Dharam Singh

ISBN (Online): 978-981-5079-18-0

ISBN (Print): 978-981-5079-19-7

ISBN (Paperback): 978-981-5079-20-3

need for a court order if at any point you breach any terms of this License Agreement. In no event will any delay or failure by Bentham Science Publishers in enforcing your compliance with this License Agreement constitute a waiver of any of its rights.

3. You acknowledge that you have read this License Agreement, and agree to be bound by its terms and conditions. To the extent that any other terms and conditions presented on any website of Bentham Science Publishers conflict with, or are inconsistent with, the terms and conditions set out in this License Agreement, you acknowledge that the terms and conditions set out in this License Agreement shall prevail.

Bentham Science Publishers Pte. Ltd.
80 Robinson Road #02-00
Singapore 068898
Singapore
Email: subscriptions@benthamscience.net

BENTHAM SCIENCE

CONTENTS

FOREWORD

As I reviewed the manuscript prior to writing this Foreword, I was fascinated by many unique features that I would like to share with you. The book can best be described as concise yet detailed. There is more useful information packed into its 12 chapters than seen in most books twice its size. Therefore, it gives me great pleasure to contribute to this foreword.

This book is an enthusiastic celebration of many Machine Learning Techniques for Engineering Applications. It is also a unique tribute to many academicians and researchers who were involved in their study and contributed to society. Still another element is provided by many interesting technical details and an abundance of illustrations in the form of figures and tables. On top of that, there are innumerable machine learning algorithms for Intelligent Systems, Computational Linguistics, Natural Language Processing, Information Retrieval, Neural Networks, Social Networks, Recommender Systems, *etc.*, indeed, to anyone with a fascination with the world of machine learning. This book can be read on two different levels. First, it may be read by ordinary people with a limited, if any, scientific background. Throughout, the book has been written with this audience in mind. The second group of readers will be represented by professionals from academia, government agencies and researchers. I do feel that everybody in the scientific community agrees with the content and ideas put forth in this book, and I hope that the information and knowledge presented will become a useful guideline for the research community and scholars.

This book contains so much useful information, and the chapters contain many pearls. I hope that this book will become a primer for teachers, teacher educators, and professional developers, helping teachers across the world to learn, teach, and practice machine learning techniques for various applications.

Sangeeta Sonania
Software Developer
Sydney
Australia

PREFACE

Machine learning deals with the issue of how to build programs that improve their performance at some tasks through experience. Machine learning (ML) plays a major role in the fourth industrial revolution, and we see a lot of evolution in various machine learning methodologies. AI techniques are widely used by practicing engineers to solve real-world problems. Industry 4.0 refers to the introduction of digital technologies and the development of skills, resources, and high-tech for the evolution of Industrial Factories. The concepts of Artificial Intelligence (AI), Machine Learning, and its applications in Industry 4.0 are popular among researchers. Several industrial applications are being designed and deployed. Herein, we share a few examples of machine learning that we use every day and perhaps have no idea that they are driven by ML-like Virtual Personal Assistants, Predictions, Videos Surveillance, Social Media Services, Email Spam and Malware Filtering, Online Customer Support, Search Engine Result Refining, Product Recommendations, and Online Fraud Detection. Besides, numerous researchers from diversified domains are working towards the amalgamation of these technologies.

The chapters of this book are organized into five parts, Machine Learning Essentials, Applied Machine Learning, Surveillance Systems, Machine Learning in IoT and Cyber Security, and Intelligent Systems. Machine learning algorithms have proven to be of great practical value in a variety of application domains. Not surprisingly, the field of software engineering turns out to be a fertile ground where many software development and maintenance tasks could be formulated as learning problems and approached in terms of learning algorithms. This book deals with the subject of applying machine learning methods and engineering. In these books, we first provide the characteristics and applicability of some frequently utilized machine learning algorithms. We then summarize and analyze the existing work and discuss some general issues in this niche area. Finally, we offer some guidelines on applying machine learning methods to software engineering tasks.

This book describes the most common Artificial Intelligence (AI), Machine Learning and its applications in Industry 4.0, including Bayesian models, support vector machines, decision tree induction, regression analysis, and recurrent and convolutional neural networks. It first introduces the principles of machine learning; it then covers the basic methods, including the mathematical foundations. The biggest part of the book provides common machine learning algorithms and their applications. Finally, the book gives an outlook into some of the future developments and possibly new research areas of machine learning and artificial intelligence in general.

This book is meant to be an introduction to Artificial Intelligence (AI), Machine Learning, and its applications in Industry 4.0. It does not require prior knowledge in this area. It covers some of the basic mathematical principles but intends to be understandable even without a background in mathematics. It can be read chapter-wise and intends to be comprehensible, even when not starting in the beginning. Finally, it also intends to be a reference book.

Key Features

• Describes real-world problems that can be solved using Machine Learning.

• Provides methods for directly applying Machine Learning techniques to concrete real-world problems.

• Research outputs require working in Industry 4.0 platforms, including the use and integration of AI, ML, Big Data, NLP, and the Internet of Things (IoT).

• We welcome new developments in statistics, mathematics, and computing that are relevant to the machine learning perspective, including foundations, systems, innovative applications, and other research contributions related to the overall design of machine learning and models and algorithms that are relevant for AI.

Prasad Lokulwar
Associate Professor Department of Computer Science and Engineering, G H Raisoni College of Engineering, Nagpur, India

Basant Verma
Professor in Emerging Technology (AI/ML, Data Science, Cyber Security) Panipat Institute of Engineering and Technology, India

N. Thillaiarasu
Associate Professor School of Computing and Information technology REVA University, Banglore, India

Kailash Kumar
Assistant Professor College of Computing and Informatics Saudi Electronic University, Riyadh, Kingdom of Saudi Arabia

Mahip Bartere
Department of Computer Science and Engineering, P. R. Pote Patil College of Engineering and Management, India

&

Dharam Singh
Senior Developer, Machine Learning and BI, Wallmart, USA

List of Contributors

Abdulaziz Albesher — College of Computing and Informatics, Saudi Electronic University, Saudi Arabia,

Avinash S. Kapse — Anuradha College of Engineering, Chikhli, Amravati University, India,

D.N. Pandit — Department of Zoology, Veer Kunwar Singh University, Ara, India

H.R. Deshmukh — Shri R. R. Lahoti Science College, India

Karthik Srinivasan — College of Computing and Informatics, Saudi Electronic University, , Saudi Arabia,

M. Chandraprabha — Galgotias College of Engineering and Technology, Galgotias University, Greater Noida, India

Md. Alimul Haque — Department of Computer Science, Veer Kunwar Singh University, Ara, India

Makram Soui — College of Computing and Informatics, Saudi Electronic University, , Saudi Arabia,

Mangala S. Madankar — Assistant Professor, Department of Computer Science and Engineering, G H Raisoni College of Engineering, Nagpur, India

Manoj Chandak — Ramdeobaba College of Engineering and Management, Nagpur, India,

P. Sasikumar — Malla Reddy Institute of Engineering & Technology, Secunderabad, India

Pallavi Hiwarkar — Assistant Professor, Department of Computer Science and Engineering, G H Raisoni Institute of Engineering & Technology, Nagpur, India

Pawan Bhalandhare — G H Raisoni College of Engineering, Nagpur, India

Pranay Saraf — G H Raisoni College of Engineering, Nagpur, India

Pratik Dhoke — G H Raisoni College of Engineering, Nagpur, India

Rahul Agrawal — G H Raisoni College of Engineering, Nagpur, India

Rajesh Kumar Dhanaraj — Galgotias College of Engineering and Technology, Galgotias University, Greater Noida, India

Ritu Aggarwal — Maharishi Markendeshwar Engineering College, Maharishi Markendeshwar Institute of Computer Technology and Business Management Mullana, Ambala, Haryana, India, 133207

Samah Alhazmi — College of Computing and Informatics, Saudi Electronic University, Riyadh, Kingdom of Saudi Arabia

Sana Zeba — Jamia Millia Islamia University, New Delhi, India

Shameemul Haque — Al-Hafeez College, Ara, India

Shruti J. Sapra Thakur — Department of Computer Science and Engineering, Amravati University, India

Suneet Kumar — Maharishi Markendeshwar Engineering College, Maharishi Markendeshwar Institute of Computer Technology and Business Management Mullana, Ambala, Haryana, India, 133207

T. Saravanan   GITAM University, Bengaluru, India

Yogadhar Pandey   Associate Professor, Technocrats Institute of Technology (Excellence), India

CHAPTER 1

Cutting Edge Techniques of Adaptive Machine Learning for Image Processing and Computer Vision

P. Sasikumar[1,*] and **T. Saravanan**[2]

[1] *Malla Reddy Institute of Engineering & Technology, St. Martin's Engineering College, Secunderabad, India*

[2] *GITAM University, Bengaluru, India*

Abstract: Computers, systems, applications, and technology, in general, are becoming more commonly used, advanced, scalable, and thus effective in modern times. Because of its widespread use, it undergoes various advancements on a regular basis. A fast-paced life is also associated with modern times. This way of life necessitates that our systems behave similarly. Adaptive Machine Learning (AML) can do things that conventional machine learning cannot. It will easily adjust to new information and determine the significance of that information. Adaptive machine learning uses a variety of data collection, grouping, and analysis methods due to its single-channeled structure. It gathers, analyses, and learns from the information. That is why it is adaptive: as long as new data is presented, the system can learn and update. This single-channeled device acts on any piece of input it receives in order to improve potential forecasts and outcomes. Furthermore, since the entire process happens in real-time, it can immediately adjust to new actions. High efficiency and impeccably precise accuracy are two of AML's main advantages. The system does not become outdated or redundant because it is constantly running in real-time. So, incorporating the three core concepts of agility, strength, and efficiency better explains AML.

Agility helps systems to respond rapidly and without hesitation. The systems achieve new levels of proficiency and accuracy as a result of their power, and they can find new ways to operate flawlessly at lower costs as a result of their performance. This chapter covers the preparation, regularisation, and structure of deep neural networks such as convolutional and generative adversarial networks. New information in the reinforcement learning chapter includes a description of t-SNE, a standard dimensionality reduction approach, as well as multilayer perceptrons on auto encoders and the word2vec network. As a consequence, these suggestions will assist readers in applying what they have learned.

---

[*] **Corresponding author Sasikumar P:** Malla Reddy Institute of Engineering & Technology, Secunderabad, India; Tel: +91- 8883209920; E-mail: sasi.mca@gmail.com

Prasad Lokulwar, Basant Verma, N. Thillaiarasu, Kailash Kumar, Mahip Bartere and Dharam Singh (Eds.)

Keywords: Autoencoders, Automatic Learning, Contourlet and orthogonal transforms, Disparity, Domain Methods, Stereo Face Images.

INTRODUCTION

One of the technologies that will flourish in the next years is adaptive machine learning, also known as adaptive automated learning. Using online machine learning models, this technology allows for continuous learning in real-time. This capability enables machine learning models to adapt to the ever-changing environment. This technology is particularly useful for autonomous car training because of its high adaptability. These vehicles must be capable of integrating new data in real-time, analysing it, and making decisions based on it. However, the technology's use is not limited to self-driving vehicles (which Gartner expects to see in the next 10 years or so). Real-time adaptive autonomous learning necessitates efficient reinforcement learning, or how an algorithm must continuously communicate with its environment in order to maximise its reward. Agriculture, web marketing, smart cities, financial institutions, and any other industry that uses the Internet of Things could benefit from these algorithms [1]. Since it must be retrained and make decisions in real-time, it is difficult to gather all produced data, organise and calculate it, and train a "traditional" machine learning model in these changing environments.

Extraction of relevant functionality from massive, potentially heterogeneous images is a critical challenge for many end-user communities. Picture segmentation is the method of partitioning a digital image into several newline segments based on sets of pixels in computer vision. Researchers may use collection platforms that run in a wide range of spectral bands. With modern delivery systems and data formats making data distribution increasingly cheaper and simpler, the availability of appropriate analysis tools is now more than ever the bottleneck to effective data exploitation. Image processing is a computationally expensive undertaking since it involves multiple low-level (pixel-level) operations on an image to complete a task, such as edge detection, edge connecting, noise reduction, dilation, erosion, and filtering. In this sense, machine vision has been successfully applied to a number of tasks such as sorting and assembling a group of machined parts, inspecting an automobile door panel for microscopic defects, and so on. Machine vision applications in manufacturing have been the subject of extensive study, as they provide the advantages of being non-contact and quicker than contact methods. Machine Vision (information gathered using an array of sensors) may be used to calculate and analyse [2] the area of a surface, allowing the user to make application-specific intelligent decisions. (Fig. **1**) shows how conventional computer vision compares to modern computer vision. The benefit of using computer vision to grab photos from the internet is that it ignores factors such as machine tool noise and vibrations. Computer vision systems must be able to capture images, collect data using vision sensors, and make educated decisions. Image denoising is the process of manipulating image data in order to create a visually high-quality image. The filtering process [3] has been found to be the most effective when the image is corrupted. Quality control and output testing have been critical components of the operation. Surface finish is crucial in a number of engineering applications, such as the surface quality of any machined component. By simply looking at a 2D image, the human brain unconsciously and automatically perceives its 3D form. However, using a computer to reconstruct 3D face from 2D images is a difficult and time-consuming process. Face recognition is one of the most basic ways for humans to communicate with one another.

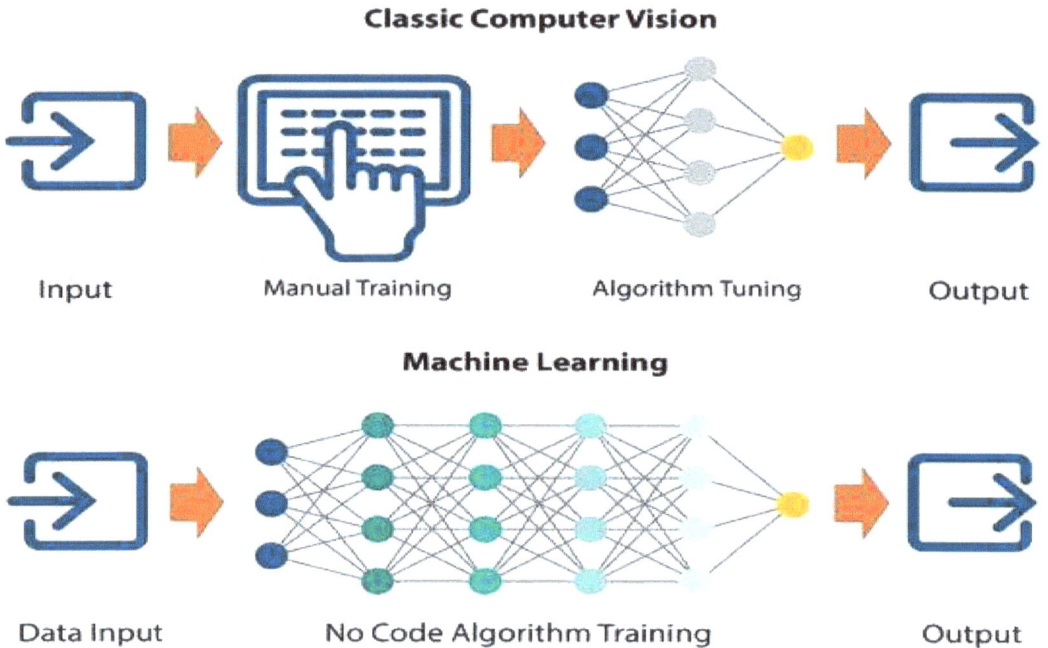

Fig. (1). Classic CV *vs* Machine Learning [18]

Law enforcement, civil applications, and security systems are only a few of the applications for face recognition. Since the human face is highly deformable and its appearance changes dramatically, face recognition is a difficult issue [4].

Where there is a shift in the posture, the facial appearances change drastically. Variations in lighting and variations in facial expression have complex effects on the appearance of a face picture. As a consequence, this chapter focuses on computer vision and pattern recognition methods for dealing with these problems.

Techniques for Improvising Images

Image improvement techniques are a set of techniques aimed at improving the visual appearance of an image or converting it into a medium suitable for human or computer study. In contrast to image reconstruction, there is no concerted effort in an image improvement process to improve the fidelity of a reproduced image in relation to any ideal form of the image. The image enhancement stops short of knowledge extraction for image analysis [5]. High-frequency filtering can be used by an image enhancement device to highlight the edge outline of objects in an image. This edge-enhanced image would then be fed into a computer, which would trace the edges' outline. The image enhancement processor will highlight important aspects of the original image while also making the data extraction machine's job easier.

The artefacts are known as grey values or regions of constant radiance. Then, by averaging the grey values within the object, you can get adequate mean values. This system, of course, necessitates a basic image content model. Consistent grey values that are clearly different from the context and/or other objects are needed for the objects of interest [6]. However, in real-world implementations, this expectation is rarely met. In general, there may be some differences in the intensities. These variations may be induced by the image forming process or be an intrinsic feature of the picture. Noise, non-uniform light, and an inhomogeneous atmosphere are common examples.

It is difficult to differentiate objects from the context in complex cases using only one function. Then computing multiple feature images from a single image may be a legitimate method. The effect is a multicomponent or vectorial function image [7]. The same thing happens when more than one image is taken from a scene, just as it does with colour photographs or some other kind of multispectral image. As a result, the averaging task must now include vectorial images. In image sequences, averaging is generalised into the time coordinate, resulting in spatiotemporal averaging.

Image enhancement is a technique for improving the interpretability of information in images for human audiences while also providing better input for other automatic image processing techniques. The main aim of image enhancement is to adjust the characteristics of an image to make it more appropriate for a particular role and observer. One or more image attributes are changed during this process [8]. The attributes chosen by a task and how they are modified are specific to that task. Furthermore, observer-specific factors such as the human visual system and the observer's perception will introduce a lot of subjectivity into the image enhancement process collection. There are a variety of methods that can be used to improve a digital picture without ruining it. The following two categories can be used to categorise enhancement methods:

• Spatial-Domain

• Frequency-Domain

Spatial-Domain Method

The picture pixels are specifically addressed by spatial domain techniques. To achieve the desired enhancement, the pixel values are manipulated. The picture is first converted to the frequency domain in frequency domain methods [9]. The image's Fourier transform is used to perform all enhancement operations, and the resulting image is generated using the Inverse Fourier transform. In the frequency domain, image enhancement techniques are based on altering the image's Fourier transform. The principle of filtering is easier to visualise in the frequency domain. As a consequence of the transformation function applied to the input values, the pixel size (intensities) of the output image will be changed.

Frequency-Domain Method

The following basic steps are applied for filtering an image in frequency domain:

• Calculate F (u, v), the input image's DFT (Discrete Fourier Transform).

• Multiply F (u, v) by H (u, v) to get G (u, v) = H (u. v) F (u,v).

• Using the inverse Fourier transform, compute the result's inverse DFT.

• Get the inverse DFT's real element.

(Eg). 2D (Fig. **2**: Stereo copy of images)

Statue

Magazine

Teddy

Modern Art

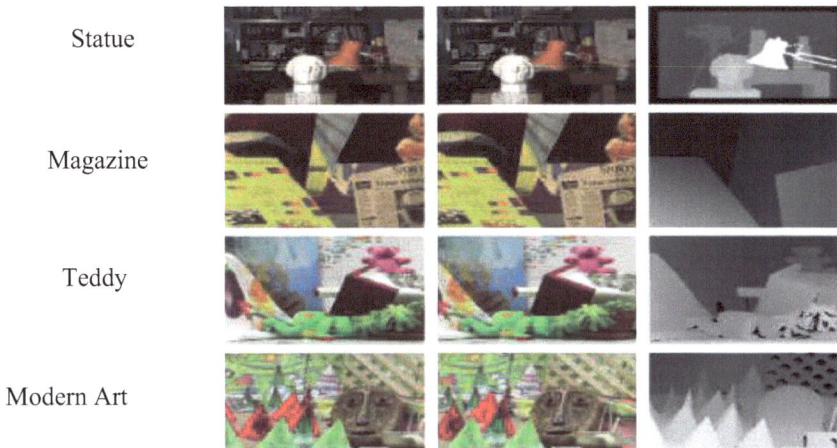

Fig. (2). Stereo copy of images [7]

Images are not nearly as complicated as they once were:

• Similarly, brightness along a line may be reported as a series of values taken at evenly spaced intervals or as a collection of spatial frequency values.

• A frequency variable is a name given to each of these frequency values.

• A picture is a two-dimensional array of pixel measurements on a flat grid.

• This data can be represented using a two-dimensional grid of spatial frequencies.

• The contribution of data that changes with defined x and y spatial frequencies is now specified by a given frequency variable.

TRANSFORMS: IMAGE IMPROVEMENT

The basic benefits of transform image improvement procedures are: 1) The importance of orthogonal transforms in optical signal/image processing, where they are used in stages including filtering, coding, detection, and restoration analysis; and 2) the low complexity of computations. Image transformations provide spectral knowledge about an image by decomposing it into spectral coefficients that can be modified (linearly or nonlinearly) for enhancement and visualisation. The effect is that the frequency composition of the picture can be easily viewed and manipulated without relying on spatial details.

Image enhancement is the process of transforming an image f into an image g using T (where T is the transformation). The letters g and p represent pixel values in images f and g, respectively. The expression connects the pixel values g and p.

$$p = T(g) \tag{1}$$

T is a transformation that converts pixel value g to pixel value p. The grey scale spectrum is mapped into the effects of this transformation (when dealing with grey scale digital images). As a result, the results are mapped out into the range [0, L-1], with L = 2k being the number of bits in the image under consideration and k being the number of bits in the image under consideration.

To enhance images in some way, several different (often elementary) operations are used. Of course, the issue is not well known since there is no objective measure of image quality. In this research, a few recipes are investigated and shown to be useful for both human and computer recognition. These methods are not problem-solving; a technique that fits well in one case might not be appropriate in another. The following are the types of enhancements that can be made with the basic level transformations function:

• Linear transformations, such as image negatives and piecewise linear transformations

• Non-linear transformations, such as logarithm and power law transformations.

A single image approach typically fails to provide the required improvements due to design or observational constraints. Another alternative is to use the information obtained from different images to develop image features. Typical image enhancement operations include (but are not limited to) the following:

• Intensity, hue, and saturation changes

• Density slicing

• Density slicing

• Edge enhancement

• Rendering optical mosaics

• Simulated stereo picture development

• contrast enhancement

Wavelet-Transform Oriented Image Improvement

The Wavelet transform is a useful tool for representing images. It allows for image processing at different resolutions. This transform's goal is to extract useful information from an image. Because of its ability to adjust to human visual features, the wavelet transform has gotten a lot of attention in the field of image processing. The signal is broken down into several parts, each of which corresponds to a different frequency band.

A new image resolution enhancement approach based on intensive inter-subband correlation is described in this paper, in which the sampling process in DWT is considered using an interpolation architecture filter. In addition, correlations between all sub-bands [10] in the lower level of separate sampling phases are examined and added to the higher level's correlated sub-bands. The filter coefficients in DWT are calculated based on the assumption that the correlations between two sub-bands in the higher level are equal to those in the lower level.

The noisy image is first converted to the wavelet domain in the general method of wavelet dependent denoising. Four sub-bands appear in the transformed image (A, V, H, and D). The 2D discrete wavelet transform, based on the level of decomposition 'j,' decomposes approximate coefficients at level 'j' into four components, namely the approximation at level 'j+1' and information in level 'j'details in three orientations (Horizontal, Vertical and Diagonal). The three higher bands may contain the noisy components due to their high frequency, and a proper threshold should be applied to smooth the noisy wavelet coefficients. The denoised image can then be reconstructed using the inverse 2D-DWT. The choice of the best threshold is key to the denoising algorithm's success. The picture and noise priors, such as mean and variance, are used to determine the threshold as denoted in eqn. 2.

$$((x, y), (a, b)) = (\psi x - a)^2 + (\psi y - b)^2 \qquad (2)$$

Wavelet-based approaches improve image resolution by calculating the retained high-frequency information from given images. They are founded on the logical premise that the image to be improved is in the wavelet-transformed sub-bands of the original image's low-frequency sub-band, and that the aim is to approximate the wavelet transform's high-frequency sub-bands. However, since the research filter bank of the wavelet transform has a low-frequency characteristic, such as a wide transition field, some information from the high-frequency band ends up in the low-frequency band.

Scaling and Translation

Scaling and Translations are two basic considerations in wavelet representations. A wavelet family is made up of scaled and translated wavelets of the same basic wavelet shape. Wavelets have the following features.

(i) As the duration of a signal event shrinks, the time or space resolution increases.

(ii) Wavelets have a band limit. They are made up of a large number of frequencies with a narrow range of frequencies.

(iii) They have high fluctuating amplitudes for a short period of time and very low or null amplitudes outside of that time period.

(iv) They are both frequency and time localised.

(v) They show sensitivity to a wide variety of waveform constitutions at full scale.

(vi) They provide efficient signal time-frequency decomposition over a spectrum of characteristic frequencies, allowing individual signal components to be separated.

IMAGE IMPROVEMENT WITH FILTERS

The design of evolved operators (EO) based filters was the subject of the first phase of this research. This background allows for noise reduction, shape, character, and object identification, as well as enhancement, restoration, texture classification, spatial and intensity sampling, and rate conversion. Additional constraints must be added to the filter in order to build it from a realistically sized training set [11 - 14]. Optimization schemes are used in this paper to significantly reduce the size of the training set necessary, making filter design simpler.

DENOISING OF IMAGES

Three different transforms are used in the second step to denoise an image. When it comes to picture denoising, it is crucial to keep the edges intact. Wavelet transformations are useful for image coding since the majority of the energy in a transformed image is distributed in the pattern transform coefficients rather than the variance coefficients. Without causing image loss, the fluctuation coefficients can be grossly quantized. This energy compression property can also be used to reduce noise. The wavelet transform coefficients are quantized, so the probably noisy, low-amplitude variables are set to zero. A minimum mean-squared error estimation approach is used to denoise the irregular coefficients. The first threshold distinguishes large magnitude coefficients, while the second distinguishes spatial periodicity coefficients, which are then chosen for restoration.

Frontward Transform

The Laplacian pyramid is used first to catch point discontinuities in the contourlet transform, followed by a directional filter bank to connect point discontinuities into linear structures. A contourlet transform is the end product, which uses basic images, including contour segments and is applied by a pyramidal directional filter bank. The Laplacian pyramid (LP) is used to decompose an image into a number of radial sub-bands, and the directional filter banks (DFB) decompose each LP information sub-band into a number of directional sub-bands. The contourlet transform incorporates directional information, which yields the best definition of all the salient information in both test images. As a result, the composite image is more complete and natural-looking, with minimal noise. It is assumed that using the composite image would boost the efficiency of the subsequent processing tasks. This process reorganises knowledge by combining it. As a consequence, the three-dimensionless output can be stored more efficiently and interpreted more quickly. The composite image improves [15 - 17] precision and reliability by using redundant information, and the method also improves interpretation capabilities for subsequent tasks by using complementary information. As a result, the data is more reliable, the utility is improved, and the output is more consistent. The contourlet transform accurately reflects the image's salient features, such as edges, lines, and contours, so the fusion process does not distort the original image as in Fig. (**3**).

IMAGE IMPROVEMENT WITH PRINCIPAL COMPONENT PCA FOR 2D

The computer's decision-making capabilities are used to define and classify pixels based on their digital signatures:

• Using principal components to create images

• Multispectral data classification

• Take pictures that can spot changes

This thesis proposes a new algorithm based on the contourlet transform 2D-PCA transformation. In image denoising, this algorithm outperforms the wavelet algorithm, particularly when it comes to removing speckle noise. PSNR is one of the parameters used to compare the wavelet and contourlet transforms. The Laplacian Pyramid (LP) has an advantage over other compact representation techniques, such as wavelet and sub-band coding, which allows for more flexibility in the configuration of the decimation and interpolation filters.

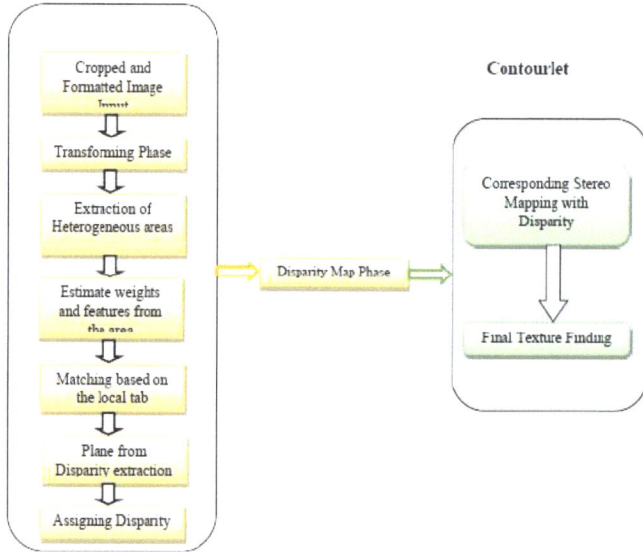

Fig. (3). Flow of image improvisation to predict texture.

The principal component analysis (PCA) rotates the axes of image space along the lines of maximum variance using a linear transformation. The image is rotated using the orthogonal eigenvectors of the covariance matrix formed from a set of image data from the input channels. The eigenchannels are a new group of image channels generated by this transformation. PCA can be used to isolate such inter-band correlation into components and fix it (layers). The knowledge content of the components created with layers of information is special.

PCA also allows for the extraction of redundant data from each input band and the compression of the data into fewer bands after reducing the data's dimensionality. The key goal of PCA is to reduce the dimensionality of a data set while retaining as much detail as possible. It calculates and produces a data set definition that is both compact and optimal.

A transformation is applied to a correlated collection of multispectral data to perform PCA analysis. When the transformation is applied to correlated data, it creates a new uncorrelated multispectral data set with ordered variance properties. The correlation and quality of information associated with the bands are indicated by the spread or variation of the distribution of points in the feature space. If the data points are concentrated in a small area, it will most likely yield very little information. The initial measurement coordinate axes may not be the best arrangement in multispectral feature space for analysing the data. The original axes can be translated and rotated using PCA analysis, resulting in the original brightness values being redistributed (reprocessed) into a new set of axes.

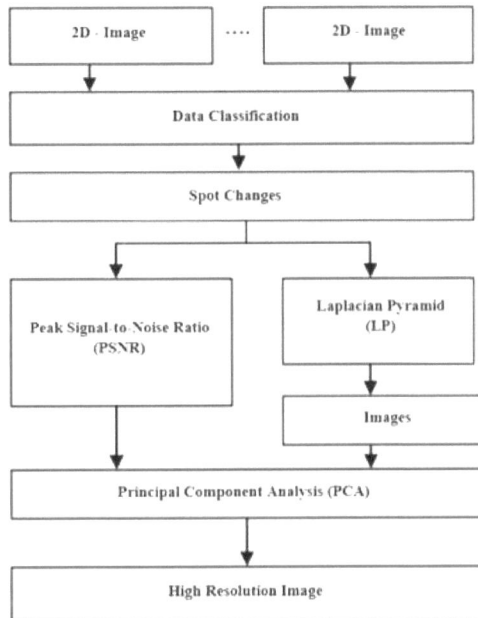

Fig. (4). Framework of PCA component for 2D image improvement [19].

A principal component analysis is a multivariate technique for projecting maximal variances onto the axes by rotating the results. In other words, a set of correlated variables is transformed into a set of uncorrelated variables, which are then sorted by reducing heterogeneity. The uncorrelated variables are all linear combinations of the original variables, with the last one being substituted with the least amount of real data loss.

The first and most critical factor is a set of variables that describes the most variance. The second principal variable, which is independent of the first, determines the next largest amount of variance. There are as many variables as there are principal elements. It can be compared to repositioning the existing axes in a vacuum.

The original variables were used to describe the parameters. There will be no association between the new variables identified by the rotation in this new rotation. The first new variable contains the greatest amount of variation; the second new variable, which is unexplained by the first and orthogonal to it, contains the greatest amount of variation.

Implementing 2D-PCA

Principal component analysis can be performed using a number of algorithms. With one exception, they will produce the same results if given the same starting data. If two or more potential rotations have the same 'maximum' variation at any stage, the choice of which one to use is indeterminate. Instead of an ellipse, the data cloud would appear as a circle in two dimensions. In a circle, every rotation is equal. The first component of an elliptical data cloud, on the other hand, would run parallel to the ellipse's main axis. This can be thought of as finding a projection of the observations onto orthogonal axes embedded in the space defined by the initial variables. The following are the parameters for selecting axes: (i) The first axis 'contains' or 'accounts' for the maximum amount of variation, (ii) The maximum amount of variation orthogonal to the first axis is found on the second axis, and the maximum amount of variation orthogonal to the first and second axes is found on the third axis, and so on before the last new axis includes the last amount of variation orthogonal to the first and second axes, as well as the last amount of variation remaining.

Principal components analysis is similar to another statistical method known as factor analysis, and it can be used to convert a series of image bands into uncorrelated principal components that are organised by the amount of image variation. As a result, the components are a statistical abstraction of the original band set's intrinsic variability.

SELECTION AND EXTRACTION OF FEATURES

This research investigates optimal and suboptimal search strategies for function selection (selecting a subset of the initial variables for classifier design). Feature extraction looks for a linear or nonlinear transformation of the original variables into a smaller set. Techniques for expressing data in a reduced dimension are known as ordination methods or geometrical methods in the multivariate analysis literature. Principal component analysis and multidimensional scaling are examples of these techniques. They are known as feature selection and feature extraction methods in the pattern recognition literature, and they include linear discriminant analysis (LDA). Dimensionality reduction can be accomplished in one of two ways given a collection of measurements. The first step is to decide which variables are irrelevant to the classification mission. In a segregation problem, factors that do not correspond to class separability are overlooked. As a result, the job is to identify observable d features among the p measurements (the number of features d must also be determined). In the measurement space, this is referred to as feature selection or simply features selection.

The second approach entails determining a transition from p dimensions to a lower-dimensional feature space. The term for this is feature extraction or feature selection in transformed space. This transformation can be supervised or unsupervised, and it can be a linear or nonlinear combination of the original variables. In the supervised case, the aim is to find the transformation that maximises a certain class separability criterion. There are two basic strategies for selecting function subsets:

1) Optimal methods: Exhaustive search methods, which are only feasible for very limited problems, and quick search methods, which can lead to a globally optimal solution but are computationally expensive, are two examples.

2) Suboptimal methods: The optimality of the above strategies is traded for numerical efficiency. While the computational criteria are based on the optimality criteria, the approach used in this study is independent of it.

Criteria for Selecting Features

A method of measuring a feature set's ability to differentiate accurately between two or more classes is necessary in order to choose a good feature set. This is achieved by defining a class separability metric that is optimised in terms of the subsets that are feasible. The feature set is chosen in one of two ways:

1) Create a classifier with the reduced feature set on a different test/validation set and choose the feature sets on which the classifier performs best. In this step, the feature set is selected to match the classifier. A different classifier range will result in a different feature set.

2) The second approach entails calculating the variance between the data distributions and prioritising function sets with the least amount of overlap (that is, maximise separability). This is independent of the final classifier used, and it has the advantage of being relatively inexpensive to implement. However, the assumptions used to determine the overlap are always crude, resulting in a poor estimation of discriminability.

Linear Criteria for Extracting Features

The method of transforming raw data (including all variables) into a data set with fewer variables is known as feature extraction. During function extraction, all available variables are used, and the data is converted (*via* a linear or nonlinear transformation) into a reduced-dimension space. As a consequence, the aim is to use a smaller collection of underlying variables to replace the initial variables. Feature extraction is useful for a variety of reasons:

1) To minimise the input data's bandwidth (resulting in faster processing and lower data requirements).

2) To provide a relevant collection of features to a classifier, resulting in improved efficiency, particularly for simple classifiers.

3) To cut down on redundancy.

4) To find new, useful underlying variables or features that describe the data, resulting in a better understanding of how the data is produced.

5) To create a low-dimensional representation (ideally in two dimensions) with minimal information loss, allowing the data to be interpreted easily and relationships and structure in the data to be defined.

Discontinuity Handling

To obtain a globally smooth field, a global smoothness restriction is introduced to allow for all discontinuities. As a consequence, methods for accurately detecting and modelling discontinuities must be established. There are two methods that can be used to integrate discontinuities

Integration Part: Limitations

One way to solve the problem of discontinuities in function f is to use the integration field. Incorrect values are obtained if the integration region contains discontinuities. As a result, algorithms must be developed that search for edges in f and, as a result, restrict the integration area to the segmented regions. Without a question, this is a complicated iterative process. First, the image's borders do not necessarily correspond to the function's edges. Second, only sparse information is available before calculating the function field f, rendering partitioning impossible.

Alteration of Smoothness Terminology

Another way to solve the discontinuity problem is to adjust the smoothness concept. Where a discontinuity is assumed, the smoothness restriction may be reduced or even removed. This is yet another iterative algorithm. In the smoothness term, a control function that flips the smoothness constraint in suitable circumstances must be used (controlled smoothness).

CONCLUSION

To summarise, adaptive machine learning is the next wave of conventional machine learning – newer, faster, and better. Even though conventional machine learning has progressed significantly, adaptive machine learning now better suits everyone's needs. Adaptive AI improves at forecasting, decision-making, and many other tasks as a result of the continuous flow of data, modified systems, and constant learning. As a result, the above strategies will outperform the ability to reliably record and represent both low-frequency and high-frequency components (such as image backgrounds) and transients (such as image edges). It can also decompose variable resolution with almost uncorrelated coefficients. Hence a researcher can achieve a progressive transmission's ability to promote the reception of a picture in various quality levels with the knowledge of this chapter.

CONSENT FOR PUBLICATION

Not applicable.

CONFLICT OF INTEREST

The authors declare no conflict of interest, financial or otherwise.

ACKNOWLEDGEMENT

Declared none.

REFERENCES

[1]   Z. Li, H. Yao, and F. Ma, "Learning with small data", *Proceedings of the 13th International Conference on Web Search and Data Mining,* 2020pp. 884-887
[http://dx.doi.org/10.1145/3336191.3371874]

[2]   A. Behura, "The cluster analysis and feature selection: Perspective of machine learning and image processing", *Data Analytics in Bioinformatics: A Machine Learning Perspective.,* pp. 249-280, 2021.

[3]   M. Marsot, J. Mei, X. Shan, L. Ye, P. Feng, X. Yan, C. Li, and Y. Zhao, "An adaptive pig face recognition approach using Convolutional Neural Networks", *Comput. Electron. Agric.,* vol. 173, 2020.105386

[http://dx.doi.org/10.1016/j.compag.2020.105386]

[4]   A. Kumar, *An Overview on Deep Learnings and its Accomplishments in Computer Vision.*.

[5]   B. Iyer, A.M. Rajurkar, and V. Gudivada, *Applied Computer Vision and Image Processing.* Springer Singapore, 2020.
[http://dx.doi.org/10.1007/978-981-15-4029-5]

[6]   M. Leo, P. Carcagnì, P.L. Mazzeo, P. Spagnolo, D. Cazzato, and C. Distante, "Analysis of facial information for healthcare applications: A survey on computer vision-based approaches", *Information (Basel),* vol. 11, no. 3, p. 128, 2020.
[http://dx.doi.org/10.3390/info11030128]

[7]   R.A. Hamzah, and H. Ibrahim, "Literature survey on stereo vision disparity map algorithms", *J. Sens.,* vol. 2016, pp. 1-23, 2016.
[http://dx.doi.org/10.1155/2016/8742920]

[8]   T. Saravanan, and N.S. Nithya, "Modeling displacement and direction aware ad hoc on-demand distance vector routing standard for mobile ad hoc networks", *Mob. Netw. Appl.,* vol. 24, no. 6, pp. 1804-1813, 2019.
[http://dx.doi.org/10.1007/s11036-019-01390-9]

[9]   N. Thillaiarasu, "ChenthurPandian, S. A novel scheme for safe-guarding confidentiality in public clouds for service users of cloud computing", *Cluster Comput.,* vol. 22, pp. 1179-1188, 2019.
[http://dx.doi.org/10.1007/s10586-017-1178-8]

[10]   T. Saravanan, and P. Sasikumar, "Assessment and Analysis of Action Degeneracy Due to Blackhole Attacks in Wireless Sensor Networks", *Proceedings of 6th International Conference on Recent Trends in Computing,* 2021pp. 345-355
[http://dx.doi.org/10.1007/978-981-33-4501-0_33]

[11]   N. Shyamambika, and N. Thillaiarasu, "A survey on acquiring integrity of shared data with effective user termination in the cloud", *2016 10th International Conference on Intelligent Systems and Control (ISCO), Coimbatore.,* 2016pp. 1-5
[http://dx.doi.org/10.1109/ISCO.2016.7726893]

[12]   T. Saravanan, and N. Thillaiarasu, "Optimal Grouping and Belief based CH selection in mobile ad-hoc network using Chunk Reliable Routing Protocol", *2021 International Conference on Advance Computing and Innovative Technologies in Engineering (ICACITE),* 2021pp. 933-940
[http://dx.doi.org/10.1109/ICACITE51222.2021.9404631]

[13]   N. Thillaiarasu, S.C. Pandian, and V. Vijayakumar, "Designing a trivial information relaying scheme for assuring safety in mobile cloud computing environment", *Wirel. Netw.,* 2019.
[http://dx.doi.org/10.1007/s11276-019-02113-4]

[14]   S. Ranjithkumar, and N. Thillaiarasu, *"A survey of secure routing protocols of mobile adhoc network." SSRG International Journal of Computer Science and Engineering.* vol. Vol. 2. SSRG-IJCSE, 2015.

[15]   M. S. Hamid, N. Abd Manap, R. A. Hamzah, and A. F. Kadmin, "Stereo Matching Algorithm based on Deep Learning: A Survey", *Journal of King Saud University-Computer and Information Sciences.,* 2020.

[16]   Y. Zhu, Z. Wu, W.D. Hartley, J.M. Sietins, C.B. Williams, and H.Z. Yu, "Unraveling pore evolution in post-processing of binder jetting materials: X-ray computed tomography, computer vision, and machine learning", *Addit. Manuf.,* vol. 34, 2020.101183
[http://dx.doi.org/10.1016/j.addma.2020.101183]

[17]   J.A. Gnanaselvi, and G.M. Kalavathy, "Detecting disorders in retinal images using machine learning techniques", *J. Ambient Intell. Humaniz. Comput.,* pp. 1-10, 2020.

[18]   https://www.qualitymag.com/articles/96138-simplifying-ai-deployment-for-quality-inspection

[19] S. Sutarti, A.T. Putra, and E. Sugiharti, "Comparison of pca and 2dpca accuracy with k-nearest neighbor classification in face image recognition", *Scientific Journal of Informatics,* vol. 6, no. 1, pp. 64-72, 2019.
[http://dx.doi.org/10.15294/sji.v6i1.18553]

## CHAPTER 2

Algorithm For Intelligent Systems

Pratik Dhoke[1,*], Pranay Saraf[1], Pawan Bhalandhare[1], Yogadhar Pandey[2], H.R. Deshmukh[3] and **Rahul Agrawal[1]**

[1] *G H Raisoni College of Engineering, Nagpur, India*

[2] *Associate Professor, Technocrats Institute of Technology (Excellence), India*

[3] *Principal, Shri R. R. Lahoti Science College, India*

Abstract: In the 21st-century, machines are becoming more and more intelligent. Terms like artificial intelligence, automation, robotics, *etc.*, are becoming the new normal in today's tech-savvy world. All of this is made possible because of complex programs (algorithms) which are able to perform such difficult tasks.

Intelligent systems are self-taught machines intended for a particular task. Intelligence is the ability to learn and use new information and skills. As the person learns from past data, the system can be programmed using various algorithms to make it intelligent.

In this chapter, we will be discussing some of the algorithms in brief, like- Reinforcement learning, Game theory, Machine Learning, Decision Tree, Artificial Neural Networks, Swarm Intelligence, and Natural Language Processing and its applications.

Keywords: Algorithm, Clustering, Game Theory, Machine Learning, Neural Network, Regression, Reinforcement Learning, Swarm Intelligent, Swarm Robots.

INTRODUCTION

Intelligent systems (IS) give a normalized methodological way to tackle significant and fairly unpredictable issues and acquire steady and solid outcomes. Obtaining from different word references, intelligence implies the potential to grasp, comprehend and benefit from the experience. As a matter of fact, there are, obviously, different meanings like the capacity to gain and hold the information, mental capacity, the capacity to react rapidly and effectively to a new circumstance, and so on.

The meaning of intelligent systems is a troublesome issue and is dependent upon a lot of discussions. From the point of view of calculation, the insight of a

* **Corresponding author Pratik Dhoke:** G H Raisoni College of Engineering, Nagpur, India;
E-mail: dhoke_pratik.cs@ghrce.raisoni.net

Prasad Lokulwar, Basant Verma, N. Thillaiarasu, Kailash Kumar, Mahip Bartere and Dharam Singh (Eds.)

framework can be described by its adaptability, versatility, learning, memory, thinking, temporal dynamics and the capacity to oversee imprecise and uncertain data.

The rapid growth of the internet and other technologies generates a lot of data. Domo, Inc. is a cloud software company that works on business intelligence tools and data visualization. It released a report stating that "Over 2.5 quintillion bytes of data is generated every single day, and it is only going to grow from there. By 2020, it is estimated that 1.7MB of data will be created every second for every person on earth" [1].

This data can be put to use by creating different kinds of algorithms in various domains, which could later be used in designing an algorithm to create a powerful, intelligent system to help tackle a real-world problem.

Reinforcement Learning

Learning is a subset of machine learning that uses trial and error techniques to learn in an interactive environment by using feedback from its own experiences and actions. It examines the prediction and control of events of perceptual importance with regards to psychological and neural rules for adaptation. These RL models are given a set of actions they can perform in a specific environment, and a goal to pursue. One of the algorithms in reinforcement learning is-

Q-Learning

Q learning is a straightforward method of learning with the help of an agent which learns in a controlled environment [2]. Agents get rewarded whenever the action is correct. The Q-learning basic structure shown in Fig. (**1**) solves problem by trial and error method having two agents.

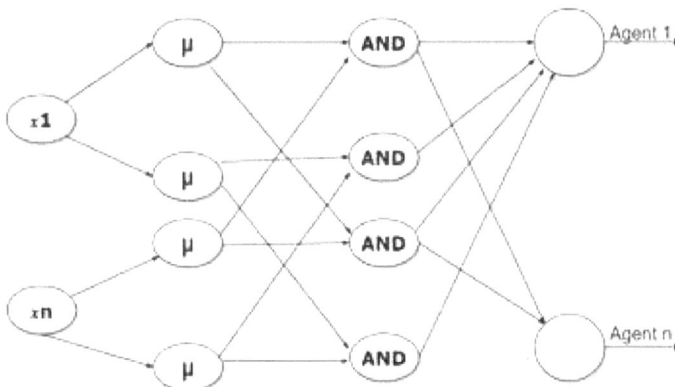

Fig. (1). Q-Learning: agents solve the problem using the trial-and-error method [3]

Game Theory

The practical applications of the Game theory are in statistical decision making, linear programming, and operation re-search.

Game theory lessens the intricacy of variations in calculations in enormous networks. It answers to decentralized cross-functional frameworks, like the players of the game, under fractional recognisability suspicions. Games can be competitive or cooperative. In a competitive game, each player is fundamentally worried regarding their own result, and due to this reason, every one of its choices is made seriously. In cooperative games, every player is worried regarding their complete advantages, while not being extremely stressed over their very own advantage.

Here, Bayesian analysis can be utilized to justify the cost dependent on perceptions of steps being undertaken. Moreover, on the ac-count of a non-zer--sum game, equilibrium may occur. It is likewise restricted by the number of players that the game has, considering the investigation of the strategies of the game ends up being more and more complex. Quite possibly, the central constraint here is that everyone should recognize the cost function of their fellow players.

Thus, in addition to labeled training data, game theory needs a prior understanding of the system. The players require information on various specifications like SINR, base station costs, and powering. (Fig. **2**) shows an illustration of rock paper scissors.

Fig. (2). Game Theory- image depicting the game of rock-paper-scissors [4]

Machine Learning

In 1959, Arthur Samuel described ML as the "field of study that allows computers to learn without being explicitly programmed".

Few Machine Learning Algorithms everyone should know-

Decision Tree

Decision trees are used to determine features and extract patterns in large databases necessary for classification and prediction modeling [13]. These features are grouped with their intuitive interpretation. This algorithm in machine learning is perhaps the most well-known algorithm being used today; that is utilized for classifying problems that come under supervised learning. It functions admirably while classifying both continuous dependent variables and categorical variables. In this algorithm, we split the populace into at least two homogeneous sets dependent and independent variables/significant attributes. (Fig. 3) shows an illustration of a decision tree with dependent and independent variables.

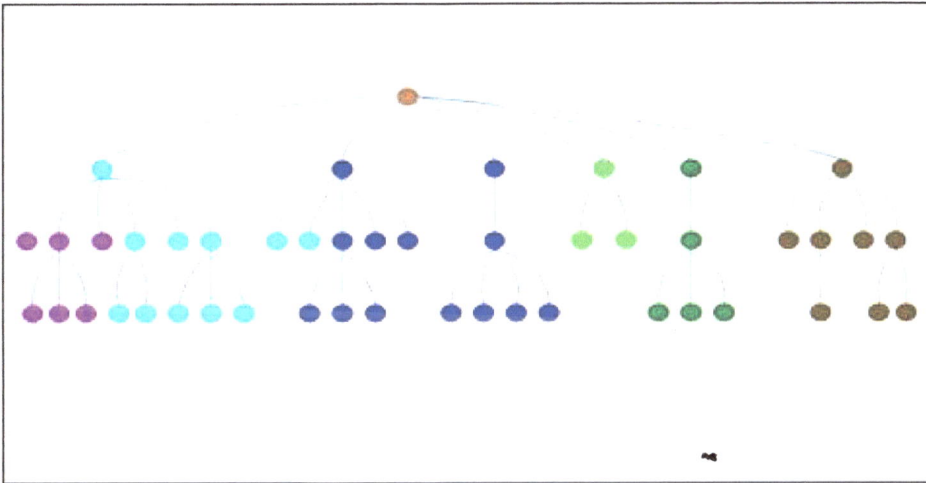

Fig. (3). Decision Tree- split the populace into at least two homogeneous sets dependent and independent variables/significant attributes [5].

Logistic Regression

Logistic Regression is another supervised learning algorithm that is very much like linear regression; the contrast between these two is that linear regression is used to solve prediction problems, logistic regression, on the other hand, is utilized to solve classification problems. When given a set of independent variables, the output prediction should be the categorical dependent variable. It can be used to classify a continuous dependent variable given different independent variables [6, 7]. Logistic regression example graph is shown in

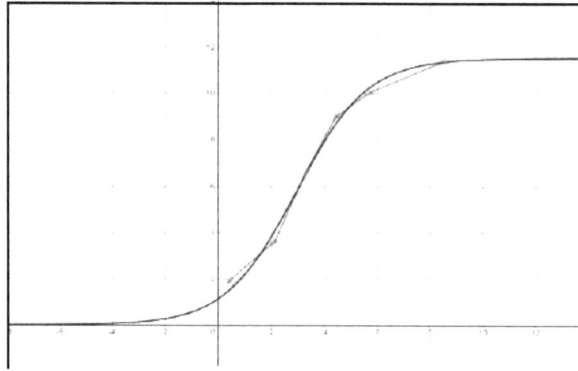

Fig. (4). Logistic Regression Graph, the dependent variable is grouping type, a usual approach is a logistic regression, and it gets its name from the type of curve it made to fit variables [8].

Linear Regression

Linear regression is a supervised ML algorithm, the simplest form of regression analysis, which is used to find the relationship between two variables. As the name suggests, a linear relationship should exist between the predictor and the target variable. To simply this, let's under-stand this with the help of an example. Lets think about a regression problem in which a continuous response of a single output variable Y is to be calculated on a linear combination on the input variable X [9]. The Linear Regression line can be seen in Fig. (**5**), graph of linear regression.

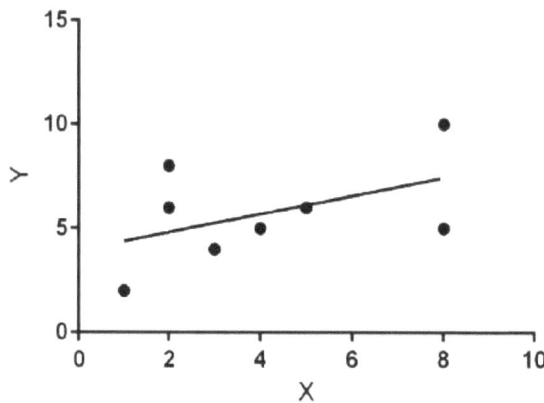

Fig. (5). Linear Regression Graph continuous response of a single output variable Y is to be calculated on a linear combination on the input variable X [9]

K-Means Clustering

Clustering is a task of finding populated groups of data points in a given data set and creating a group of similar or clustered data groups [10]. Each of these groups is called a cluster and can be defined as an area where the tightness of data points is higher than the other area in the region.

K-means clustering in an unsupervised learning algorithm that is extremely popular among ML enthusiasts. As the name suggest, this creates different clusters from the unlabeled datasets given; after inputting the unlabeled dataset in the algorithm, the complete dataset is split into k-number of clusters and repeats the process to meet the right clusters, for which the value of k should be predetermined. (Fig. **6**) shows scatter graph with an example of k means clustering example.

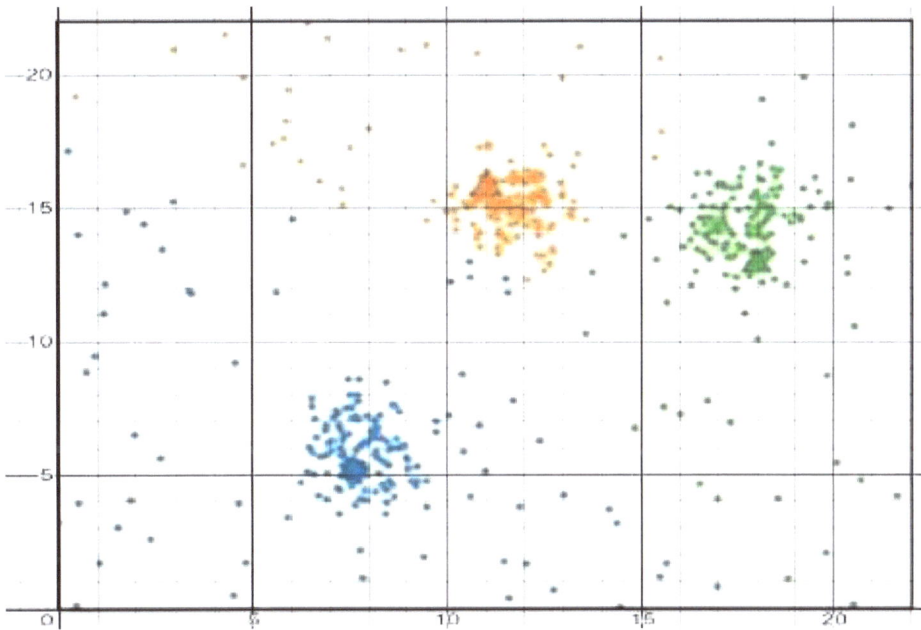

Fig. (6). Scatter graph of K-means Clustering [10]

Artificial Neural Network (ANN)

Since the 1980s, research on the ANNs has made extraordinary advancements, and ANNs are used a lot in the industry [11, 12]. Artificial Neural Networks are nonlinear information processing systems that combine countless processing units called synapses connected in a network with a sequence of features. ANN is the pinnacle of artificial intelligence, which is designed to replicate the way the human brain functions, processes and analyzes data. It works exactly like the human brain. ANN has neurons that are interconnected by nodes; these neurons are called the processing units.

An ANN goes through supervised training to learn and recognize information and understand its pattern; during this phase, it is taught what it is that needs to be looked up for producing a certain output with the help of yes/no questions. (Fig. **7**) shows the example of ANN.

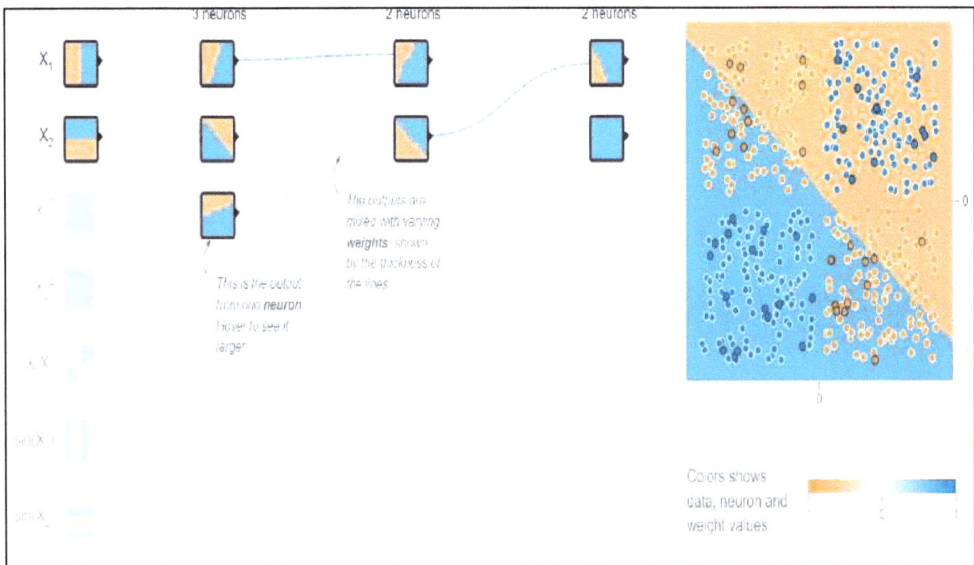

Fig. (7). Sample Example of ANN using: https://playground.tesnorflow.org [13]

Swarm Intelligence

Science is derived from nature. Science proved how nature actually works. Many great discoveries have been inspired by nature, for example Velcro, SONAR, gravitation, *etc.*

Swarm intelligence is developed from insects and animal behavior. Ants, bees, wolves, lions, *etc.* These animals and insects work in swarms, and getting inspired from that Gerado Beni & Jing Wang introduced swarm intelligence in the context of cellular robotic systems in 1989 [14]. Nature's illustration of a swarm of birds is shown in Fig. (**8**).

Fig. (8). Swarm of Animals shows this concept of swarm can be put into robotics and decision-making algorithms [15].

Swarm Robots

This principle of swarm can be used in robotics to create groups of robots intended to do an identical task and coordinating with other robots. These swarm robots can be very efficient compared to traditional robots [15]. Multiple swarm robots are small in size and simple in design compared to traditional robots that are bulkier and more complex. Each robot in swarm robots has a specific task; they communicate locally among themselves and do the task using different types of sensors embedded in them. Swarm robots are decentralized and traditional robots are centralized control.

There are many applications in various domains, for example - Military, Healthcare, search and rescue, *etc.* (Fig. **9**) shows swarm robots in the military used for surveillance.

Fig. (9). Swarm Robots for military surveillance [15]

Swarm Intelligence in Decision Making Algorithm

The principle of swarm can be used in decision making. Swarm intelligence can help to take quick and optimized solutions to the tasks such as polls, surveys, *etc.* Swarm intelligence in decision making is like taking votes in a much-optimized way with a feedback loop by interacting with the swarm to make a decision. The algorithm assesses the real-time behavior to take the most optimized solution. (Fig.**10**) shows an illustration of decision-making algorithm by making an outcome by the voting system and assigning weights to every answer, and calculating it.

What should we order for our lunch ?

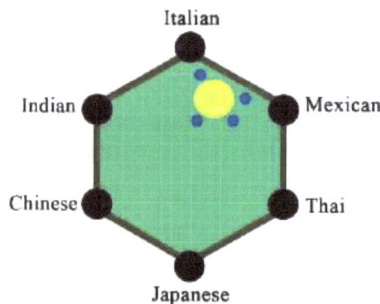

Fig. (10). Decision making algorithm in Swarm intelligence solving a problem for "What should we order for lunch from given options" [16]

Natural Language Processing

People communicate with each other with the help of language, but we can't directly communicate with computers [17]. Computers are unable to understand our natural language. In order to make them understand our natural language, Natural language processing (NLP) was introduced. NPL started in the late 1950s as a section of artificial intelligence & linguistics [18]. In this 21st century, we see NLP everywhere, for example, google assistant, amazon alexa, google translator, google home, speech recognition, speech-to-text, *etc.* So, how does NLP work?

Syntactic and Semantic are the major parts of NLP, to understand the meaning and grammar of the text or natural language [19]. There are various processes to make NLP more efficient and clean-

Data preprocessing- Data is cleaned before processing with the help of various data preprocessing algorithms.

Tokenization- breaks the text into smaller chunks or units.

Part of speech tagging - joining words to create syntactic meaning.

Lemmatization - reducing to their root form

Stop word removal - filtering word that has no unique meaning. Example - preposition and article in Fig. (**11**) show the NLP.

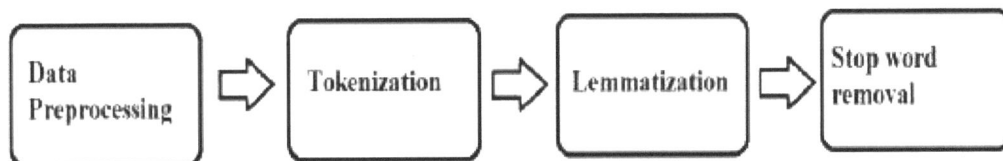

Fig. (11). Natural Language Processing steps [20]

CONCLUSION

In this chapter, we have covered a few algorithms for intelligent systems very briefly. Since there is Continuous research and advancement going on in intelligent algorithms, they are getting more complex and optimized. The algorithms we presented here do not have complete intuition but a brief description to get an overview of some of the intelligent systems.

As time passes, we hope there will be an advancement in the field of computer science and decision-making systems or intelligent systems.

FUTURE SCOPE

The aforementioned techniques may add sufficient intelligence to any system to adapt to particular challenges. Be that as it may, a broad multi-disciplinary perspective is needed to fulfill the constant need of the users. There emerges an undeniable question of how much intelligence should be added to a system. The appropriate response is, 'there are endless possibilities. The difficulties are huge and disturbing, yet shared methodologies are merging for a potential solution.

CONSENT FOR PUBLICATION

Not applicable.

CONFLICT OF INTEREST

The authors declare no conflict of interest, financial or otherwise.

ACKNOWLEDGEMENTS

Declared none.

REFERENCES

[1]   *Data Never Sleeps 6.0 [Online]. Available.*, .https://www.domo.com/learn/infographic/data-neve-
        -sleeps-6

[2]   Arthur L. Samuel, "Some Studies in Machine Learning Using the Game of Checkers", *IBM Journal of
        Research and Development.*, vol. 44, no. 1.2, pp. 210-229, 1959.
        [http://dx.doi.org/10.1147/rd.33.0210]

[3]   P.Y. Glorennec, "Fuzzy Q-learning and dynamical fuzzy Q-learning", *Proceedings of 1994 IEEE 3rd
        International Fuzzy Systems Conference,* vol. vol.1, 1994pp. 474-479
        [http://dx.doi.org/10.1109/FUZZY.1994.343739]

[4]   Rock Paper Scissors, Scissors, Stone, Cloth PNG Transparent Clipart Image and PSD File for Free
        Download [Online], Available: https://in.pinterest.com/pin/309692911878257658/

[5]   P.H. Swain, and H. Hauska, "The decision tree classifier: Design and potential", *IEEE Trans. Geosci.
        Electron.,* vol. 15, no. 3, pp. 142-147, 1977.
        [http://dx.doi.org/10.1109/TGE.1977.6498972]

[6]   J. Lever, M. Krzywinski, and N. Altman, "Logistic regression", *Nat. Methods,* vol. 13, no. 7, pp. 541-
        542, 2016.
        [http://dx.doi.org/10.1038/nmeth.3904]

[7]   N. Altman, and M. Krzywinski, "Simple linear regression", *Nat. Methods,* vol. 12, no. 11, pp. 999-
        1000, 2015.
        [http://dx.doi.org/10.1038/nmeth.3627] [PMID: 26824102]

[8]   J. Lever, M. Krzywinski, and N. Altman, "Logistic regression", *Nat. Methods,* vol. 13, no. 7, pp. 541-
        542, 2016.
        [http://dx.doi.org/10.1038/nmeth.3904]

[9]   X. Su, X. Yan, and C.L. Tsai, "Linear regression", *Wiley Interdiscip. Rev. Comput. Stat.,* vol. 4, no. 3,
        pp. 275-294, 2012.
        [http://dx.doi.org/10.1002/wics.1198]

[10]   A. Likas, N. Vlassis, and J.J. Verbeek, "The global k-means clustering algorithm", *Pattern Recognit.,*
        vol. 36, no. 2, pp. 451-461, .
        [http://dx.doi.org/10.1016/S0031-3203(02)00060-2]

[11]   S. Ding, H. Li, C. Su, J. Yu, and F. Jin, "Evolutionary artificial neural networks: a review", *Artif.
        Intell. Rev.,* vol. 39, no. 3, pp. 251-260, 2013.
        [http://dx.doi.org/10.1007/s10462-011-9270-6]

[12]   W.S. McCulloch, and W. Pitts, "A logical calculus of the ideas immanent in nervous activity", *Bull.
        Math. Biophys.,* vol. 5, no. 4, pp. 115-133, 1943.
        [http://dx.doi.org/10.1007/BF02478259]

[13]   Henrik Hoeiness, Axel Harstad, and Gerald Friedland, "From Tinkering to Engineering:
        Measurements in Tensorflow Playground", *Peer-reviewed by and presented at ICPR 2020.,*
        2021.http://arxiv.org/abs/2101.04141

[14]   *Beni, Gerardo.* vol. 3342. From Swarm Intelligence to Swarm Robot-ics, 2004, pp. 1-9.Lecture Notes
        in Computer Science
        [http://dx.doi.org/10.1007/978-3-540-30552-1_1]

[15]   Vedant Bahel, Atharva Peshkar, and Sugandha Singh, "Swarm Intelli-gence-Based Systems: A
        Review", *Proceeding of International Con-ference on Computational Science and Applications..*

[http://dx.doi.org/10.1007/978-981-15-0790-8_16]

[16]   L. Metcalf, D.A. Askay, and L.B. Rosenberg, "Keeping Humans in the Loop: Pooling Knowledge through Artificial Swarm Intelligence to Improve Business Decision Making", *Calif. Manage. Rev.,* vol. 61, no. 4, pp. 84-109, 2019.
[http://dx.doi.org/10.1177/0008125619862256]

[17]   A. Chopra, A. Prashar, and C. Sain, "Natural Language Processing", *International Journal of Technology Enhancements and Emerging Engineering Research,* vol. 1, pp. 131-134, 2013.

[18]   P.M. Nadkarni, L. Ohno-Machado, and W.W. Chapman, "Natural language processing: an introduction", *J. Am. Med. Inform. Assoc.,* vol. 18, no. 5, pp. 544-551, 2011.
[http://dx.doi.org/10.1136/amiajnl-2011-000464] [PMID: 21846786]

[19]   R. Wolff, *What Is Natural Language Pro-cessing & How Does It Work? monkeylearn.,* 2020.https://monkeylearn.com/blog/what-is-natural-language-processing

[20]   N. Indurkhya, and F. Damerau, *Handbook of Natural Language Processing.* CRC Press, 2010.
[http://dx.doi.org/10.1201/9781420085938]

## CHAPTER 3

Clinical Decision Support System for Early Prediction of Congenital Heart Disease using Machine learning Techniques

Ritu Aggarwal[1,*] and **Suneet Kumar**[2]

[1] *Maharishi Markendeshwar Engineering College, Maharishi Markendeshwar Institute of Computer Technology and Business Management Mullana, Ambala, Haryana, India, 133207*

[2] *Maharishi Markendeshwar Engineering College, Mullana, Ambala, Haryana, India, 133207*

Abstract: One of the main reasons for deaths in children or low-age kids is congenital heart disease detected by CDSS (clinical decision support system). If it's diagnosed at an early stage, the significant results can be obtained for life-saving. The practitioners are not equally qualified and skilled so the detection of the disease and the proper diagnosis is delayed. The best prevention is the early detection of the symptoms of this disease. An automated medical diagnosis system is made to improve the accuracy and diagnose the disease. CHD expands the heart deformation as in newborn babies. Early detection of CHD is necessary to detect and diagnose this disease. Due to this, the life of a newborn child is in danger. By different detection methods, CHD could be accomplished by its clinical information using CDSS and it is also detected by its non-clinical data. In pregnant ladies, CHD is diagnosed by their non-clinical data by applying it to the newborn baby that is in their womb. Due to this, different machine learning algorithms, including K-NN and MLP, are explored. For CHD detection, dataset selection is a big issue, and it is utilized by the Support Vector Machine and random forest, K-NN, and MLP algorithms. This proposed work develops a decision support system to detect congenital heart disease. In this proposed work, the data mining techniques and the machine learning algorithms are used to gain insight into the system for their accuracy rate. This proposed work is designed and developed by the Python jupyter notebook to implement MLP. This paper presents an analysis using the machine learning algorithm to develop an accurate and efficient model for heart disease prediction. The MLP models have a high accuracy of 97%.

Keywords: CHD (Congenital heart disease), DSS (decision support system), K-NN (K-nearest neighbor), Machine learning, MLP (Multilayer Perception), SVM (support vector machine).

* **Corresponding author Ritu Aggarwal:** Maharishi Markendeshwar Engineering College, Maharishi Markendeshwar Institute of Computer Technology and Business Management Mullana, Ambala, Haryana, India, 133207; E-mail: errituaggarwal@gmail.com

Prasad Lokulwar, Basant Verma, N. Thillaiarasu, Kailash Kumar, Mahip Bartere and Dharam Singh (Eds.)

INTRODUCTION

Clinical theory in heart detection using DSS (Decision Support System) is a set of tools that are based on computerized information programs based on discernment, resolution, and the action of courses in the organization or

business [1]. DSS helps in identifying what actions should be taken if a particular condition is satisfied. DSS provides the capability to solve problems by providing specific information. DSS can also provide suggestions based on information stored in it [2]. Suggestions were given by DSS to help the people to make decisions. It is useful for solving unstructured and semi-structured problems. It analyzes the huge amount of data for comprehensive data preprocessing, which is used to solve problems that help decision-making [3]. Mostly DSS used information such as E-government, health care, marketing, and inventory operation-related data [4]. It solves different queries and must be easy to interact with DSS. DSS can retrieve required information, perform analysis, make decisions, produce reports, and estimate the effects of decisions [5]. ADSS represents information graphically and an expert system or artificial intelligence (AI). It works together with knowledge workers and business executives [6, 7]. Typical information that a decision support application might gather and present would be:

(a) Accessing all information assets, including legacy and relational data sources;

(b) Comparative data figures;

(c) Projected figures based on new data or assumptions;

(d) Consequences of different decision alternatives, given experience in a specific context.

DSS is suitable for semi-structured problems and man/machine systems. DSS is very important for any manager to solve problems andmake decisions accordingly. If a CBIS is used, then we need a large database with some criteria that is given below [8].

1. Data manipulation means a large amount of computation.

2. Relationships between complex information systems [9].

3. At the different stages, analysis and judgment are required.

4. Communication *via* DSS tools [10].

The problem with DSS is that it is not suitable for unstructured problems, and it works on structured problems because it is based on CBIS. DSS needs to manage these problems and requires a large database. Examples are spreadsheets, Analysis packages, Expert systems, and Modeling [11]. It acts as a goal seeker for managers to complete a certain goal [12]. DSS is an individual or group of individuals that use decision-making called GDSS, which supports a group of decisions. GDSS is a well-integrated system, which is interactive, and a support group facilitator for decision making [13]. Antenatal decency is the major reason for increasing the rate of newborn decency [14] such as underweight Childs, contagious diseases, undernourishment, and congenital birth defects. The defects due to the congenital birth are common in newborns. In china, the newborns are widely affected by this disease. The estimated range is 2 to 5 which means 2 out of the 5 children are suffering from congenital birth defects. The Antenatal defect due to CHD is higher as compared to other diseases [15]. If these symptoms are recognized earlier, these diseases could be treated very well .Sometimes the medical practitioners have a lack of knowledge and experience as comapred to subject specialists [16]. These diseases could be reduced by diagnosing it at an earlier stage by developing the predictive model for congenital heart disease using a decision support system . This model predicts the CHD during the pregnancy and is treated based on some non-clinical data. Without clinical data, it's difficult to identify congenital heart disease in a woman's womb.

RELATED WORK

In his study, Liu s *et al.* [13] projected univariate and multivariate examinations to distinguish ecological danger factors that advance the odds of CHD on medical clinic-based information containing records of 164 patients affacted with CHD. Components like infant's physiological state, the scope of earlier pregnancies, higher parcel disease in anticipating moms, B-mode USG assessment, and mental pressure all through early maternity were investigated. Detrano *et al.* [20] proposed the machine learning classifier based on DSS that is used for heart disease prediction and classification. By using this classifier, he achieved an accuracy of 77%. B.Vanishree *et al.* [24] proposed a model to predict the newly conceived infantwho has an CHD from her mom in her womb. In this paper, predicting congenital heart diseases by 3 unique classifiers such as WSVM, Logit, and WRF was done on unequal information. In this proposed work, Edmonds *et al.* [26] used the Cleveland dataset and achieved higher precision in terms of accuracy rate. It highlights the feature section techniques for selecting the relevant features from the dataset. Gudadhe *et al.* [27]. utilized multilayer perceptron (MLP) and backing vector machine calculations for coronary illness order and proposed arrangement framework and acquired exactness of 80.41%. Kahramanli and Allahverdi *et al.* [28] planned a coronary illness characterization framework that utilized a cross-breed method wherein a neural organization incorporates a fuzzy and fuzzy neural organization. Also, the proposed arrangement framework accomplished a grouping precision of 87.4%. Palaniappan and Awang *et al.* [29], in this paper researchers, used different machine learning algorithms for diagnosing CHD. It used NB, DT, ANN classifiers for detecting disease. Its achieved accuracy performance for NB is 86.12% and in ANN 88.12%.

PROPOSED METHODOLOGY AND DATASET

The proposed work firstly took the dataset for Congenital heart disease then preprocessing of data, secondly used the specified prediction models for train and testing the samples, and finally evaluated the results by classification of CHD. This Work is implemented in jupyter notebook, python 3.7.1.

Table 1. Dataset for CHD.

Attributes	Type
Age(between 18-40)	In years
Family Relic(hereditary)	Family history
History of women illness	Suppository taken
Diet when the women are pregnant	Outside food or Unhealthy lifestyle of women

According to the Table **1**. dataset is taken for detection of CHD in which the imbalanced data is balanced by the clinical and non-clinical data tests as shown (Fig. **1**)

STEPS FOR TRAINING AND TESTING THE DATASET

This imbalanced dataset is handled by the following steps. The given dataset is equally divided into 2 data frames. Each data record is labeled with some values and considers CHD as label 1 and Non-CHD as 0. Put the label 1 CHD in data frame 1 and 0 CHD in data frame 2. Secondly, train and test these data frames. 3. At last, the training data subsets for both frames combine to form the final training set results. Finally, remove null values from the dataset and data cleaning is performed preprocessing and column-wise.

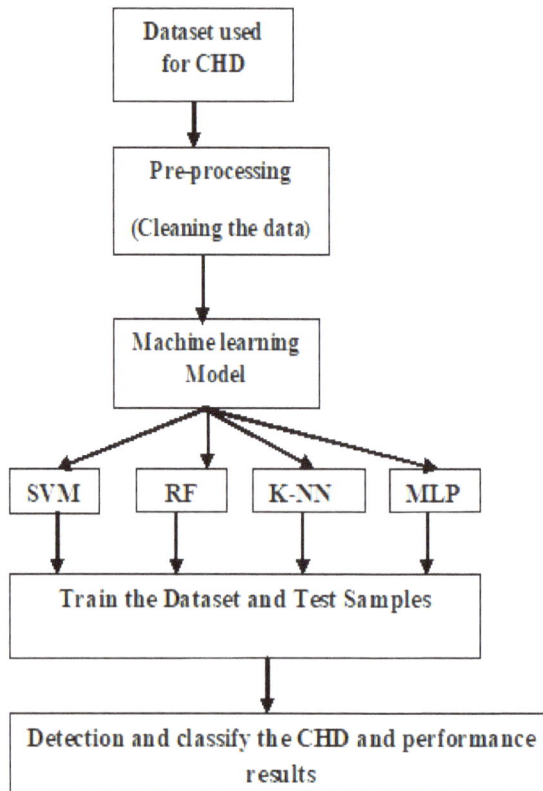

Fig. (1). Proposed Methodology

MACHINE LEARNING ALGORITHMS FOR PREDICTION

To accurately find out the accuracy and performance of congenital heart disease. Some of the following classification models of machine learning are used. These are the following prediction classification models [17].

SUPPORT VECTOR MACHINE

SVM is used for two distinct categories that are classification and regression. It separates the information point by seeking out the decision surface in these two distinct categories [18]. By adding some weighting, the parameter is used to classify the unbalanced data to give it additional class prominence. Kernel selection has persuaded to provide outcomes [19].

RANDOM FOREST

It is built by making the combination selected decision tree from the training set subset combined to form an RF classifier [20]. RF classifier works based on the vote of all the decision trees [21]. It is a voting classifier that estimates the final class to test the object for getting their results. The classification method of RF gives results according to the maximum votes given [22].

MULTILAYER PERCEPTRON

It is a neural network. MLP is made up of multiple layers and solve only linearly separable problems by the single-layer perceptron. It could not solve complex problems [23]. If one or more layers are added to a single-layer perceptron, it is called the multilayer perceptron network. The other name of MLP is a feed-forward neural network [24]. It has one or many hidden layers. MLP is used for the classification of input patterns and pattern recognition; it produces the prediction-based results according to too the input information and approximation.

It has three neurons for the input layer and three for the output layer.

INPUT LAYER

It takes the input vector (x1...XP). The range for each variable is -1 to 1. The standardized constant input values are called bias values for each hidden layer and the weight assigns multiplied and added to form a neuron [25].

HIDDEN LAYER

A weight (wij) B at each neuron n the hidden layer and weight multiplied by each input neuron.The resultant added sum uj and produced the output value hj [26].

OUTPUT LAYER

According to neuron weight wkj is multiplied by each hidden layer [27]. And the added result vj according to the weighted values. The transform function I and weighted sum vj produce output values yk [28].

K- NEAREST NEIGHBOR (K-NN)

This classification method is a supervised by classification **a**lgorithm and instance learning algorithm [29]. The classified object is dependent on the nearest point or neighbor. Using Euclidean distance is used to measure and calculate the distance of attributes. It takes the group named points and how to use them marked on another point [30]. Using K-NN fill, the missing values and data are clustered on a similarity basis among them. This algorithm is used for classification and regression .It is versatile for searching K-NN, which has provided irrelevant features and is a noisy algorithm. This classifier takes the data points for testing, and these testing data points compare with the training data points [31].On the basis of the test data point is to predict the label that is closest to the trained label class by using the distance C1 .it is calculated by the given formula [32]:

$$d1\ (c1,c2) = \sum |c1p\text{-}c2p| \qquad\qquad (1)$$

Whereas the distance points c1 and c2 are the vector representation of 1and 2, respectively [33]. $\sum$ is taken by overall points, and the d1 is the distance [34, 35].

EXPERIMENTS AND RESULTS

The results depend on how the model was trained and evaluate the metrics calculated from the confusion matrix used for every classifier used in this proposed work. The trained model obtains the best results when the testing is applied to the dataset. For a good performance evaluation of the CHD problem, various performance metrics are used, like T_pos_rate and T_neg_rate, and F1-score that were employed. These all are calculated as:

$$\text{Precision} = \text{T\_pos\_rateT\_pos\_rate+F\_neg\_rate} \qquad\qquad (2)$$

$$\text{Recall} = \text{T\_neg\_rateT-neg\_rate+F\_pos\_rate} \qquad\qquad (3)$$

$$\text{Accuracy} = \text{T\_pos\_rate+ T\_neg\_rateT-pos\_rate+ --neg+ F\_pos\_rate+ F\_neg\_rate} \qquad (4)$$

$$\text{F-score} = \text{w*T\_pos\_rate+(1-w)*T\_neg\_rate} \qquad\qquad (5)$$

Here w is the weight that is being used to adjust to an e value used for unbalanced data in machine learning [35] shown in Table **2**.

Table 2. Performance of each Classifier

Classifier	Accuracy	Precision	Recall	F-Score
SVM	0.92	0.65	0.79	0.74
RF	0.84	0.62	0.71	0.84
K-NN	0.95	0.78	0.75	0.85

(Table 2) cont.....

Classifier	Accuracy	Precision	Recall	F-Score
MLP	0.97	0.79	0.76	0.91

It used the class to maintain the accuracy for T_neg_rate there is class. Each classifier had the following table that calculates the accuracy for RF =0.94, SVM=0.92 and MLP = 0.97and K-NN=0.95. The results for each classifier are shown in Fig. (2) labelled as "graph results of each classifier".

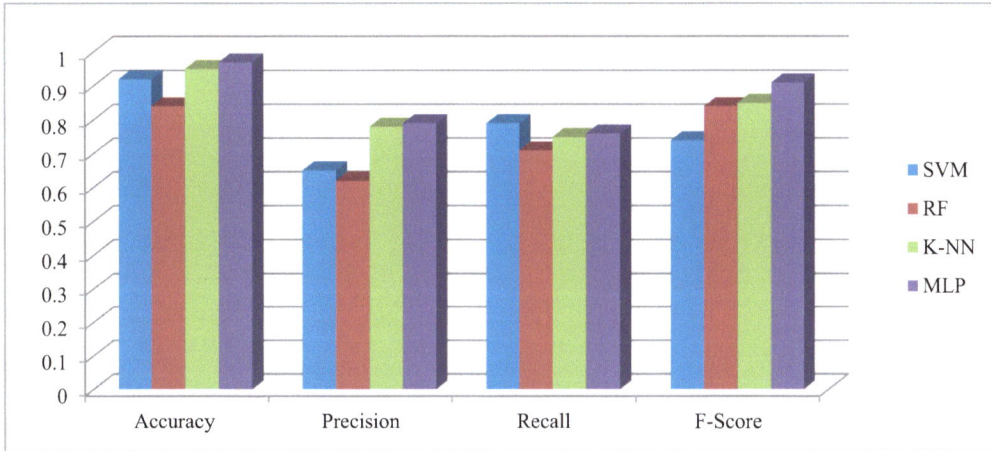

Fig. 2. By Graph Results of each classifier

The accuracy for MLP and K-NN is better than other classifiers. The performance could be increased.

Comparison Results

The given analysis Table **3** compares performance results between various Models and shows our work's results.

Table 3. Comparison Performance

Sr.No	Existing Work Performance	Accuracy
1	Detrano *et al.* [25]	SVM=77%
2	Palaniappan and Awang *et al.*	NB =86.12%,ANN =88.12%.
3	Kahramanli and Allahverdi *et al.* [28]	Fuzzy neural network=87.4%
4	**Our work**	MLP=97%

CONCLUSION

In this work, the CDSS is used to detect congenital heart disease during a child's pre-birth by using the non-clinical data of the pregnant mothers that should be collected non-presumptuously. In this work, four machine learning classifiers are used to predict CHD. This work can aid pre-birth CHD forecast in a kid, so important advances are being taken post-birth for early administration of the sickness. This work likewise energizes working for an expectation of different illnesses utilizing non-clinical data and not putting pregnant ladies under clinical equipment.

CONSENT FOR PUBLICATION

Not applicable.

CONFLICT OF INTEREST

The authors declare no conflict of interest, financial or otherwise.

ACKNOWLEDGEMENTS

I solely prepared this chapter under the guidance of Suneet Kumar.

REFERENCES

[1] AnithaSaxena, "Congenital Heart Disease in India: a Status Report", *Indian Journal of Pediatrics.,* vol. 72, pp. 595-598, 2005.

[2] R.S. Boneva, L.D. Botto, C.A. Moore, Q. Yang, A. Correa, and J.D. Erickson, "Mortality associated with congenital heart defects in the United States: trends and racial disparities, 1979-1997", *Circulation,* vol. 103, no. 19, pp. 2376-2381, 2001.
[http://dx.doi.org/10.1161/01.CIR.103.19.2376] [PMID: 11352887]

[3] Hongyan Cao, *Screening high-risk clusters for developing birth defects in mothers in Shanxi Province, China: application of latent class cluster analysis.,* p. 343, 2015.*BMC pregnancy and childbirth 15.1 (2015),* p. 343, 2015.
[http://dx.doi.org/10.1186/s12884-015-0783-x]

[4] Congenital Heart Disease Index, http://www.medicinenet.com/congenital_heart_disease/www.may

[5] D.M. Wells, D. Walrath, and P.S. Craighead, "Improvement in tangential breast planning efficiency using a knowledge-based expert system", *Med. Dosim.,* vol. 25, no. 3, pp. 133-138, 2000.
[http://dx.doi.org/10.1016/S0958-3947(00)00039-X] [PMID: 11025259]

[6] A. Goel, "Genre classification of songs using neural network", *International Conference on Computer and Communication Technology (ICCCT),* 2014
[http://dx.doi.org/10.1109/ICCCT.2014.7001506]

[7] R.G. Grabitz, M.R. Joffres, and R.L. Collins-Nakai, "Congenital heart disease: incidence in the first year of life. The Alberta Heritage Pediatric Cardiology Program", *Am. J. Epidemiol.,* vol. 128, no. 2, pp. 381-388, 1988.
[http://dx.doi.org/10.1093/oxfordjournals.aje.a114978] [PMID: 3394704]

[8] A. Hassan, and S. Fahad, "The Correlation Between Infants' Congenital Heart Defects and Maternal

Folic Acid Supplementation", *The Egyptian Journal of Hospital Medicine 31.5616,* pp. 1-6, 2018.

[9]   H. Yan, Y. Jiang, and J. Zheng, *A multi-layer perceptron based Medical Decision Support System for heart disease diagnosis* vol. 30. Expert System with Applications, 2006, pp. 272-281.

[10]   J. Kim, J. Lee, and Y. Lee, "Data-mining-based coronary heart disease risk prediction model using fuzzy logic and decision tree", *Healthc. Inform. Res.,* vol. 21, no. 3, pp. 167-174, 2015.
[http://dx.doi.org/10.4258/hir.2015.21.3.167] [PMID: 26279953]

[11]   L. Jiang, C. Li, S. Wang, and L. Zhang, "Deep feature weighting for naive Bayes and its application to text classification", *Eng. Appl. Artif. Intell.,* vol. 52, pp. 26-39, 2016.
[http://dx.doi.org/10.1016/j.engappai.2016.02.002]

[12]   H. Li, M. Luo, and J. Zheng, "An artificial neural network prediction model of congenital heart disease based on risk factors", *Medicine (Baltimore),* vol. 96, no. 6, 2017.e6090
[http://dx.doi.org/10.1097/MD.0000000000006090] [PMID: 28178169]

[13]   S. Liu, J. Liu, J. Tang, J. Ji, J. Chen, and C. Liu, "Environmental risk factors for congenital heart disease in the Shandong Peninsula, China: a hospital-based case-control study", *J. Epidemiol.,* vol. 19, no. 3, pp. 122-130, 2009.
[http://dx.doi.org/10.2188/jea.JE20080039] [PMID: 19398851]

[14]   Yanhong Luo, *Predicting congenital heart defects: A comparison of three data mining methods.,* 2017.
[http://dx.doi.org/10.1371/journal.pone.0177811]

[15]   M. Jadhav, and A. Sattikar, *REVIEW of Application of Expert Systems in the Medicine, Sinhgad Institute of Management and Computer Application.* SIMCA, 2014.

[16]   M.I. Jordan, and T.M. Mitchell, "Machine learning: Trends, perspectives, and prospects", *Science,* vol. 349, no. 6245, pp. 255-260, 2015.
[http://dx.doi.org/10.1126/science.aaa8415] [PMID: 26185243]

[17]   Sarfaraz Masood, and Madhav Mehta, "Isolated word recognition using neural network", *Annual IEEE India Conference (INDICON). IEEE,* 2015.

[18]   National Health and Family Planning Commission of PRC, *National stocktaking report on birth defect prevention,* 2012.

[19]   P.K. Anooj, "Clinical decision support system: Risk level prediction of heart disease using weighted fuzzy rules", *Journal of King Saud University - Computer and Information Sciences,* vol. 24, no. 1, pp. 27-40, 2012.
[http://dx.doi.org/10.1016/j.jksuci.2011.09.002]

[20]   R. Detrano, A. Janosi, and W. Steinbrunn, "International application of a new probability algorithm for the diagnosis of coronary artery disease", *Am. J. Cardiol.,* vol. 64, no. 5, pp. 304-310, 1989.
[http://dx.doi.org/10.1016/0002-9149(89)90524-9] [PMID: 2756873]

[21]   A.G. Rekha, M.S. Abdulla, and S. Asharaf, "Artificial Intelligence Marketing: An application of a novel Lightly Trained Support Vector Data Description", *Journal of Information and Optimization Sciences,* vol. 37, no. 5, pp. 681-691, 2016.
[http://dx.doi.org/10.1080/02522667.2016.1191186]

[22]   Yong Song, "Clinical significance of circulating microRNAs as markers in detecting and predicting congenital heart defects in children", *Journal of translational medicine.,* vol. 16.1, p. 42, 2018.
[http://dx.doi.org/10.1186/s12967-018-1411-0]

[23]   L. Tapak, H. Mahjub, O. Hamidi, and J. Poorolajal, "Real-data comparison of data mining methods in prediction of diabetes in iran", *Healthc. Inform. Res.,* vol. 19, no. 3, pp. 177-185, 2013.
[http://dx.doi.org/10.4258/hir.2013.19.3.177] [PMID: 24175116]

[24]   K. Vanisree, "Decision support system for congenital heart disease diagnosis based on signs and symptoms using neural networks", *Int. J. Comput. Appl.,* vol. 19, no. 6, pp. 6-12, 2011.
[http://dx.doi.org/10.5120/2368-3115]

[25]   S.J. Yeh, H.C. Chen, and C.W. Lu, "Prevalence, mortality, and the disease burden of pediatric congenital heart disease in Taiwan", *Pediatr. Neonatol.,* vol. 54, no. 2, pp. 113-118, 2013.
[http://dx.doi.org/10.1016/j.pedneo.2012.11.010] [PMID: 23590956]

[26]   B. Edmonds, "Using localized 'Gossip' to structure distributed learning", *Proceedings of AISB Symposium on Socially Inspired Computing,* 2005pp. 1-12 Hatfield, UK

[27]   M. Gudadhe, K. Wankhade, and S. Dongre, "Decision support system for heart disease based on support vector machine and artificial neural network", *Proceedings of International Conference on Computer and Communication Technology (ICCCT),* 2010pp. 741-745 Allahabad, India
[http://dx.doi.org/10.1109/ICCCT.2010.5640377]

[28]   H. Kahramanli, and N. Allahverdi, "Design of a hybrid system for the diabetes and heart diseases", *Expert Syst. Appl.,* vol. 35, no. 1-2, pp. 82-89, 2008.
[http://dx.doi.org/10.1016/j.eswa.2007.06.004]

[29]   S. Palaniappan, and R. Awang, "Intelligent heart disease prediction system using data mining techniques", *Proceedings of IEEE/ACS International Conference on Computer Systems and Applications (AICCSA 2008),* 2008pp. 108-115 Doha, Qatar
[http://dx.doi.org/10.1109/AICCSA.2008.4493524]

[30]   Andrew K. Ewer, *Pulse Oximetry Screening for Critical Congenital Heart Defects: A Life-Saving Test for All Newborn Babies.,* p. 14, 2019.
[http://dx.doi.org/10.3390/ijns5010014]

[31]   S.S. Lightstone, T.J. Teorey, and T. Nadeau, *Physical Database Design: the database professional's guide to exploiting indexes, views, storage, and more.* Morgan Kaufmann, 2010.

[32]   E.F. Ewen, C.E. Medsker, and L.E. Dusterhoft, *Data warehousing in an integrated health system: building the business case.* ACM, 1998, pp. 47-53.
[http://dx.doi.org/10.1145/294260.294271]

[33]   M.H. Kuo, T. Sahama, A.W. Kushniruk, E.M. Borycki, and D.K. Grunwell, "Health big data analytics: current perspectives, challenges, and potential solutions. International Journal of Big Data Intelligence. 2014; 1(1- 2): 114-26. doi: 10", *IJBDI,* vol. 2014, 1504.063835

[34]   R. Aggarwal, and P. Thakral, "Meticulous Presaging Arrhythmia Fibrillation for Heart Disease Classification Using Oversampling Method for Multiple Classifiers Based on Machine Learning", In: *Advances in Data Computing, Communication and Security. Lecture Notes on Data Engineering and Communications Technologies.,* P. Verma, C. Charan, X. Fernando, S. Ganesan, Eds., vol. Vol. 106. Springer: Singapore, 2022.
[http://dx.doi.org/10.1007/978-981-16-8403-6_9]

[35]   R. Aggarwal, and S. Kumar, "An automated perception and prediction of heart disease based on machine learning", In: *AIP Conference Proceedings* vol. 2424. Publishing LLC, 2022no. 1, .
[http://dx.doi.org/10.1063/5.0076788]

CHAPTER 4

A Review on Covid-19 Pandemic and Role of Multilingual Information Retrieval and Machine Translation for Managing its Effect

Mangala Madankar[1,*] and **Manoj Chandak**[2]

[1] *Research Scholar, G H Raisoni College of Engineering, Nagpur, India*

[2] *Ramdeobaba College of Engineering and Management, Nagpur, India*

Abstract: Novel Coronavirus disease 2019 (COVID-19) was initiated in the town of Wuhan, Hubei Province, Central China, and has multiplied speedily to 215 nations to date. Around 178,837,204 confirmed cases and 3880450 deaths had been reported across the globe till 23 June 2021. The exceptional outburst of the 2019 novel coronavirus called COVID-19 around the world has placed numerous governments in a precarious position. Most of the governments found no solution except imposing fractional or full lockdown. The laboratories grew rapidly across the globe to test and confirm the rate of disease spread. The disease had adverse effects on the global economy. This chapter focuses on using technology on languages such as NLP, Multilingual Information Retrieval Systems, and Machine Translation to evaluate the impact of covid-19 outbreaks and manage it.

Keywords: Covid 19 Pandemic, Information Retrieval, Multilingual Information Retrieval, Machine Translation, Natural Language Processing.

INTRODUCTION

Orthocoronavirinae, Order Nidovirale, is the the family of novel coronavirus. There are four types of viruses in this group *i.e.*, Alpha (α-CoV) Coronavirus, Beta (β-CoV) Coronavirus, Gamma (γ –CoV) Coronavirus and Delta (δ-CoV) Coronavirus. COVID-19 is an abbreviation for "Coronavirus-Disease-2019". This is a respiratory illness disease initiated by severe-acute-respiratory-syndr-me-coronavirus-2 (SARS-CoV-2). [1] Similar to virus influenza SARS-CoV-2 damage the human body's breathing function and causes illnesses like cough, fatigue, and fever. SARS-CoV-2 belongs to the β-CoV coronavirus family, although exact initiation of the virus is still mysterious and it derives its gene sources from rodents and bats, according to scientists. [1].

[*] **Corresponding author Mangala Madankar:** G H Raisoni College of Engineering, Nagpur, India;
E-mail: mangala.madankar@raisoni.net

In December 2019, the COVID-19 infection appeared in the city of Wuhan in China and spread to 215 countries of the world. The worst affected countries of the world by COVID-19 are shown in Fig. (**1**) . This article brings the basic analysis of COVID-19 disease and the role of current technologies such as information retrieval, machine translation, and multilingual information retrieval. How efficiently these technologies could help in providing the correct pandemic information, awareness among the people, knowledge of safety precaution, treatment, and diagnosis is the basic purpose of this article, This information would be available in native language of the user to moderate the pandemic adverse effect and save lives.

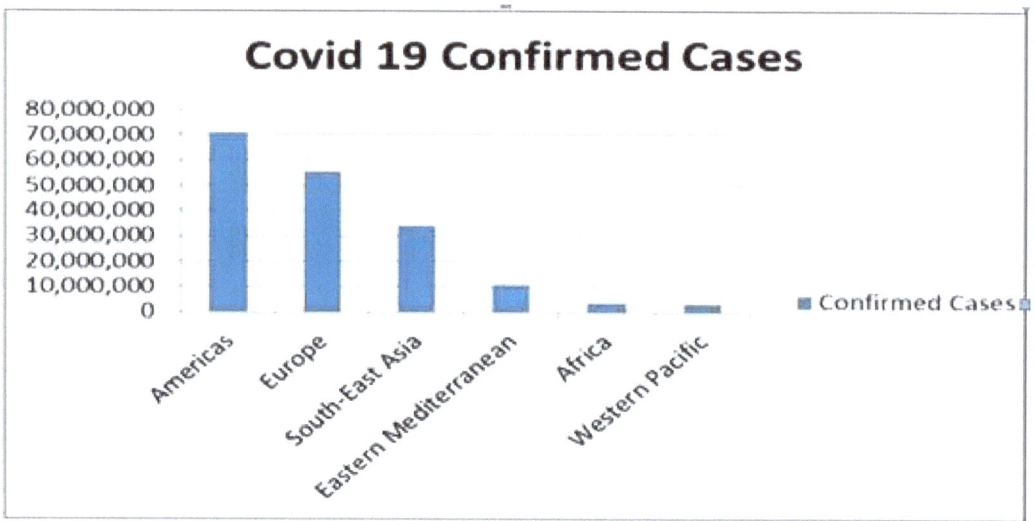

Fig. (1). Top regions affected by Covid-19 WHO Report – (23 June 2021).

This paper is organized into five sections; first section is the introduction. In section II, existing work on COVID-19 pandemic is discussed. In section III, we discuss various stages of transmission of COVID-19 disease. Section IV includes disease mechanism, the current method of diagnosis, safety precautions, treatment and preventive measures, while section V lists the progressing tools and technologies for moderating the influence of COVID-19 pandemic effectively. Finally, section 6 concludes the paper.

RELATED WORK

Viral infections, especially caused by various coronaviruses, have become a severe community health problem, according to WHO [2]. Coronaviruses are positive sense spherical RNA viruses having a diameter of 600Å-1400 Å [3], with proteins like spikes protruding structures on their surfaces. In the last two decades, we have witnessed the appearance of various viral outbreaks like coronavirus, such as the SARS-CoV outbreak in 2002-2004 [4], and in 2012 infection of (MERS-CoV) respiratory syndrome coronavirus. SARS-CoV and MERS-CoV outbreaks originated in China and Saudi Arabia, respectively. 31 December 2019, the COVID-19 outbreak occurred when 27 cases of unknown etiology pneumonia were presented at China's WHO office. The outbreak epicenter was connected to the wholesale market of exotic animals like bats, snakes, and marmots as well as other seafood of Wuhan in China [5].

A novel twists of extremely contagious SARS-CoV-2, β-coronavirus has been reasoned accountable for the quick epidemic of COVID-19. Unique distinctiveness of the virus consists of its exceptionally infectious character and comparatively extensive (1-14 days) incubation time. A human being can be contaminated by the disease without having a single symptom at all. And hence people contaminated by the disease may silently transmit the disease unknowingly. Substantial epidemic of COVID-19 has provoked a range of laboratories, researchers, scientists and organizations around the world to carry out a huge levels of investigation to come up with vaccines and other protocols to treat patients. To search out the treatment protocol for COVID-19 disease, the medical history of 138 infected patients, their demographics, signs and symptoms are assessed carefully by the scientist and the author mentioned in the paper [6]. In the paper [7], Author has published a case study of 99 patients affected by COVID-19 in Wuhan, China. In this study, the patient's clinical, epidemiological and radiological characteristics of the disease have been mentioned. Their study mentioned that 17% developed acute respiratory syndromes and 11% died due to multiple organ dysfunction syndromes. In the paper [8] author Fang *et al.* have presented treatment and outline of clinical features of COVID-19. In paper [9] author reviewed the Google scholar, PubMed and Elsevier platform for tomography characteristics of COVID-19. Paper [10 - 13] provide transitory outline of clinical aspects, diagnosis and treatment of COVID-19 outbreak. Paper [14] presents an adaptive immune reaction against SARS-CoV-2 virus. Also, the author studied the generation of monoclonal antibodies by antibody generating cells while caring for and after acute infection. Author Vinay Chamola at el. in paper [1] present the role of Artificial Intelligence, Drones, Internet of Things, Block chain, and 5G technologies in managing the COVID-19 pandemic.

OUTBREAK STAGE OF COVID 19

At the time of writing this research paper, a huge amount of research in the domain of COVID-19 disease has been published worldwide. But no effort in the present works attempts to review the role of emerging skills such as information retrieval, multilingual information retrieval, and machine translation for managing the situatioduring the COVID-19 pandemic as well as carrying out research after the pandemic. Covid-19 pandemic is classified into four different stages according to WHO. This classification of transmission remains constant all over the world. Due to this classification, many countries like India have decided to lockdown at the early stage to prevent the outbreak. In India, from 16 march, all school, colleges, malls and cinema halls shut their doors, and even travel bans. Following are the four stages of transmission of COVID-19 disease.

Travel history from infected countries

The initial step of the Covid-19 outbreak is when cases of infected people are imported from affected countries. In this case, local transmission is not activated. The disease is limited to the patient only who has a travel history.

Local Transmission

Local transmission is the second step of the outbreak of COVID-19. At this stage, people who come across direct contact with the infected person may be infected. The disease may be limited at this stage by contact tracing of infected person and by quarantining and social distancing measures from the patient.

Geographical Cluster of Cases

The geographical cluster is the third phase of the outbreak of COVID-19. At this stage, the virus infects the individual neither in contact with someone who does nor has a history of travel. At this stage, finding the origin of the virus spread is difficult. A sealed geographical area is highly recommended to prevent the disease.

Community Transmission

Fourth and last stage of COVID-19 pandemic is related to community transmission. At this level extremely high number of positive cases and death have been reported. Outbreak gets out of control at this stage and vaccine or cure is the only solution to fight the disease's impact. Country like India is currently in the fourth stage *i.e.*, community spreading.

CURRENT SITUATION IN INDIA

Now a Full-blown Community Transmission is happening in Bangalore, Karnataka and Maharashtra, India. The virus is more widespread across India. The SARS-CoV-2 virus is roaming wild, often not leaving any trace to create the sequence of transmission. The pandemic is in different phases in different states of India; hence it difficult to overhaul the policy altogether.

TREATMENT

Disease COVID-19, triggered by SARS-CoV-2, a novel coronavirus, has steered the globe into an exceptional state of alarm. Neither exact nor definite treatment for COVID-19 yet exists, not a preventive vaccine. Many scientists are working on the preventive vaccine, and this is in testing mode itself.

According to the WHO, two types of patient categories for COVID-19, symptomatic and asymptomatic, are having symptoms like dry cough, fever, headache, sore throat, loss of taste or smell and tiredness; these are the most common symptoms. Some serious symptoms include shortness of breath or difficulty breathing, chest discomfort, and loss of taste, speech and movement. Asymptomatic patients do not have any symptoms.

The treatment protocol for COVID-19 is almost symptomatic, the kind of treatment advised is totally based on the exact symptoms shown by the patients. Maximum cases of COVID-19 disease are asymptomatic, as mild and patients recover by themselves without the need for extra supportive care from the health system; therefore, home isolation is preferred in this case.

However, critical and serious cases of COVID-19 require hospitalization. In this case, patients who experience a high fever and difficulty in breathing may require additional oxygen *via* ventilators. Other problems may occur in the patients due to destabilized immune system by the coronavirus. These patients can be treated with antifungals and antibiotics on individual basis. Kidney can also be affected by Coronavirus And kidney replacement treatment may be need in some cases [15].

Whichever the case of COVID-19 diagnosed patient, one should be in strict isolation to prevent further transmission of the disease. Currently, no antivirus medicine and vaccine is available in the commercial market.

Many pharmaceutical organizations have developed possible medicines as a treatment to cure from coronavirus, but yet none of these medicine is accepted globally. WHO does not endorse self-medication with any drugs, including antibiotics as a treatment for COVID-19. Hydroxy choloroquine has the potential characteristics to fight pathological inflammation connected with COVID-19. Hydroxy chloroquine has been hypothesized to benefit controlling different effects of COVID-19 infection. This drug advises parallel antiviral and antiinflammatory properties having fewer side effects, signifying the finest choice for treating COVID-19 [16]. The next section shows the illness severity caused by COVID-19.

ILLNESS SEVERITY

The severity of COVID-19 diseases is shown in the statistics of Table **1**.

Table 1. Division of COVID-19 cases.

Sr. No	Various Cases of COVID-19	In %
1	Asymptomatic Cases	50 to 60 %
2	Symptomatic Cases	40 to 50 %
3	Mild to moderate Category (out of 40 to 50 % symptomatic Cases)	81%
4	Sever Category (hypoxia, dyspnea or > (50%) lung involvement on CT Scan (out of 40 to 50 % symptomatic Cases)	14%
5	Critical Category (Shock, respiratory failure or multi organ system dysfunction) Scan (out of 40 to 50 % symptomatic Cases)	5 %
6	Secondary attack rate	6%-(10 to 20 %)

Statistics show that nearly 50-60% of infected patients are asymptomatic. It totally depends on the immune system of the body and how the body treats this virus. Risk Factors for Severe Illness show age-related mortality risk as below Table **2**:

Table 2. Age related mortality risk.

Sr. No	Age(years)	Mortality Risk
1	80 and above-	14.8%
2	70–79	8.0%
3	60–69	3.6%
4	50–59	1.3%
5	40–49	0.4%
6	<40	0.2%

Case fatality was higher for patients with comorbidities like heart disease, diabetes, high BP, Cancer *etc.*: 6% to 10.5% [17]. Convalescent plasma (CP), or immune plasma, is one of the best treatments.

ANTIBODY AND PLASMA THERAPY

The patients who have already fought with COVID-19 disease and recovered from it can help in curing others by donating plasma against COVID-19. It gives a favorable outcome in acute patients. To neutralize COVID-19, the generation of recombinant human being monoclonal antibodies is a straight forward path. Convalescent plasma is first collected from the recovered person from COVID-19. This plasma is also called the Human-Anti-SARS-CoV-2 plasma. Later it is transfused into the patients suffering from infection *via* post-exposure prophylaxis. Plasma derived monoclonal antibodies are just like immunoglobulin (IgG) derived antibodies. CP is an inactive antibody treatment that exhibited some achievement as a deactivating antibody in contradiction to other coronavirus epidemics [18].

VACCINE

Co-vaccine from Bharath biologicals from Hyderabad, India.

- Oxford vaccine developed by Astra Zeneca,
- mRNA-1273 by Moderna and
- Russian vaccine- WHO

PREVENTIVE MEASURE

Prevention is always better than cure. As we know, countries fall sick with COVID-19 must take effective prevention to diminish the probability of flattering further victim. If persons and society adapt the practices for presentencing coronavirus, the globe may soon observe a compressed COVID-19 curve. The devastation of the arch indicates down the line the transmission of the COVID-19 infection to the scope of wherever accessible healthcare amenities can sufficiently hold the influence of the infection.

   i. Wash your hands regularly with water and soup or rub your hands with sanitizer containing more than 70% alcohol.
   ii. Practice for a safe distance of at least 2 meters from others.
  iii. Wear a mask whenever you go out. If you are using a washable mask, clean it carefully; otherwise, ensure proper disposal if you use and throw the mask.
   iv. Stay at home is safe, except it is absolutely essential to go out. Persons older than 60, citizens with fundamental physical condition, and pregnant ladies are particularly guided to reside away from community gatherings.
   v. Without systematic sanitization of your hands, do not touch your nose, mouth and eyes.
   vi. Commonly used things such as doorknobs, light switches, laptops and phones should be routinely disinfectant as well as touched surfaces and desks should be cleaned regularly.

vii. Cover your nose and mouth with your bent elbow or tissue while sneezing and coughing.

viii. Stay at home if you are not feeling well.

ix. If you have tiredness, cough, fever and difficulty breathing, take medical treatment immediately [19].

COVID-19 outbreak emphasizes subsequent good practices in maintaining hygiene's. It is essential to note that good eating habits and regular exercise should be followed in daily life to maintain good immune system of the body not only for COVID situation but also after it.

Myths

Some myths are there that drinking hot water and gargling can prevent coronavirus infection; in reality, COVID-19 can indeed cause a sore throat and gargle with hot and salty water may get feeling better, but it has not a direct effect on the virus.

Another myth is that "steam inhaling is a good treatment for COVID-19 infection" This is not true. There is no evidence that the virus can kill by inhaling steam. When a person is infected with a virus, the virus is present inside human cells, hence inhaling steam will not affect it [20].

EMERGING TECHNOLOGY FOR MITIGATING THE EFFECT OF THE COVID-19 PANDEMIC

Since December 2019, the novel coronavirus COVID-19 has continued its attack across the world. World is facing this pandemic's effects on health issues, psychology, and the crazing economy due to the long lockdown period in many countries. Billions of individuals are suffering from the threat of this infection. In every second, deaths are recorded worldwide. Circumstances are not likely to get well again in the upcoming days. However, to handle the COVID-19 pandemic's enormous use of technological approaches is emerging.

Various e-technologies play an important role in the COVID-19 pandemic to improve public health [1].

The first step in this pandemic is to provide awareness regarding COVID-19 disease and its preventive measures in people's native languages all over the world. In the following section, we are listing the digital technologies which can use to mitigate the effect of the COVID-19 pandemic.

Infodemic and Natural Language Processing

In the COVID-19 pandemic, people are fighting not only with the epidemic but also with the infodemics; infodemics are an excessive quantity of information about the problem, making it complex to recognize the clarification. This refers to fake news that spreads faster and more easily than the virus [21]. Much misinformation regarding the COVID-19 pandemic has been posted on social media. To control the spread of such false rumors and offer verified material, skill companies like YouTube, Facebook, and Google have employed NLP techniques.

With the help of natural language processing techniques, one can counter the spread of rumors and misinformation, such as hot weather kills the virus and high consumption of ginger and garlic can prevent the coronavirus; misinformation creates difficulty in searching for accurate lifesaving information related to hygiene, physical distancing, quarantine and preventive measures must reach to everyone to save the life's in this pandemic. Paper [22] presents how data extraction is carried out by using Natural Language Processing techniques.

Arogya Setu App

Aarogya Setu App, or a contact tracing App, is designed and developed by the National Informatics Centre, India's Department of IT and Electronics, in 11 native languages of India to benefit the people curb the transmission of COVID-19 disease in the country. Any citizen of India can download this mobile application to use the various services by registering their mobile number. On installing this application from the play store, firstly, it gives the option to the user to select the language, so the user can be comfortable interacting with the application and use Bluetooth and GPS for tracking data. The App is available for both Android and iOS users. The App also provides a database of all the relevant public information about the novel Coronavirus [23].

On launching the App Aarogya Setu, it became immediately famous among the people. In just 5days of its release, 10 million Indian public get it downloaded. The government of India (GoI) has guaranteed the public that any other task will not use data collected by app except contact tracing and it is encrypted form always.

Issues of Languages all Over the World and Machine Translation

Languages matter in pandemics like the covid-19. Language is the fundamental part of gaining and understanding the knowledge of an individual. It is an intrinsic part of human rights and fundamental freedom of use. Table **3** shows the top 30 languages used worldwide with their native users. In this pandemic, correct information such as life-saving information, healthcare information, preventive measures, and myths should reach the individual in their native languages. Language translation in the medical field matters a lot because accurately translated information may save the life of an individual.

Table 3. Top 30 Languages by Number of Native Speaker.

Sr. No.	Language	Approximate # of Speakers
1	Mandarin Chinese	NATIVE: 873 million
		2nd: 178 million
		TOTAL: 1.051 billion
2	Hindi	NATIVE: 370 million
		2nd:120 million
		TOTAL: 490 million
3	Spanish	NATIVE: 350 million
		2nd: 70 million
		TOTAL: 420 million
4	English	NATIVE: 340 million
		TOTAL: 510 million
5	Arabic	NATIVE: 206 million
		2nd: 24 million
		TOTAL: 230 million
6	Portuguese	NATIVE: 203 million
		2nd: 10 million
		TOTAL: 213 million
7	Bengali	NATIVE: 196 million
		TOTAL: 215 million
8	Russian	NATIVE: 145 million
		2nd: 110 million
		TOTAL: 255 million
9	Japanese	NATIVE: 126 million
		2nd: 1 million
		TOTAL: 127 million
10	German	NATIVE: 101 million
		2nd: 128 million
		TOTAL: 229 million

(Table 3) cont.....

Sr. No.	Language	Approximate # of Speakers
11	Panjabi	Western: 60 million
		Eastern: 28 million
		TOTAL: 88 million
12	Javanese	76 million
13	Korean	71 million
14	Vietnamese	NATIVE: 70 million
		2nd: 16 million
		TOTAL: 86 million
15	Telugu	NATIVE: 70 million
		2nd: 5 million
		TOTAL: 75 million
16	Marathi	NATIVE: 68 million
		2nd: 3 million
		TOTAL: 71 million
17	Tamil	NATIVE: 68 million
		2nd: 9 million
		TOTAL: 77 million
18	French	NATIVE: 67 million
		2nd: 63 million
		TOTAL: 130 million
19	Urdu	NATIVE: 61 million
		2nd: 43 million
		TOTAL: 104 million
20	Italian	61 million
21	Turkish	NATIVE: 60 million
		2nd: 15 million
		TOTAL: 75 million
22	Persian	54 million
23	Gujarati	46 million
24	Polish	46 million
25	Ukrainian	39 million
26	Malayalam	37 million

(Table 3) cont.....

Sr. No.	Language	Approximate # of Speakers
27	Kannada	NATIVE: 35 million
		2nd: 9 million
		TOTAL: 44 million
28	Oriya	32 million
29	Burmese	NATIVE: 32 million
		2nd: 10 million
		TOTAL: 42 million
30	Thai	NATIVE: 20 million
		2nd: 40 million
		TOTAL: 60 million

[Source: https://www.vistawide.com/languages/top_30_languages.htm]

Machine translation has a key role in overcoming the translation issues of languages. Machine translation is used to translate information from the source language to its target language. Basically MT is a challenging task due to the large varieties of languages used worldwide as well as their corresponding vocabulary and different protocols of grammar. Sequences of sentences also maters for the correct translation of the input query. Paper [24] shows the various machine translation techniques used to translate one language into another. The Machine translation model in COVID-19 research is discussed in the paper [25]. Here the author has developed a multilingual and multi-domain neural machine translation model specialized for biomedical data. This model enables the translation of five languages into English, mainly French, German, Italian, Spanish and Korean.

Difficulties in Accessing Data in the Native Language

In this uncertain pandemic time of the COVID-19 outbreak, much information has been making rounds on the internet. Everyone is trying to access the data like articles on preventive measures, current cases, medical reports and much informative knowledge in their native language to understand the pandemic in a better way [26]. In this paper, the author presents a novel approach to accessing information in the user's native language. Many researchers have worked on this approach to get the information in the user's native language. For accessing the data in the native language, machine translation with information retrievals like cross-lingual information retrieval and multilingual information retrieval play a key role. C-DAC, IIT Bombay and FIRE agencies have done tremendous work in the field of Machine Translation for Indian languages. Many researchers worldwide have developed machine translation systems for their national languages. By using all these concepts of science and technology, all related information regarding COVID-19 can reach the common man in his native language. This could help in spreading awareness among people and save lives.

INFORMATION RETRIEVAL SYSTEM FOR COVID-19

New Information Retrieval System for COVID-19: TREC COVID

TREC-COVID is a new approach to information retrieval systems to design and estimate approaches to optimize search engines for the existing and speedily growing number of technical papers about Covid-19 and related subjects. Document Collection for TREC-COVID comes from the Allen Institute for Artificial Intelligence; they have developed (CORD-19) the COVID-19 Open Research dataset, a free resource of academic articles about COVID-19 and other coronaviruses [27].

CO-Search: COVID-19 Information Retrieval

Co-search is the COVID-19 information-retrieval- system with question answering, semantic search, and abstractive summarization. It is a scientific search engine over the growing corpus of coronavirus literature and publications. CO-Search is a retriever ranker semantic search engine developed to input complex questions over the literature of COVID-19, possibly helping overworked health workers search for scientific solutions during a crisis [28].

COVID-19 Dataset Search System

Information retrieval system for COVID-19-related data is created based on the document released by COVID-19 research challenge. Here ETL is used to parse the document corpus and store body text in tables and metadata in SQLite databases so that the sentence-level information can be efficiently queried. Whatever context is accessed by the database again, is converted into the user's native language. For measuring the model's performance, achieved results can be measured in terms of accuracy and precision.

The given system uses a combination of Natural Language Processing and AI techniques to find the best matching sentences. The demo URL for the search query is presented with the following link. https://telesens.co/covid-demo/main.html [29].

Role of Cross-lingual and Multilingual Information Retrieval in COVID-19 Pandemic

To access the information in the user's native language, multilingual information retrieval plays a vital role independent of in which language data is stored in a database. If information is stored in a database in one language and query in another, then it is called a cross-language information retrieval system. And suppose the information is stored in different languages in a cloud database and the information accessing query is also in more than one language. In that case, this method is called the multilingual information retrieval system.

To solve the issue of the language barrier in this pandemic, a novel model is suggested in Fig. (**2**). Global dataset of the COVID-19 pandemic is stored in a cloud environment, and end users try to access the information in their native language. Typically this model is planned for n number of native natural languages. The query input model can accept the separate queries at the input level, then translate the queries into English language and perform information retrieval process.

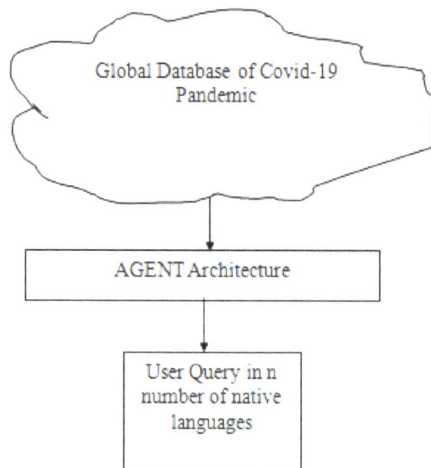

Fig. (2). Research design for multilingual information system in COVID-19 Pandemic.

Challenges in Machine Translation, Information Retrieval and MLIR system

MLIR Systems and machine translation can conceivably play a vital role in moderating the influence of the COVID-19 pandemic and related research. Currently however MLIR and MT are still at the prefatory stages. Numerous limitations and challenges hampering the applications of MLIR in COVID-19 influence managing are listed below [30, 31].

1. Natural language processing is highly complex. To yield THE accurate and reliable results of machine translation, bilingual dictionaries are needed.
2. Another limitation faced by the MT system is word translation problem, Phrase Translation problem, Syntactic Translation Problem and Semantic Translation

Problem.

3. To yield the accurate result from the MT model, statistic machine translation requires a substantial amount of training data.
4. To make an optimised search engine on special data is again a challenging task.
5. For COVID-19, the dataset varies on a daily basis, so making the IR system based on corpus is challenging.

CONCLUSION

This article discusses COVID-19 and explores the current status of COVID-19 worldwide, the top countries affected by COVID-19, outbreak stages of COVID-19, disease mechanism, transmission mechanism, the current method of diagnosis, safety precautions, treatment and preventive measures and illness severity. Further discussion focuses on emerging technologies such as machine translation, information retrieval, multilingual information retrieval and the role of language in managing the COVID-19 pandemic. This paper present the quantity of work carried out on COVID-19 pandemic in the form of information research.

CONSENT FOR PUBLICATION

Not applicable.

CONFLICT OF INTEREST

The authors declare no conflict of interest, financial or otherwise.

ACKNOWLEDGEMENT

Declared none.

REFERENCES

[1]   Vinay Chamola, Vikas Hassija, Vatsal Gupta, and Mohsen Huizani, "A Comprehensive Review of the COVID-19 Pandemic and role of IoT,Drones, AI, Blockchain and 5G in Managing its effect", *Special Section On Deep LearningAlgorithms For Internet Of Medical Things,* 2020.
        [http://dx.doi.org/10.1109/ACCESS.2020.2992341]

[2]   M. Cascella, M. Rajnik, A. Cuomo, S.C. Dulebohn, and R. Di Napoli, Features, evaluation and treatment coronavirus (COVID-19).*StatPearls.* StatPearls Publishing: Treasure Island, FL, USA, 2020.https://www.ncbi.nlm.nih.gov/books/NBK554776/ updated 2020 Apr 6 Internet [Online]

[3]   T. Singhal, "A review of coronavirus disease-2019 (COVID-19)", *Indian J. Pediatrics,* vol. 87, no. 4, pp. 281-286>, 2020.
        [http://dx.doi.org/10.1007/s12098-020-03263-6]

[4]   M. Chan-Yeung, and R. Xu, "SARS: Epidemiology", *Respirology,* vol. 8, pp. S9-S14, 2003.
        [http://dx.doi.org/10.1046/j.1440-1843.2003.00518.x]

[5]   C. Sohrabi, Alsa_, N. O'Neill, M. Khan, A. Kerwan, A. Al-Jabir, C. Iosi_dis, and R. Agha, "World

health organization declares global emergency: A review of the 2019 novel coronavirus (COVID-19)", *Int. J. Surgery,* vol. 76, pp. 71-76, 2020.

[6]   D. Wang, B. Hu, C. Hu, F. Zhu, X. Liu, J. Zhang, B. Wang, H. Xiang, Z. Cheng, Y. Xiong, Y. Zhao, Y. Li, X. Wang, and Z. Peng, "Clinical characteristics of 138 hospitalized patients with 2019 novel coronavirus_ infected pneumonia in Wuhan, China", *JAMA,* vol. 323, no. 11, pp. 1061-1069, 2020.
[http://dx.doi.org/10.1001/jama.2020.1585] [PMID: 32031570]

[7]   N. Chen, M. Zhou, X. Dong, J. Qu, F. Gong, Y. Han, Y. Qiu, and J. Wang, "Epidemiological and clinical characteristics of 99 cases of 2019 novel coronavirus pneumonia in Wuhan, China: A descriptive study", *Lancet,* vol. 395, no. 10223, pp. 507-513, 2020.

[8]   F. Jiang, L. Deng, L. Zhang, Y. Cai, C. W. Cheung, and Z. Xia, "Review of the clinical characteristics of coronavirus disease 2019 (COVID-19)", *J. Gen. Internal Med.,* vol. 35, pp. 1545-1549, 2020.
[http://dx.doi.org/10.1007/s11606-020-05762-w]

[9]   S. Salehi, A. Abedi, S. Balakrishnan, and A. Gholamrezanezhad, "Coronavirus disease 2019 (COVID-19): A systematic review of imaging _ndings in 919 patients", *Amer. J. Roentgenol.,* pp. 1-7, 2020.
[http://dx.doi.org/10.2214/AJR.20.23034]

[10]   Hidde Heesakkers, W. Devlin John, and J.C> Arjen, *Association between delirium prediction scores and days spent with delirium.* Elsevier, 2020.
[http://dx.doi.org/10.1016/j.jcrc.2020.03.008]

[11]   Simone Piva, Matteo Filippini, Fabio Turla, Sergio Cattaneo, Alessio Margola, Silvia De Fulviis, Ida Nardiello, Alessandra Beretta, Laura Ferrari, Raffaella Trotta, Gloria Erbici, Emanuele Focà, Francesco Castelli, Frank Rasulo, Michael J. Lanspa, and Nicola Latronico, *Clinical presentation and initial management critically ill patients with severe acute respiratory syndrome coronavirus 2 (SARS-CoV-2) infection in Brescia, Italy.,* .
[http://dx.doi.org/10.1016/j.jcrc.2020.04.004]

[12]   Xiya Ma, *Critical care capacity during the COVID-19 pandemic: Global availability of intensive care beds.* Elsevier, 2020.
[http://dx.doi.org/10.1016/j.jcrc.2020.04.012]

[13]   Ernest van Veen, Mathieu van der Jagt, Giuseppe Citerio, Nino Stocchetti, Jelle L. Epker, Diederik Gommers, Lex Burdorf, David K. Menon, Andrew I.R. Maas, Hester F. Lingsma, and Erwin J.O. Kompanje, "End-of-life practices in traumatic brain injury patients: Report of a questionnaire from the CENTER-TBI study",
[http://dx.doi.org/10.1016/j.jcrc.2020.04.001]

[14]   N. Jennifer, Thomas J. Manley, Emily Svejnoha, "The ImmuneRACE Study: A Prospective Multicohort Study of Immune Response Action to COVID-19 Events with the ImmuneCODE™ Open Access Database",
[http://dx.doi.org/10.1101/2020.08.17.20175158]

[15]   D. Wang, B. Hu, C. Hu, F. Zhu, X. Liu, J. Zhang, B. Wang, H. Xiang, Z. Cheng, Y. Xiong, Y. Zhao, Y. Li, X. Wang, and Z. Peng, "Clinical characteristics of 138 hospitalized patients with 2019 novel coronavirus– infected pneumonia in Wuhan, China", *JAMA,* vol. 323, no. 11, pp. 1061-1069, 2020.
[http://dx.doi.org/10.1001/jama.2020.1585] [PMID: 32031570]

[16]   X. Li, Y. Wang, P. Agostinis, A. Rabson, G. Melino, E. Carafoli, Y. Shi, and E. Sun, "Is hydroxychloroquine beneficial for COVID-19 patients?", *Cell Death Dis.,* vol. 11, no. 7, p. 512, 2020.
[http://dx.doi.org/10.1038/s41419-020-2721-8]

[17]   N. Chen, M. Zhou, X. Dong, J. Qu, F. Gong, Y. Han, Y. Qiu, J. Wang, Y. Liu, Y. Wei, J. Xia, T. Yu, X. Zhang, and L. Zhang, "Epidemiological and clinical characteristics of 99 cases of 2019 novel coronavirus pneumonia in Wuhan, China: A descriptive study", *Lancet,* vol. 395, no. 10223, pp. 507-513, 2020.
[http://dx.doi.org/10.1016/S0140-6736(20)30211-7]

[18]   A. Jaime, *Convalescent plasma: A possible treatment of COVID-19 in India.,* vol. 76, no. 2, pp. 236-

237, 2020.
[http://dx.doi.org/10.1016/j.mjafi.2020.04.006]

[19] World Health Organization, https://www.who.int/emergencies/diseases/novelcoronavirus-2019/advice-

[20] Digital Medic, Available online at: https://digitalmedic.stanford.edu/myth/myth-inhaling-steam-i--an-effective-covid-19-treatment/

[21] A. Guterres, *UN tackles 'infodemic' of misinformation and cybercrime in COVID-19 crisis,* 2020.https://www.un.org/en/un-coronavirus-communications-team/un-tacking-%E2%80%98infodemic%E2%80%99-misinformation-and-cybercrime-covid-19

[22] Sujata More, and Mangala Madankar, "Data Extractions using natural language processing tools", *Helix Internation Journal ESCI,* vol. 8, no. 5, pp. 3846-3848, 2018.

[23] TechRadar India, https://www.techradar.com/in/news/indian-government-launchesaarogya-se

[24] M. Madankar, "Dr. M.B. Chandak, Nekita Chavhan, "Information Retrieval System and Machine Translation: A Review", In: *International Conference on Information Security and Privacy (ICISP2015)*Nagpur, INDIA, 2015.

[25] A. Berard, M. Gallé, Z.M. Kim, V. Nikoulina, and L. Park, "A machine translation model for Covid-19 research", *Blog.* Available online: https://europe.naverlabs.com/blog/a-machine-translation-moel-for-covid-19-research/

[26] Mangala Madankar, "Multilingual Information Retrieval System: A Design Approach", *Helix International Journal ESCI,* vol. 8, no. 5, pp. 3863-3867, 2018.

[27] Ellen Voorhees, Tasmeer Alam Steven Bedrick, Dina Demner-Fushman, William R Hersh, Kyle Lo, Kirk Roberts; TREC-COVID: Constructing a Pandemic Information Retrieval Test Collection, Available online: https://lhncbc.nlm.nih.gov/publication/pub10054

[28] A. Esteva, A. Kale, R. Paulus, K. Hashimoto, W. Yin, D. Radev, and R. Socher, "CO-Search: COVID-19 Information Retrieval with Semantic Search, Question Answering, and Abstractive Summarization", https://arxiv.org/abs/2006.09595

[29] https://www.telesens.co/2020/06/10/building-a-information-retrieval-system-based-on-the-covid-19-research-challenge-dataset-part-1/

[30] H. Mohamed, "A Brief Study of Challenges in Machine Translation", *IJCSI International Journal of Computer Science,* vol. 14, no. 2, 2017..

[31] P. Koehn, and R. Knowles, "Six Challenges for Neural Machine Translation", *Proceedings of the First Workshop on Neural Machine Translation,* 2017pp. 28-39 Vancouver, Canada
[http://dx.doi.org/10.18653/v1/W17-3204]

[32] Vishal Dinesh kumar Soni Information Technologies: Shaping The World Under The Pandemic Covid 19", Vol 11, Issue 6,June/ 2020 Issn No: 0377-9254.

CHAPTER 5

An Empirical View of Genetic Machine Learning based on Evolutionary Learning Computations

M. Chandraprabha[1] and **Rajesh Kumar Dhanaraj**[1,*]

[1] *Galgotias College of Engineering and Technology, Galgotias University, Greater Noida, India*

Abstract: The only prerequisite in the past era was human intelligence, but today's world is full of artificial intelligence and its obstacles, which must still be overcome. It could be said that anything from cars to household items must be artificially intelligent. Everyone needs smartphones, vehicles, and machines. Some kind of intelligence is required by all at all times. Since computers have become such an integral part of our lives, it has become essential to develop new methods of human-computer interaction. Finding an intelligent way of machine and user interaction is one of the most crucial steps in meeting the requirement. The motivations for developing artificial intelligence and artificial life can be traced back to the dawn of the computer era. As always, evolution is a case of shifting phenomena. Adaptive computer systems are explicitly designed to search for problem-specific solutions in the face of changing circumstances. It has been said before that evolution is a massively parallel quest method that never works on a single species or a single solution at any given time. Many organisms are subjected to experiments and modifications. As a result, this write-up aims to create Artificial Intelligence, superior to machine learning that can master these problems, ranging from traditional methods of automatic reasoning to interaction strategies with evolutionary algorithms. The result is evaluated with a piece of code for predicting optimal test value after learning.

Keywords: Evolutionary computation, Evolutionary algorithms, Fitness stage, Genetic and Heredity, Population, Stochastic.

INTRODUCTION

Evolutionary algorithms (EAs) are a type of optimization algorithm that uses a meta heuristics approach to solve problems. Selection, mutation, and crossover are all genetic operators it goes through [1]. It iteratively expands candidate solutions set based on the survival of the fittest theorem. The methodology of the "black box"character distinguishes evolutionary algorithms from other approaches

---

[*] **Corresponding author Rajesh Kumar Dhanaraj:** Galgotias College of Engineering and Technology, Galgotias University, Greater Noida, India; E-mail: sangeraje@gmail.com

Prasad Lokulwar, Basant Verma, N. Thillaiarasu, Kailash Kumar, Mahip Bartere and Dharam Singh (Eds.)

that are often referred to as evolutionary optimization methods. It also relies on very few conclusions regarding the objective functions that underpin it. Even the concept of an objective function is simple since it excludes systemic problems from the problem at hand and allows for the creation of an admissible heuristic by individuals. These features improve the efficiency of evolutionary algorithms across a wide variety of problem domains. (Fig. **1**) illustrates the fundamental steps to be followed while applying the evolutionary-based algorithms for the applications [2]. This chapter will cover the fundamental concepts and properties of evolutionary algorithms, as well as probability theory and stochastic processes. Before reading this novel, it is presumed that the reader has taken a simple probability and statistics course. As a result, the aim is to assist the reader in refreshing their memory and establishing a common language and set of notations through the evolutionary procedure in deep learning. Random processes will be briefly analyzed [3], and some basic principles will be stated, in addition to probability and random variables. Finally, basic concepts and properties relevant to knowledge theory will be summarized at the end of the chapter. This chapter can be skipped by readers who are familiar with all of these concepts.

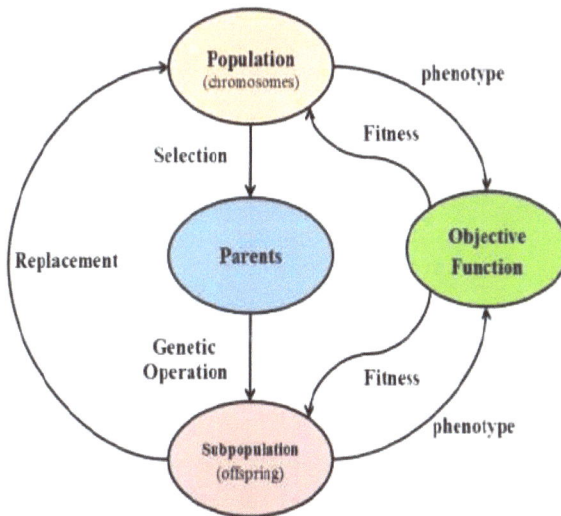

Fig. (1). Basic notions of evolutionary algorithms

Preamble of Evolutionary Algorithms (EA)

Evolutionary Algorithms (EA) are heuristic search techniques focused on artificial reproduction of the processes that underpin living organism evolution. Natural selection and genetics are the two primary pillars. In his book "Origin of Species by Means of Natural Selection," Charles Darwin describes natural selection for the first time in his own words, " [4]... if variations useful to any organic being occur, individuals thus characterized will almost certainly have the best chance of surviving in the fight for life; and, due to the strong theory of inheritance, they will almost certainly produce offspring similarly characterized. For the sake of brevity, I've dubbed this preservation theory Natural Selection."

Biological evolution has created autonomous, highly complex living beings capable of solving difficult problems such as continuous adaptation to an unpredictable and ever-changing world. The wide variety of settings in which life achieves integration demonstrates that the evolutionary process is resilient and capable of solving complex problems. Indeed, EA has been used to solve difficult problems where other optimization algorithms [5] have failed to deliver satisfactory results. Three core ideas underpin all evolutionary algorithms: Individuals with differences that better match them to the world are more likely to have more offspring.

Heredity: Children mimic their parents but are never identical to them.

Variability: Minor differences in offspring can have a major impact on survival chances.

Both evolutionary algorithms adopt the working structure depicted in Fig. (**2**) and advance in the following manner:

1. First, a population Pop of individuals p is generated with a random genome p g.

2. For each candidate solution p. x in Pop, the values of the fitness functions f are computed. This assessment can include complex simulations and calculations.

3. The utility of the different features of the solution candidates has been determined using the fitness functions, and a fitness value v (p) has been measured.

4. A subsequent screening procedure eliminates solution candidates in poor physical condition, allowing those in good physical condition to reach the mating pool with a higher probability. Since fitness can be enhanced, the lower the v (p. x)-values are, the higher the (relative) utility of the person to whom they belong [6].

5. Offspring are generated in the reproduction process by adjusting or combining the genotypes p. g of the selected individuals' p Mate using the search algorithm. Search Op $\in$ Op (which are called reproduction operations in the context of EAs).

After that, the offspring are reintroduced into the population.

6. If the termination conditions are met, the evolution will come to a halt at this stage. If not, the algorithm moves on to step 2.

There is no such thing as "sex" in evolutionary algorithms. Any member of the mating pool has the ability to be recombined with every other member [7].

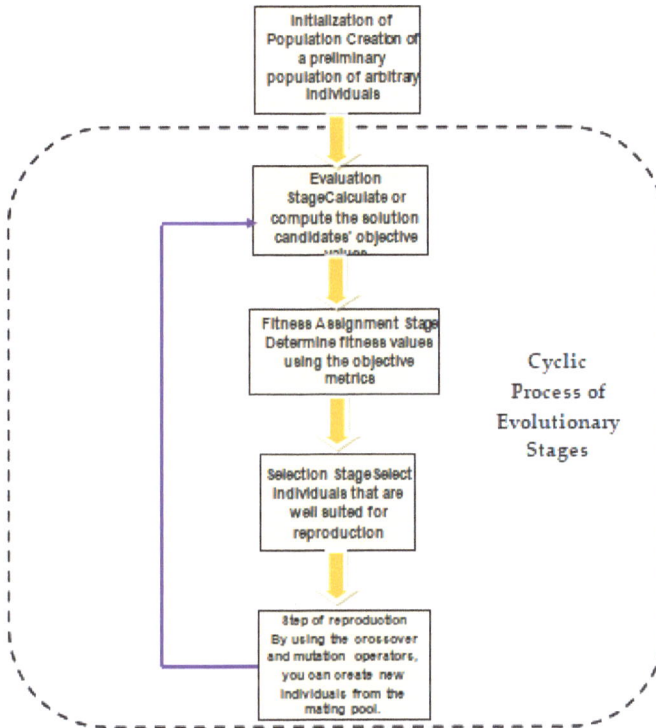

Fig. (2). Cycle of Evolutionary Stages

Contextual Parameters of EA

Individuals who apply evolution laws are candidate solutions in the EA sense, offering a more or less successful response (reply) to a specific issue. These answers fit into a search space defined by the exam issue. The EA method aims to enhance individual output in an iterative, step-by-step manner [8]. The first step is to create a new population made up of N randomly created individuals. The fitness function then begins the assessment process and assigns a performance degree or fitness value to each person. The concept of the fitness function is dependent on the objective function, and it is not always an easy task that differs by domain. After that, this population evolves for a number of generations [9] before it meets a termination criterion. Individuals can reproduce, survive, or disappear from the population in each generation, depending on the actions of two selection operators:

Selection for reproduction: This means that solutions with above-average output can be included in the reproduction phase more frequently. According to Darwin's theory [10], the healthier a person is, the better his/her chances of survival are.

The variation operators process the selected solutions (copies) after that. Selection for replacement: decides which individuals must be removed [11] from the population in order to maintain constant population size or, in certain cases, to regulate population size according to a specific strategy.

It is important to transform individuals using a collection of variation operators in order to find better solutions than those found in the current population (or genetic operators). Mutation and replication are the two primary variation operators in EAs [12] (also called recombination or crossover). Crossover exchanges certain characteristics of a group (usually two) individuals to produce offspring that are a combination of their parents.

Mutation changes a small part of the individual's structure, while crossover changes a large part of the individual's structure. The expertise gained in the field of genetics has influenced these operators. Since it introduces new genetic material into the population, the mutation operator may be called an invention operator [13]. Conversely, Crossover is a conservation operator since it only redistributes genetic material already present in the population. These variation operators aim to create better individuals through stochastic changes in their structure. Genotype refers to an individual's syntactical structure, which is a basis for genetic knowledge. The genotype is decoded into phenotype, which can be related to the climate. i.e., the topic to be addressed. Selection works on the phenotype, changing the likelihood of genetic information scattering in subsequent generations based on the degree of adaptation. Variation operators such as mutation and recombination, on the other hand, operate on the genotype.

CLASSIFICATION OF EVOLUTIONARY ALGORITHMS

The evolution is geared toward environmental adaptation. Randomness (mutation, recombination operators) and selection combine to form the evolutionary scheme (which directs the choice of the genotypes involved in the next generation). The disorder arises from randomness, while order arises from the selection.

The Family of Evolutionary Algorithms

As seen in Fig. (**3**), the evolutionary algorithm family consists of five members:

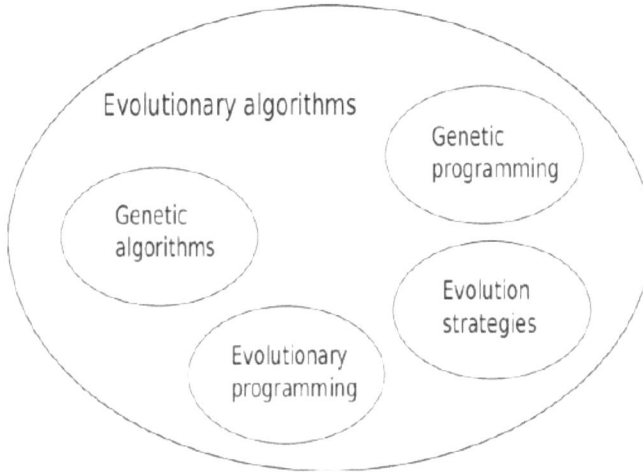

Fig. (3). Members of EA

1. Genetic programming (GAs). All evolutionary algorithms with bit strings are referred to as GAs.

2. Evolution Strategies refer to a group of evolutionary algorithms that look into the space of real vectors X Rn.

3. Genetically Modified Species (GMS/GP). There are two options for definitions: GP includes all evolutionary algorithms that evolve programmes, algorithms, and the like. Second, all EAs that produce tree-shaped individuals use Genetic Programming.

4. Online learning methods that assign output values to specified input values are known as Learning Classifier Systems (LCS). They use genetics on the inside.

5. Evolutionary programming (EP) is a progression strategy that considers genome events as distinct organisms rather than individuals. It has largely merged into Genetic Programming and other evolutionary algorithms over the years.

The EA is usually divided into four main classes, which are presented in the following subsections in order from oldest to most recent:

- Genetic Algorithm

- Genetic Programming

- Evolutionary Programming

- Genetic Algorithm

The representations of individuals and, as a result, the meanings of the genetic operators working on them are the key differences between these methods.

FITNESS FUNCTION & PROBABILITY

The documentation of a "fitness function," which calculates how close each chromosome gets to solving the problem at hand, is a critical step in applying evolutionary algorithm computation. The fitness function is also used to handpick which chromosomes would be involved in producing offspring. The behavior and performance of the GA in seeking a solution are strongly affected by the fitness function's specific characteristics. Many studies have centered on the idea of epistasis, which is a form of fitness mechanism in which the fitness of a chromosome is determined by the interaction between gene values at different locations on the chromosome.

- Population size: This option determines the population size.

- Parameters: This choice determines how many parameters are used in the computer's evaluation feature.

- Number of games per match: This choice defines the number of games played between two Evaluation functions during a match.

- Survivor Probability: This choice determines the likelihood of the total number of Evaluation Values being passed on to the next Generation. The percentage is 10% in this case.

- Crossover Probability: This option specifies the likelihood of crossover; it can only be used in combination with the classic style algorithm.

- Mutation Probability: This choice specifies the mutation rate in terms of the number of bits mutated.

- Classic style fitness: Only the classic style algorithm is supported by this option. At each generation, it determines the "fitness giver" Evaluation function.

• Use fitness sorting per generation: This choice specifies whether the population's Evaluation mechanism should be sorted according to their fitness, in some way, just before all mutation/recombination occurs at each generation.

• Generations: This parameter specifies the number of generations to simulate. The number −1 denotes infinity.

The fact that GAs do not promise to find the best possible solutions for a problem is important and striking, but they are usually good at seeking suitable solutions in a fair period of time. Many board games that require a significant amount of search space have this requirement GA assigns appropriate coding (or representation) for the problem; a fitness function is needed, which assigns merit to each encoded solution; and it is critical to define the selection and reproduction laws, which are genetic operators. A collection of parameters or genes represents each potential solution to a problem. The genes are fused to form a chromosome, which is a string of values. The binary string type is the most common representation because it is simple and easy to manipulate by genetic operators.

SHORT-TERM MEMORY THRESHOLDING (STM)

We consider using the thresholding method to monitor the short-term memory, which measures the frequencies of the solutions selected from the current population, to minimize the sampling bias caused by the population's small size and the sampling procedure. The thresholding procedure applies an adjustable threshold to the peak frequency and distributes the additional counts equally across the remaining frequency [14]. As a result, oversampling will be stopped, and the solution with the largest frequency will no longer dominate the probability model. The adaptive threshold is calculated by the number of feature experiments completed, which shows how much of the expected evolution has happened. Let FEC and FET stand for the cumulative number of feature and functional evaluations, respectively. The following formula, Eq. (**1**) is used to measure the current adaptive threshold value:

$$Threshold_x = Threshold_{x-1} + C\ [FE_C/FE_T] \qquad (1)$$

The adaptive threshold's current Threshold x value is calculated by applying an increment to the previous Threshold x-1 value. This increase is proportional to the percentage of overall evolution attained, where C is a constant that represents the relative scaling of the number of function evaluations and the threshold value. As a result, the adaptive threshold value, like the increasing rate, increases incrementally as the evolution process progresses. By limiting the sample solution's highest frequency, this architecture allows the evolution to focus on exploration at an early stage. The adaptive threshold value rises incrementally as the evolution progresses, allowing the evolution to move from discovery to exploitation of promising solutions in Fig. (4).

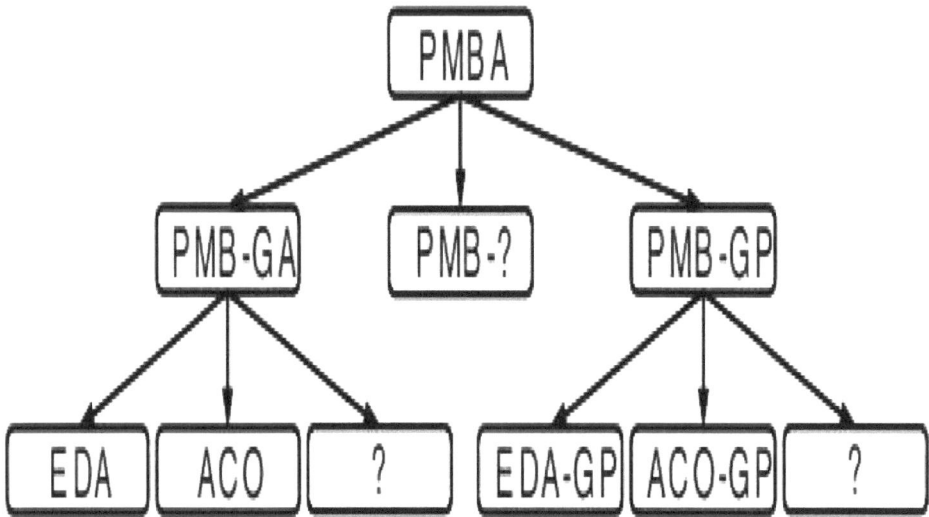

Fig. (4). Terminologies of PMB

Where, PMBA - Probabilistic Model-Building Algorithm

EDA - Estimation of Distribution Algorithm

ACO –Ant, Colony Optimization

GA – Genetic Algorithm

GP – Genetic, Programming

INCLUSION OF PROBABILISTIC AND STOCHASTIC PROCESSES (PSP) IN EA

Integrating probabilistic and stochastic processes into evolutionary algorithms allows for learning a probability distribution over entities. The end aim is to converge to a degenerate distribution representing the best solutions to the problem, but this isn't always said explicitly.

For functional reasons, this objective is typically adjusted in realistic systems (symmetry breaking—not all solutions are retained; exploration—so that full degeneracy is avoided).

Since the search spaces are infinite or enormously broad, exhaustive and arbitrary searches are impossible. As a result, hypotheses are needed to guide the search and provide a cost-effective description of where it is now. Almost all non-random search methods rely on a space-wide distance metric and the premise that variations in fitness between points are proportional to their distance. PMBAs typically depend on one more assumption: that humans are made up of components and that the health of people who share a component is linked.

As a consequence, PMBA models attempt to link these elements to exercise. Specific systems parameterize these structures in several ways, imposing external limits on the search space's layout (unimodality, symmetry, and so on).

The algorithm in Table **1**, which can be thought of as a generalization of crossover to recombination of the entire population, replaces the step in the traditional GA where variation operators (crossover and mutation) are applied to individuals with a model update and sampling procedure, which can be thought of as a replacement for the step in the traditional GA where variation operators (crossover and mutation) are applied to individuals. It is hoped that if the models are sufficiently descriptive, all possible configurations will be sampled. If the model representation is suitable for the problem, PMBAs may prevent the loss of essential building blocks during evolution. This was a major motivator for EDA efforts.

Table 1. Typical PMB algorithms

Algorithm 1: A classic PSP for EAs
Using an initial likelihood model, generate N individuals at random (termination condition is satisfied) Test people depending on their health level. Choose the most eligible people. Using the chosen people, update the stochastic model. Although sampling new people from the model propagation end

OPTIMIZING EAS

The optimization technique is used in the majority of academic CIG studies. This means that a game's feature is regarded as an optimization problem, and an optimization algorithm is applied to it. Anything that can be represented as a set of parameters [15] and where success can be evaluated in any way can be conveniently cast as an optimization challenge.

The parameters may be board location values in a board game or the weight values of a neural network controlling an agent in almost any game. A global optimizer, such as an evolutionary algorithm, a type of local search, or some other problem-specific heuristic, may be used as the optimization algorithm.

The key feature of the optimization method is that we know what we want from the game in advance (for example, the best score or the ability to defeat as many enemies as possible), and we use the optimization algorithm to get it.

Machine learning algorithms are tested using games for computational intelligence. There are several examples of various computer games being used to measure the performance of CI algorithms, either by contrasting unlike algorithms or, more generally, by actually presenting that a specific algorithm should be used to learn to play (or optimize the playing of) a particular game. There are some examples of using both evolutionary algorithms and td-learning to learn assessment functions for board games [16], but there are also interesting experiments using only evolutionary approaches, such as Fogel's Blondie24, where evolution learned to play Checkers at a very high stage.

This isn't to suggest that CI algorithms can't be used to make these games more enjoyable. It's not out of the realm of possibilities to develop game parameters for a game in order to make it more enjoyable, with the fitness function being either human expert knowledge or any kind of optimization metric. However, efforts to evolve full control schemes are discussed in the Innovation section below.

Imitation

In the imitation method, supervised learning is used to replicate a game's function. The player's behavior, the behavior of an alternate game agent, or the mechanics of a board game move may all be learned. While supervised learning is a large and active research subject in machine learning [17], with several efficient algorithms built, it is also a challenging task; this does not appear to have spawned research in the imitation method to CIG.

Unlike optimization and reinforcement learning algorithms, supervised learning algorithms tend to have relatively little published study. The key explanation is that there are almost inadequate high-quality datasets for evaluating supervised learning algorithms that are now publicly available. Using games to test these algorithms would be useful only if the algorithm being studied was a tweaked version of one specifically designed for the game in question; otherwise, one of the existing datasets might be used [18].

Innovation

The distinction between optimization and innovation methods is hazy. Essentially, the distinction is that the optimization method involves determining what kind of behavior, design, or arrangement is expected and then using CI strategies to achieve the desired effect in the most efficient manner possible. When following the creative strategy, the researcher is uncertain about what he is searching for. He or she may have a formula for scoring or valuing good outcomes over negative, however, they are looking for lifelike, complicated, or merely curious actions, arrangements, or systems rather than ideal ones. An evolutionary algorithm [19] is usually used, but it is used here mostly as a method for search-based programming rather than as an optimizer.

This may be the real reason why evolutionary simulations have failed to produce a truly complex general behavior or "actual intelligence." Computer games, especially complex agent games, are being used as a serious substitute for evolutionary simulations in the creative approach to games for computational intelligence. Such video games have a lengthy list of benefits that address many of the abovementioned issues.

FUNCTIONALITY OF GA

The functionality of GA relies on mutation and cross-over for producing chromosomes from the initial population. The generated chromosome gives the highest fitness value where the other leaves (fall out). These highest fitness values are attained in successive generations, and the cross-over process is successively carried out. The mutation process is carried out to give optimal value and maximal global search. It specifies the chosen feature subset and guarantees that this feature subset needs to be fulfilled with subset requirements [20]. Here, 'd' is set as a constraint value. The extracted feature that breaks out this constraint is considered the penalty. Hence, the chromosome is expressed in Eq. (**2**), Eq. (**3**) & Eq. (**4**), with the penalty term derived from the auto-encoder.

$$Cf=JXcKL(ñ|ñjXc \tag{2}$$

$$Cf=JXcñ \ Inñññj+ \ 1-ñIn(1-ñ1-rhoj)(Xc) \tag{3}$$

Here, is a feature subset of C_f, and the penalty is expressed as in Eq. (**4**):

$$KL\ (\ ñ|ñjXc= W*|Xc- d| \tag{4}$$

Here, w is determined as the weighted sparsity in auto-encoder and penalty co-efficient in GA. The simplest form of GA is considered to resolve the optimization issue. The exploration is fulfilled; however, the parameter works in a weaker state over the local optimum points. Hence, the auto-encoder is merged with the GA to enhance the parameter functionality by fine-tuning GA's capabilities. In conventional GA, the optimal values are derived from the mutation step, and a local searching operation is performed to evaluate the fitness value of the feature subset.

However, with the adoption of an auto-encoder, there is a substitution from the previous values. The feature subset acquires a chance to enhance the GA functionality locally. Therefore, it gains a better fitness value when provided for further computation.

This process is continued until the auto-encoder with the genetic algorithm attains a better optimal value and determines the internal layers used in the classifier model [21 - 24]. Therefore, the optimal values can handle the optimization issue and improve the system performance, as in Fig. (5).

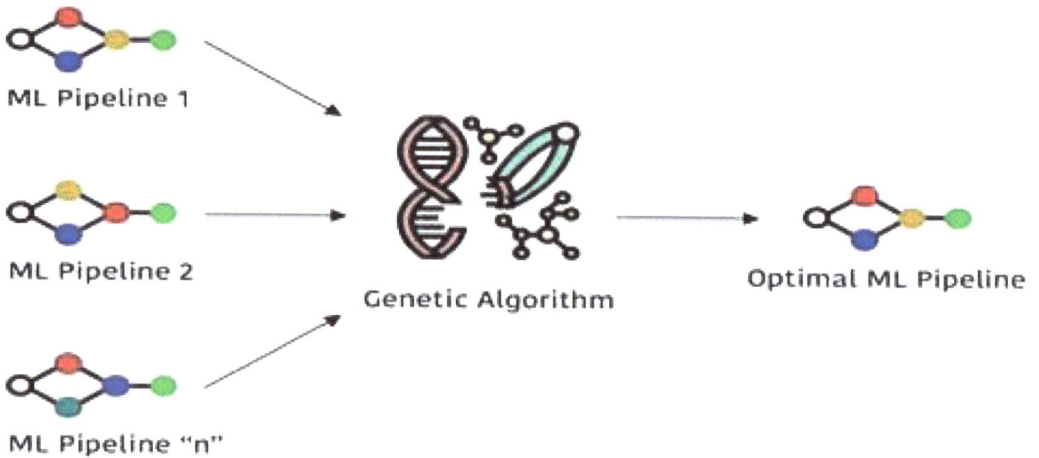

ML Pipeline 1

ML Pipeline 2

Genetic Algorithm

Optimal ML Pipeline

ML Pipeline "n"

Fig. (5). Optimization through GA

SAMPLE CODE OF EA TO FIND OPTIMAL RESULT OF A TEST

Table **2** shows the sample code of evolutionary algorithms that helps to find the optimal result of a test and its results.

Table 2. Sample EA Code & Results

```
pop_size=5
n_gen=15
#fix random seed
np.random.seed(1)
#initialization
X = np.array([initialize() for _ in range(pop_size)])
F = np.array([evaluate(x) for x in X])
# for each generation, execute the loop until termination for k in range(n_gen):
# select parents for the mating parents = select(pop_size, 2)
# mating consisting of crossover and mutation
_X = np.array([mutate(crossover(X[a], X[b])) for a, b in parents])
_F = np.array([evaluate(x) for x in _X])
# merge the population and offspring
X, F = np.row_stack([X, _X]), np.concatenate([F, _F])
# perform a duplicate elimination regarding the x values
I = eliminate_duplicates(X)
X, F = X[I], F[I]
# follow the survival of the fittest principle
I = survival(F, pop_size)
X, F = X[I], F[I]
# print the best result for each generation
print(k+1, F[0], X[0].astype(np.int))
```

Executing the code will results:
1 0.9951847266721969 [1 0 0 0 1 0 0 0]
2 0.9951847266721969 [1 0 0 0 1 0 0 0]
3 0.9951847266721969 [1 0 0 0 1 0 0 0]
4 0.9951847266721969 [1 0 0 0 1 0 0 0]
5 0.9951847266721969 [1 0 0 0 1 0 0 0]
6 0.9996988186962042 [1 0 0 0 0 0 1 0]
7 0.9996988186962042 [1 0 0 0 0 0 1 0]
8 0.9996988186962042 [1 0 0 0 0 0 1 0]
9 0.9996988186962042 [1 0 0 0 0 0 1 0]
10 0.9996988186962042 [1 0 0 0 0 0 1 0]
11 0.9996988186962042 [1 0 0 0 0 0 1 0]
12 0.9999247018391445 [1 0 0 0 0 0 0 1]
13 1.0 [1 0 0 0 0 0 0 0]
14 1.0 [1 0 0 0 0 0 0 0]
15 1.0 [1 0 0 0 0 0 0 0]

Table **2** explains the steps followed in genetic algorithms.

1. Initialization of population

2. Mating of Parents

3. Selection

4. Cross over and Mutation

5. Merge the population and offspring

6. Perform a duplicate elimination

7. Print the result of each generation

The np. randomseed() generates a new set or repeats pseudo-random numbers, and it is a numerical value.

CONCLUSION

This chapter clarified the relationship between evolutionary algorithms in deep learning with PSP and its threshold with STM, as well as the core desires of machine learning. In genetic programming, probabilistic model building has a lot to promise. It's difficult to say what type will ultimately succeed, but we hope that the systematization we've attempted here, as well as the open questions we've posed, will help to stimulate the field and lead to more oriented research. Finally, deep learning is surrounded by a variety of domain-specific jargon. Finally, evolution has worked out a way to arrive at a solution that is identical to the optimum we calculated analytically earlier in this section. For real-world problems, you may not even know what the best solution is and be surprised by what your genetic algorithm might come up with. As a result, the chapter's goal has piqued the interest of the evolution principle to optimization problems while enduring deep learning research. Many technical terms are borrowed from other fields, but be mindful that familiar terms can refer to something entirely different in the context of deep learning.

CONSENT FOR PUBLICATION

Not applicable.

CONFLICT OF INTEREST

The authors declare no conflict of interest, financial or otherwise.

ACKNOWLEDGEMENT

Declared none.

REFERENCES

[1]   A. Slowik, and H. Kwasnicka, "Evolutionary algorithms and their applications to engineering problems", *Neural Comput. Appl.,* vol. 32, no. 16, pp. 12363-12379, 2020.

[http://dx.doi.org/10.1007/s00521-020-04832-8]

[2]   X. Ma, Y. Yu, X. Li, Y. Qi, and Z. Zhu, "A survey of weight vector adjustment methods for decomposition-based multiobjective evolutionary algorithms", *IEEE Trans. Evol. Comput.,* vol. 24, no. 4, pp. 634-649, 2020.
[http://dx.doi.org/10.1109/TEVC.2020.2978158]

[3]   V. Santucci, M. Baioletti, and A. Milani, "An algebraic framework for swarm and evolutionary algorithms in combinatorial optimization", *Swarm Evol. Comput.,* vol. 55, p. 100673, 2020.
[http://dx.doi.org/10.1016/j.swevo.2020.100673]

[4]   J.G. Falcón-Cardona, and C.A.C. Coello, "Indicator-based multi-objective evolutionary algorithms: a comprehensive survey", *ACM Comput. Surv.,* vol. 53, no. 2, pp. 1-35, 2021. [CSUR].
[http://dx.doi.org/10.1145/3376916]

[5]   J.M. Moyano, E.L. Gibaja, K.J. Cios, and S. Ventura, "Combining multi-label classifiers based on projections of the output space using Evolutionary algorithms", *Knowl. Base. Syst.,* vol. 196, p. 105770, 2020.
[http://dx.doi.org/10.1016/j.knosys.2020.105770]

[6]   M. Parol, T. Wójtowicz, K. Księżyk, C. Wenge, S. Balischewski, and B. Arendarski, "Optimum management of power and energy in low voltage microgrids using evolutionary algorithms and energy storage", *Int. J. Electr. Power Energy Syst.,* vol. 119, p. 105886, 2020.
[http://dx.doi.org/10.1016/j.ijepes.2020.105886]

[7]   A. Thakkar, and R. Lohiya, "Role of swarm and evolutionary algorithms for intrusion detection system: A survey", *Swarm Evol. Comput.,* vol. 53, p. 100631, 2020.
[http://dx.doi.org/10.1016/j.swevo.2019.100631]

[8]   A. Rajabi, and C. Witt, "Self-adjusting evolutionary algorithms for multimodal optimization", *Proceedings of the 2020 Genetic and Evolutionary Computation Conference,* 2020pp. 1314-1322
[http://dx.doi.org/10.1145/3377930.3389833]

[9]   B. Case, and P.K. Lehre, "Self-Adaptation in Nonelitist Evolutionary Algorithms on Discrete Problems With Unknown Structure", *IEEE Trans. Evol. Comput.,* vol. 24, no. 4, pp. 650-663, 2020.
[http://dx.doi.org/10.1109/TEVC.2020.2985450]

[10]   G. Sadeghi, M. Najafzadeh, and M. Ameri, "Thermal characteristics of evacuated tube solar collectors with coil inside: An experimental study and evolutionary algorithms", *Renew. Energy,* vol. 151, pp. 575-588, 2020.
[http://dx.doi.org/10.1016/j.renene.2019.11.050]

[11]   Thillaiarasu and S. ChenthurPandian, "Enforcing security and privacy over multi-cloud framework using assessment tech-niques", *International Conference on Intelligent Systems and Control (ISCO).,* 2016pp. 1-5
[http://dx.doi.org/10.1109/ISCO.2016.7727001]

[12]   N. Thillaiarasu, "ChenthurPandian, S. A novel scheme for safe-guarding confidentiality in public clouds for service users of cloud computing", *Cluster Comput.,* vol. 22, pp. 1179-1188, 2019.
[http://dx.doi.org/10.1007/s10586-017-1178-8]

[13]   N. Shyamambika, and N. Thillaiarasu, "A survey on acquiring integrity of shared data with effective user termination in the cloud",
[http://dx.doi.org/10.1109/ISCO.2016.7726893]

[14]   L. Krishnasamy, T. Ramasamy, R. Dhanaraj, and P. Chinnasamy, "A geodesic deployment and radial shaped clustering (RSC) algorithm with statistical aggregation in sensor networks", *Turk. J. Electr. Eng. Comput. Sci.,* vol. 29, no. 3, 2021.

[15]   S. Ranjithkumar, and N. Thillaiarasu, *"A survey of secure routing protocols of mobile adhoc network." SSRG International Journal of Computer Science and Engineering.* vol. Vol. 2. SSRG-IJCSE, 2015.

[16]   BaressiŠegota, "S., Anđelić, N., Lorencin, I., Saga, M., & Car, Z. Path planning optimization of six-degree-of-freedom robotic manipulators using evolutionary algorithms", *Int. J. Adv. Robot. Syst.,* vol. 17, no. 2, p. 1729881420908076, 2020.

[17]   S. Hosseini, and B.M.H. Zade, "New hybrid method for attack detection using combination of evolutionary algorithms, SVM, and ANN", *Comput. Netw.,* vol. 173, p. 107168, 2020.
[http://dx.doi.org/10.1016/j.comnet.2020.107168]

[18]   J.J. Bird, E. Wanner, A. Ekárt, and D.R. Faria, "Optimisation of phonetic aware speech recognition through multi-objective evolutionary algorithms", *Expert Syst. Appl.,* vol. 153, p. 113402, 2020.
[http://dx.doi.org/10.1016/j.eswa.2020.113402]

[19]   Q. Xu, Z. Xu, and T. Ma, "A Survey of Multiobjective Evolutionary Algorithms Based on Decomposition: Variants, Challenges and Future Directions", *IEEE Access,* vol. 8, pp. 41588-41614, 2020.
[http://dx.doi.org/10.1109/ACCESS.2020.2973670]

[20]   A.N. Sloss, and S. Gustafson, "2019 Evolutionary Algorithms Review", *Genetic and Evolutionary Computation,* vol. XVII, pp. 307-344, 2020.
[http://dx.doi.org/10.1007/978-3-030-39958-0_16]

[21]   S. Boonstra, K. van der Blom, H. Hofmeyer, and M.T.M. Emmerich, "Conceptual structural system layouts via design response grammars and evolutionary algorithms", *Autom. Construct.,* vol. 116, p. 103009, 2020.
[http://dx.doi.org/10.1016/j.autcon.2019.103009]

[22]   M.N. Jahromi, Z. Gomeh, G. Busico, R. Barzegar, N.N. Samany, M.T. Aalami, D. Tedesco, M. Mastrocicco, and N. Kazakis, "Developing a SINTACS-based method to map groundwater multi-pollutant vulnerability using evolutionary algorithms", *Environ. Sci. Pollut. Res. Int.,* vol. 28, no. 7, pp. 7854-7869, 2021.
[http://dx.doi.org/10.1007/s11356-020-11089-0] [PMID: 33040292]

[23]   B. Doerr, "Lower bounds for non-elitist evolutionary algorithms *via* negative multiplicative drift"., *International Conference on Parallel Problem Solving from Nature,* 2020pp. 604-618
[http://dx.doi.org/10.1007/978-3-030-58115-2_42]

[24]   M. D. Ramasamy, K. Periasamy, L. Krishnasamy, R. K. Dhanaraj, S. Kadry, and Y. Nam, "Multi-Disease Classification Model using Strassen's Half of Threshold (SHoT) Training Algorithm in Healthcare Sector", *IEEE Access.*.
[http://dx.doi.org/10.1109/ACCESS.2021.3103746]

CHAPTER 6

High-Performance Computing for Satellite Image Processing Using Apache Spark

Pallavi Hiwarkar[1,*] and **Mangala S. Madankar**[2]

[1] *Assistant Professor, Department of Computer Science and Engineering, G H Raisoni Institute of Engineering & Technology, Nagpur, India*

[2] *Assistant Professor, Department of Computer Science and Engineering, G H Raisoni College of Engineering, Nagpur, India*

Abstract: High-Performance Computing is the aggregate computing application that solves computational problems that are either huge or time-consuming for traditional computers. This technology is used for processing satellite images and analysing massive data sets quickly and efficiently. Parallel processing and distributed computing methods are very important to process satellite images quickly and efficiently. Parallel Computing is a computation type in which multiple processors execute multiple tasks simultaneously to rapidly process data using shared memory. In this, we process satellite image parallel in a single computer. In distributed computing, we use multiple systems to process satellite images quickly. With the help of VMware, we are creating a different operating system (like Linux, windows *etc*.) as a worker. In this project we are using cluster formation for connecting master and slave: apache spark is one of the important concepts in this project. Apache spark is one of the frameworks and Resilient Distributed Datasets are one of the concepts in the spark, we are using RDD for dividing dataset on the different node of the cluster.

Keywords: Satellite images, Apache spark, python, Image processing, VMware, Parallel Computing, Distributed Computing.

INTRODUCTION

Remote sensing is one of the important concepts in this project. With the support of high-performance computing and apache spark, we can process and display satellite information quickly [1]. Satellite sensors capture images of the earth: in these images, we can see the population on the earth, the water on the earth, the greenery and the land on the earth.

---

* **Corresponding author Pallavi Hiwarkar:** Assistant Professor, Department of Computer Science and Engineering, G H Raisoni Institute of Engineering & Technology, Nagpur, India; E-mail: pallavi.hiwarkar@ghru.edu.in

Prasad Lokulwar, Basant Verma, N. Thillaiarasu, Kailash Kumar, Mahip Bartere and Dharam Singh (Eds.)
All rights reserved-© 2022 Bentham Science Publishers

High Performance Computing is the aggregate computing framework that solves computational problems that are either huge or time consuming for traditional computers. This technology is used for processing satellite images and analysing massive data sets quickly and efficiently [1]. This technology concentrates on executing and performing parallel and distributive methods parallelly and distributedly for solving difficulties. Parallel processing and distributed computing methods are very important to process satellite images quickly and efficiently. Parallel Computing is a computation type in which multiple processors execute multiple tasks simultaneously for rapid execution of data using shared memory. In this, we process satellite images parallelly in a single computer. In distributed computing, we use multiple systems to process satellite images quickly [1].

Apache spark supports multiple languages like scala, python and java. With the help of spark, we can develop a project in different languages. HPC technology is used for processing satellite images and analysing massive data sets quickly and efficiently. HPC provides high computation Power that's why we can process a large number of data quickly, and HPC improves the computational speed: in this project, we are using apache spark with HPC [1]. . Apache spark is a framework Resilient Distributed Datasets is one of the concepts in the spark we are using RDD for dividing dataset on the different node of the cluster it may be computed. We are using python for programming purposes [3].

RDD have the capacity to divide a large number of data into small pieces based on the key, in previous projects, a large amount of data took additional time to display and execute, but now we are using RDD for executing large data fastly: multiple nodes are available in RDD to execute a large number of data. In RDD, multiple executors are present. Each executor executes different jobs.VMware is one of the useful software in this project which is used for creating multiple operating systems that we are using as workers in this project; we are performing cluster formation: and in the cluster formation we are connecting servers and clients. Each worker communicates with each other: if we enter any command from the server, the worker performs the task, and it processes the image fastly. We create a server in our main machine, and workers in a virtual machine.

Parallel Computing

Parallel processing is one of the important parts of high performance computing. Parallel computing is one of the computation types in which the number of processors execute multiple tasks simultaneously to rapidly process data using shared memory. In this, we process satellite images parallelly in a single computer. With the help of parallel processing, we can display and process satellite images quickly. We can process satellite images in parallel shown in Fig. (**1**).

Parallel Computing

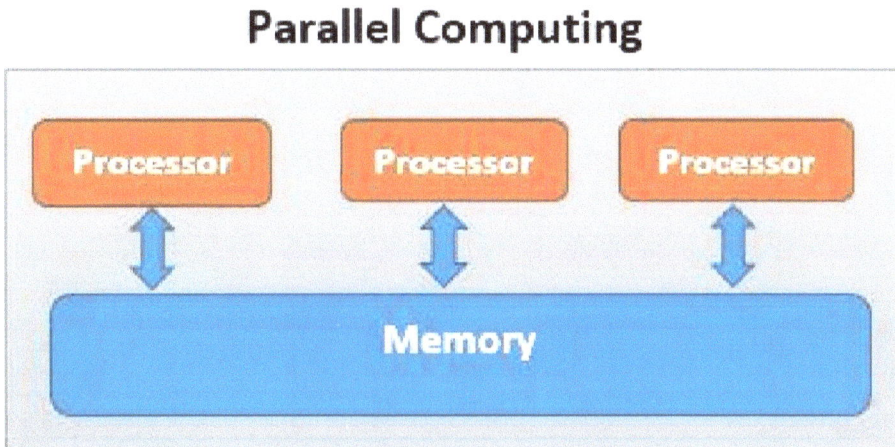

Fig. (1). Parallel Computing.

In parallel processing, multiple processors perform the task with a single computer. To perform any task, we required multiple processors.

(https://subscription.packtpub.com/book/application_development/9781787 126992/1/ch01lvl1sec10/parallel-versus-distributed-computing)

Benefits Of Parallel Computing

1. It saves money and time than other methods.
2. Taking care of bigger issues on sequential computing it can be unfeasible.
3. When the local resources are finite, it can exploit non-neighbourhood assets.
4. It solves large problems in a short time.
5. It executes multiple tasks simultaneously.

Distributed Computing

Distributed Computing is one of the important parts of high performance computing. Distributed computing uses multiple systems to quickly process satellite images, as shown in Fig. (**2**).

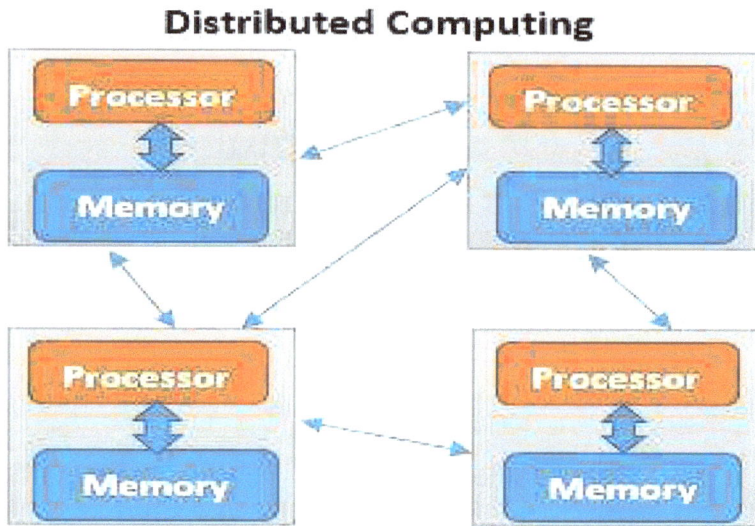

Fig. (2). Distributed Computing.

First, this system creates a different OS like Linux and windows. Each system has its own memory.

To create different OS, we are using VMware; with the help of VMware we create multiple systems as a worker. Each worker has its own memory and each worker performs a task simultaneously. Because of that, it performs a task quickly and efficiently.

(https://subscription.packtpub.com/book/application_development/97817871269 92/1/ch01lvl1sec10/parallel-versus-distributed-computing)

Benefits Of Distributed Computing:

1. In this different nodes shared data with each other easily.
2. If one node fails because of some error, it cannot affect other nodes.
3. Every node has its own memory, so there is more space to store data.
4. Flexibility is more than in other systems.

Virtual Machine Software (VMware Workstation Pro)

As shown in Fig. (**3**), VMware workstation pro is the computer software; this is one of the important software we are using in this project. With the help of VMware, we can create multiple systems like Linux OS, windows. We consider this system as a worker that is connected with a server. Each worker has its own memory. Each worker communicates with the other through a network. If one worker fails because of some error, it cannot affect another.

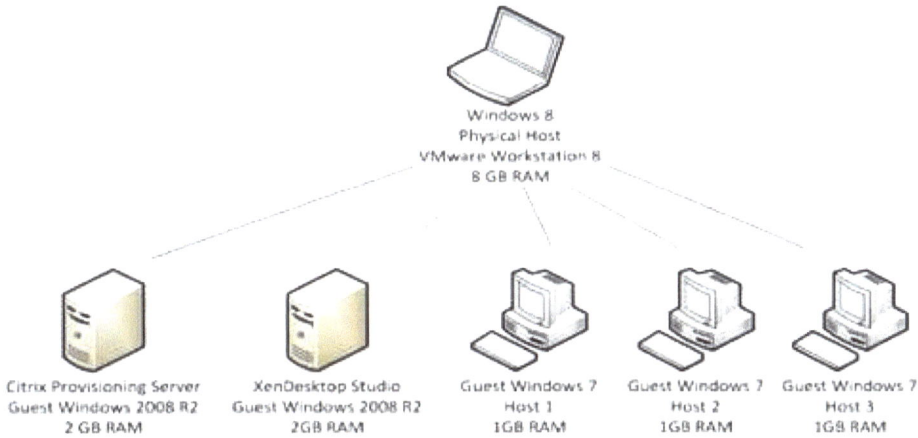

Fig. (3). VMware Workstation Pro System.

We can install VMware software in our single physical system; after that, we can create different OS in the Vmware. Then we use these virtual machines simultaneously with our actual system. So we are using VMware for operating multiple systems simultaneously.

(https://virtualizedgeek.com/2013/03/01/physical-*vs*-virtual-virtualization-lab/)

Apache Spark

Apache spark is simple to use than other frameworks and open source means this is free to use. Without paying any amount, we can use it easily and efficiently. SQL Machine Learning (ML) and diagram process has mostly used this framework. One of the main features and concepts of apache spark is cluster computing, which increases the processing speed of an application. Spark programs will run a hundred times faster than Hadoop programs.

Apache spark processes efficiently and provide result quickly. For display the image quickly and efficiently, we need parallel computing, distributed computing and apache spark. In this experiment, we are using python with apache spark; in the spark, some in-memory processing capability is present, but the spark doesn't store all data in the memory. We can process and display the data efficiently and quickly with the help of apache spark; spark is one of the important concepts in this project. In previous years, satellite data was processed and displayed slowly, but now in this experiment, we are using apache spark for processing and displaying that data speedily and efficiently. One of the main processes in the spark is Resilient Distributed Datasets (RDD). The Resilient Distributed Datasets is used for distributing the datasets and for the repetitious algorithm, with the help of workers, it distributes the datasets.

Features of Apache Spark

• *Speed*

Spark also allows it to run in Hadoop cluster applications many times faster in memory than other frameworks, and ten times faster as compared to performing on disk [9]. Apache spark provides a high speed for executing and displaying the data fastly, apache spark provides a high speed. Speed is one of the main features of apache spark.

• *Supports multiple languages*

It supports many languages like python, scala and java in the spark. With the help of this, we can implement the task in many languages [9].

• *Reusability*

For batch-processing we can reuse the spark code; reusability is also an important feature in the apache spark

Components Of Spark

Spark is an autonomous approach. It has its own cluster management and is not dependent on any application. Apache Spark is faster than other frameworks, and easy to use [4]. The Fig. (**4**) shows differentparts of the apache spark.

• *Apache Spark Core*

Apache spark is provided in-memory computation, and functionalities are constructed on the top of the spark. To delivers speed, the spark core is the groundwork [5]. Spark Core and RDD are inserted together, RDD is in the middle of the concepts of Spark, *and RDD* is separate from the dataset.

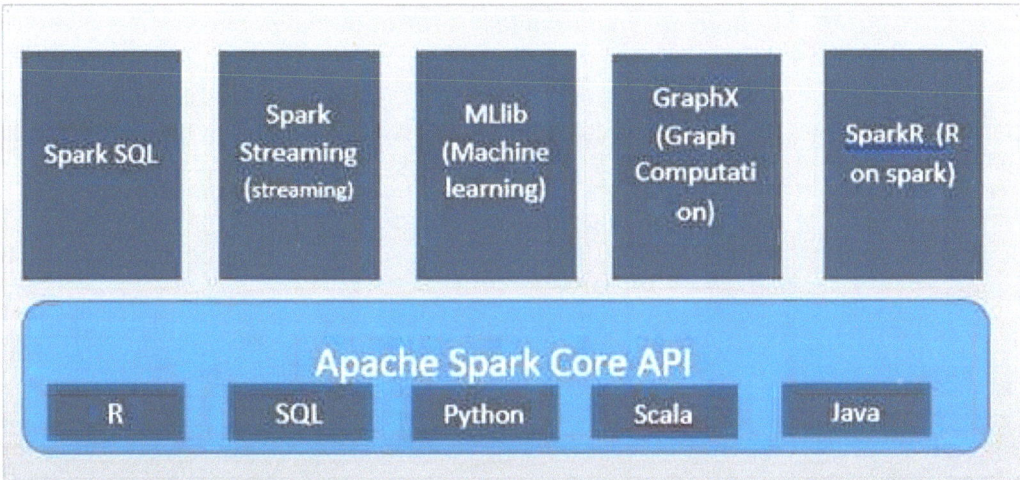

Fig. (4). Component of Apache Spark.

(https://data-flair.training/blogs/apache-spark-ecosystem-components/)

• *Spark SQL*

The spark SQL is also A concept present in the spark core that introduces Schema RDD; the novel data abstraction is nothing but the organized and semi-organized information which provides support [6]. Spark SQL is structured data processing for spark module

• *Spark Streaming*

Spark streaming is one of the concepts present in apache spark architecture and apache spark; in data streaming, the infinite sequence of information arrives continuously. For future use, it divides input information into discrete units [3].

• *MLlib (Machine Learning Library)*

It is a distributed background in apache spark; it is mostly used in the machine learning system [7].

• *GraphX*

In apache spark, the graphX is one of the graph processing frameworks used for developing graphs.

Spark Architecture Overview

(https://www.edureka.co/blog/spark-architecture/)

As shown in Fig. (**5**), there are spark context, cluster manager and worker present; spark context work like a driver node in the spark context, having some basic functions and these functions are worked with cluster manager. The cluster manager is connected with spark context and executors; cluster manager allocates task to the executors; after that, a large amount of tasks is divided into smaller tasks.

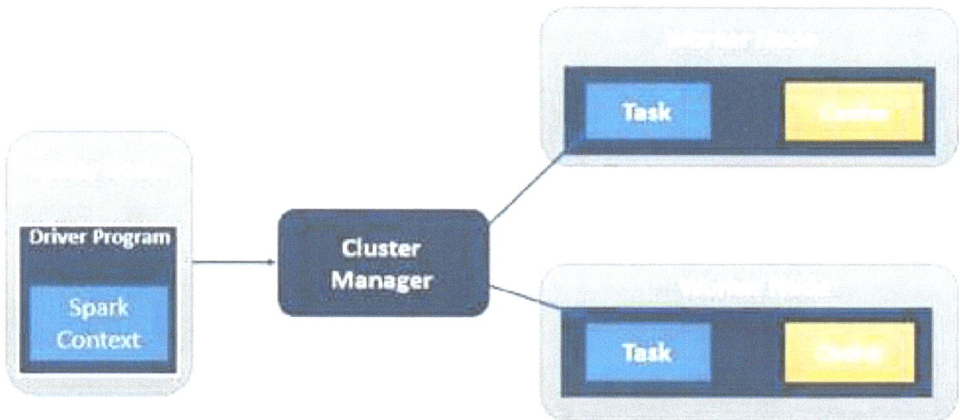

Fig. (5). Apache Spark Architecture.

As shown in Fig. (**6**), The cluster manager assigns the task to the executors; there are n number of executors present in this architecture cluster that provide the task to every executor, and then executors perform that task quickly. If one executor fails in this system, they could not affect other executors; executors execute the work and then return to the spark context.

Resilient Distributed Dataset (RDD)

In spark application, RDDs are one of the main building blocks; RDD meaning in basic:

- Resilient: error is present in the task, it removes that error and rebuilds the data.
- Distributed: in a cluster, multiple nodes are present, and each has distributed data.
- Dataset: a group of partitioned data.

(https://intellipaat.com/blog/tutorial/spark-tutorial/programming-with-rdds/)

Fig. (6). Successfully connected master with workers.

Over the distributed collection, it is a level of abstracted data. Now we can see it working in Fig. (7) . The data present in RDD is divided into large pieces based on a key. RDDs are extremely resistant, in previous years the big amount of data takes additional time to execute, but with the help of RDD, we can process large data quickly [10]. RDD divides large data into small pieces and process large amount of information quickly. RDD has multiple nodes to execute a large number of data. In RDD, every executor performs a different task; if one executor fails, it doesn't affect other executors and they will still process data [10].

In the distributed system, every dataset present in the RDD is separated into logical pieces [10]; there are different nodes present in the RDD; every nodes partition the data set in the form of small pieces. Due to this, we can execute action and transformation on the whole data parallel. Also, we don't need to worry about data distribution, spark takes care of data distribution.

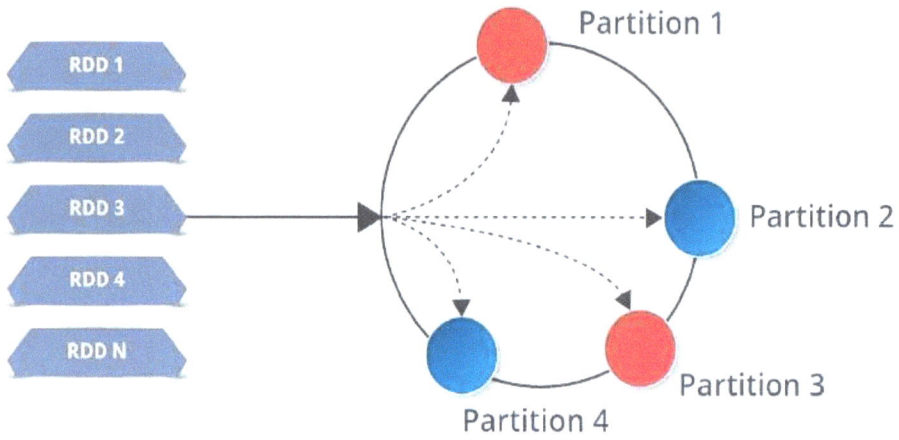

Fig. (7). Resilient Distributed Dataset (RDD).

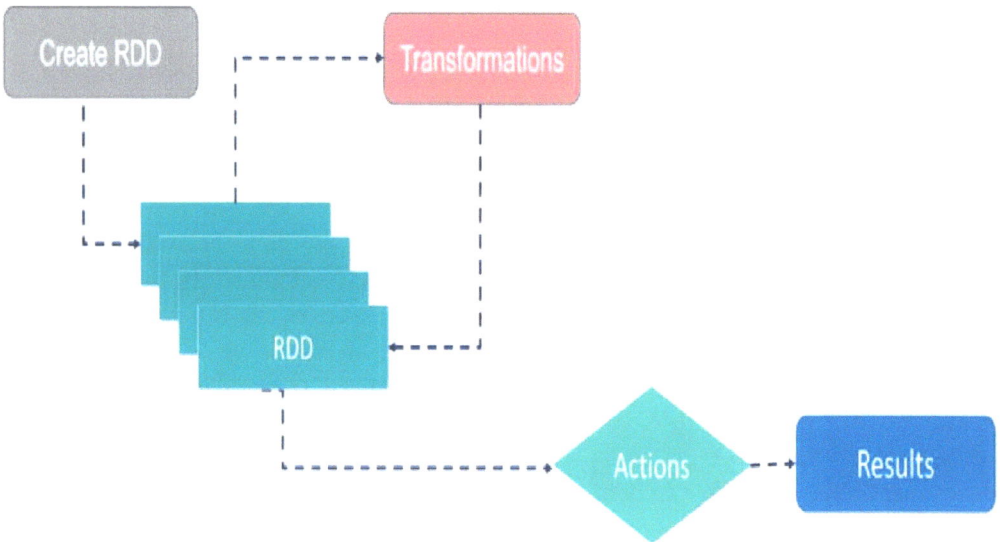

Fig. (8). Workflow of RDD.

(https://www.edureka.co/blog/spark-architecture/)

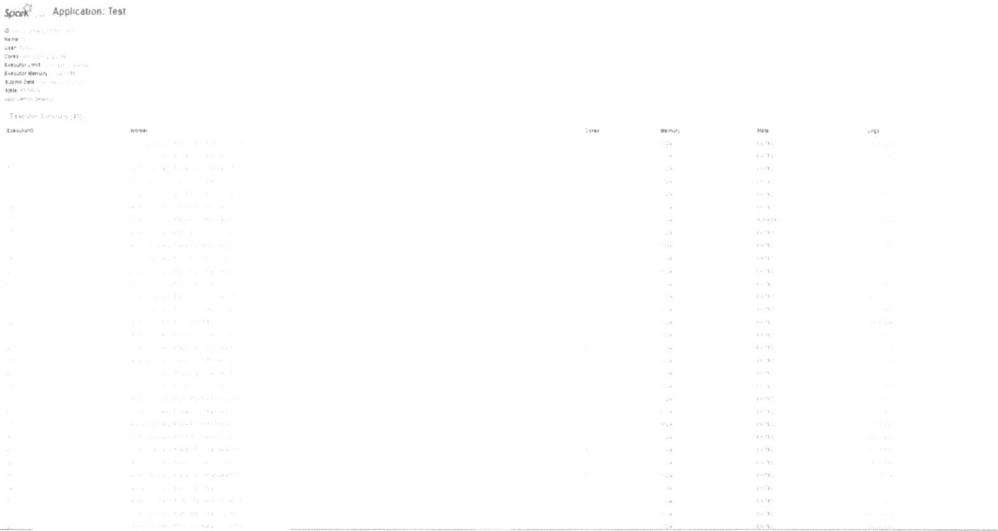

Fig. (9). Multiple worker perform a task.

Methodology

Fig. (**10**) shows how this project works. So firstly, we have to install Apache spark; for installing apache spark, some software are required like java, scala, and Eclipse.

Cluster formation:-in cluster formation, we are connecting the master with the slave; master is nothing but the server and the slave is nothing but the workers, so we are connecting the server with workers with the help of some commands, for cluster formation we are creating workers in VMware.

Parallel computing:- after cluster formation, we process the image parallelly for fast processing, with the help of a number of processors and one server [1].

Distributed Computing:- after cluster formation, we process the image distributedly; in the distributed processing number of workers process and display the image quickly [1].

Processing multiple images:- with the help of parallel and distributed processing, we are processing multiple images quickly and efficiently.

Cluster Manager:- The cluster manager assigns the task to the executors; there are n number of executors present in this architecture cluster that provide the task to every executor and then the executors performs that task quickly.

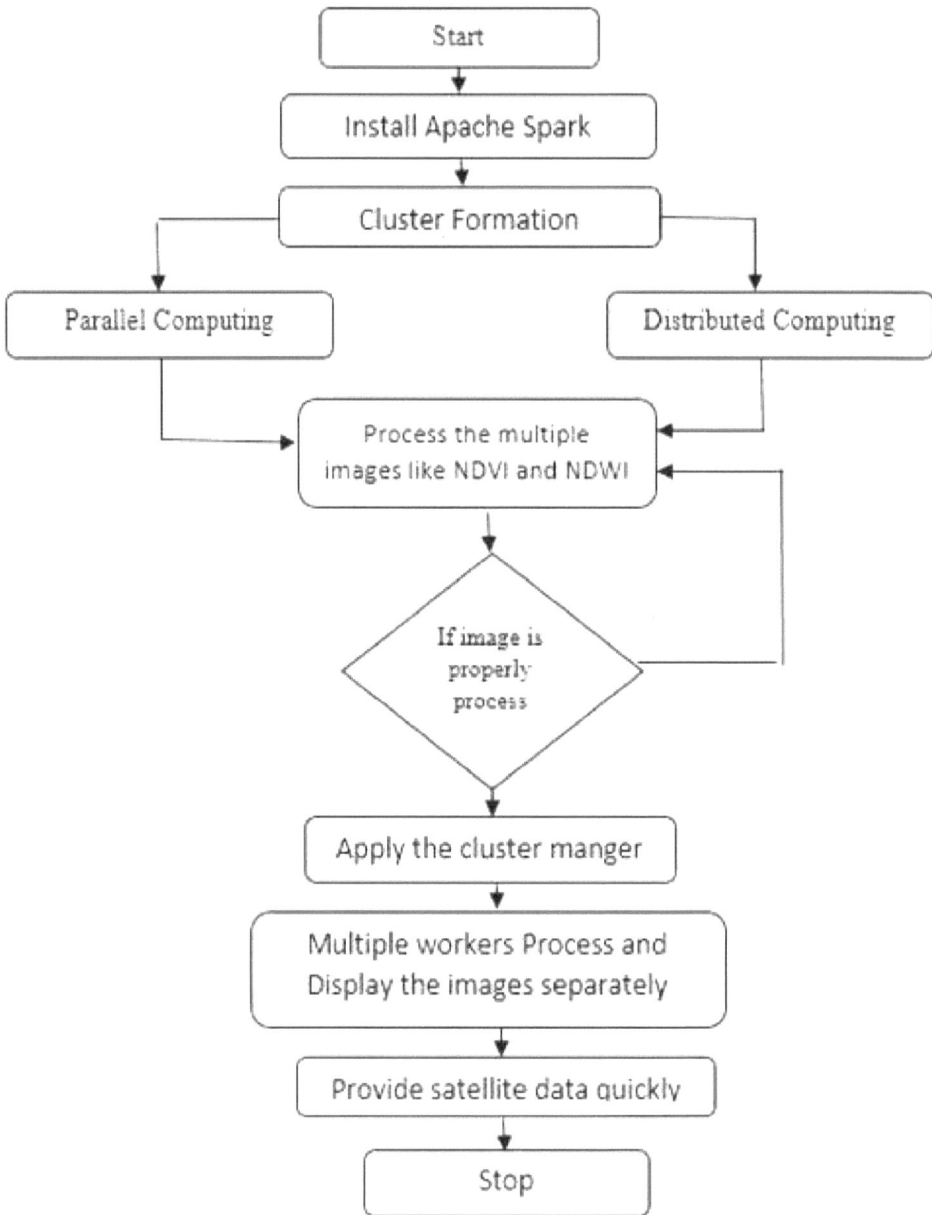

Fig. (10). Workflow of Project.

NDVI (Normalized Difference Vegetation Index)

In this project, we used NDVI algorithm; with the help of this algorithm, we can identify and detect remote sensing dimensions from space; for analysing RS dimensions, we are using the graphical indicator NDVI. With the help of NDVI, we can observe green contains vegetation.

For quickly and simply identifying green vegetation areas, the NDVI is one of the popular algorithms, it also detects the live green plant area in multispectral remote sensing data. The satellite has some sensors that detect and click some earth photographs; in that data, we are applying NDVI for identifying green vegetation areas [11].

The NDVI calculation formula is as following Fig. (**11**):

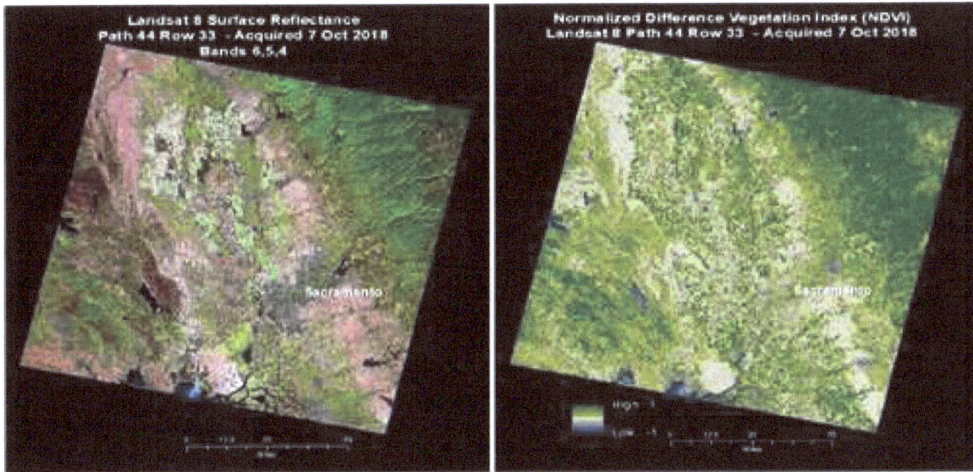

Fig. (11). NDVI Image.

In this project, we used NDVI algorithm. In this algorithm, we used NIR and Red band, which employed Landsat 5 images, so the NIR is the fourth band and Red is the third band in LANDSAT 5. NIR is nothing but the near-infrared region, and red stands for red band. With the help of 3rd and 4th bands, we can calculate NDVI algorithm. NDVI is calculated between -1.0 and +1.0, and they take values between 0 to 1.

The NDVI image is given below; it shows that NDVI calculated only the green portion of the earth.

Proposed Plan Work

High Performance Computing is the collection of applications that solve computational problems that are either massive or time consuming for traditional computers [1].Parallel computing is helpful in processing data parallelly and quickly. Distributed processing is also helpful in processing and displaying the data quickly. In distributed computing, we use multiple systems to process satellite image quickly; in distributed computing, we can perform a task on a different system. For this, firstly, we create a different OS like Linux and windows. Each system has its own memory. With the help of VMware, we are creating a different operating system (like Linux, windows *etc.*) as a worker. In this project, we are using cluster formation for connecting master and slave. Apache spark is one of the important concepts and framework in this project.

The core reason behind outstanding performance of apache spark is Resilient Distributed Datasets we are using RDDs are extremely resistant; in previous years the big amount of data took more time to process, but with the help of RDD, we could process large data quickly. RDD divides large data into small pieces and quickly processes large amounts of information..we are using python for programming spurposes.

RESULT

In this project, we aim to process and display a large amount of images in a shorter time than normal time. Normally processing satellite images may take more time, but with the help of apache spark and high-performance computing, we get a huge amount of data in a short time, in some seconds. The reason is we are processing data parallelly and distributedly.. With the help of parallel and distributed computing, we are quickly processing and displaying a large amount of data. The following result shows that images are run and displayed quickly and efficiently.

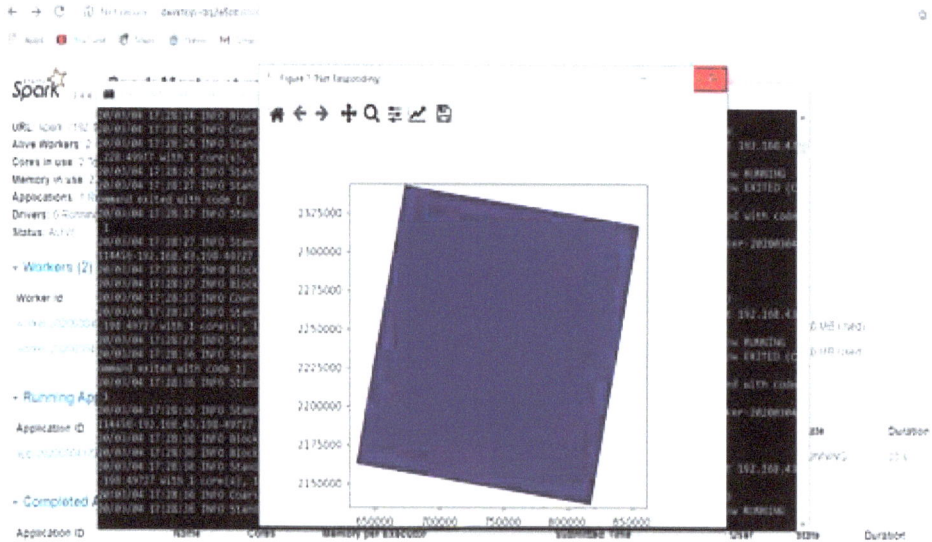

Fig. (12). Image is display.

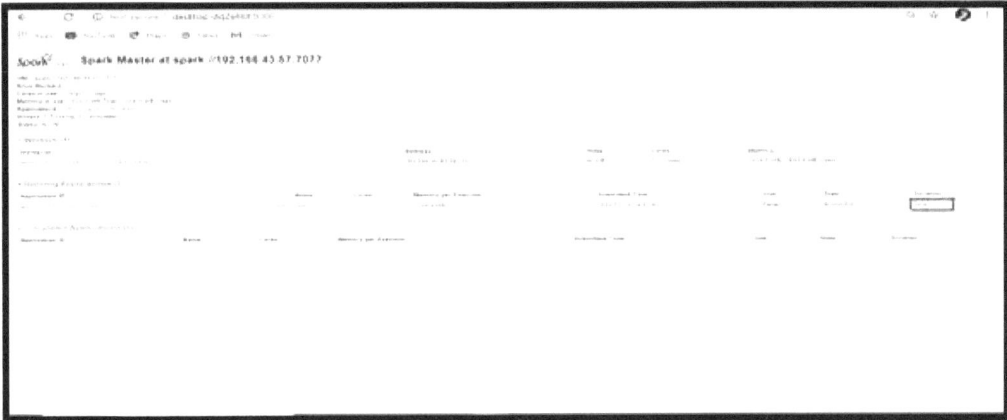

Fig. (13). Result.

CONCLUSION

Distributed computing and parallel computing are among high-performance computing methods. In this project, we are trying to improve the speed of data, display and process it quickly. We used apache spark with distributed and parallel computing. With the help of these two methods, we easily process and display a large number of satellite images. We used Landsat 5 images in this project for fast computation and python with a spark. In the spark, all the information is not stored in memory, It has some in-memory capabilities in remote sensing research work, the HPC methods play a very important role. We are using RDD to divide large data into small pieces and process a large amount of information quickly; in the spark, there is capability to distribute data automatically with the help of RDD.

CONSENT FOR PUBLICATION

Not applicable.

CONFLICT OF INTEREST

The authors declare no conflict of interest, financial or otherwise.

ACKNOWLEDGEMENT

Declared none.

REFERENCES

[1]   M. Bhojne, A. Pallav, and A. Chakravarti, "High Performance Computing for Satellite Image Processing and Analyzing", *International Journal of Computer Applications Technology and*

Research., vol. 2, pp. 424-430, 2013.4

[2]   https://www.tutorialspoint.com/apache_spark/apache_spark_tutor ial.pdf

[3]   https://www.tutorialspoint.com/apache_spark/apache_spark_introduction.htm

[4]   https://www.enterprisesearchblog.com/machine-learning/

[5]   https://www.oreilly.com/library/view/scala-andspark/9781785280849/5fe3b50f-3042-4-bd-9255372050ef1117.xhtml

[6]   https://quizlet.com/216060966/hadoop-internshipterms-flash-cards/

[7]   http://studentlearning.in/big-data/https://databricks.com/glossary/what-are-sparkapplications

[8]   https://www.researchgate.net/publication/220346431_Automatic_Cloud_Detection_and_Removal_Al gorithm_for_

[9]   https://www.oreilly.com/content/hadoop-with-python/

[10]   https://www.edureka.co/blog/spark-architecture/

[11]   https://www.linkedin.com/pulse/ndvi-ndbi-ndwi-calculation-using-landsat-7-8-tek-bahadur-kshetri/

## CHAPTER 7

Artificial Intelligence and Covid-19: A Practical Approach

Md. Alimul Haque[1,*], Shameemul Haque[2], Samah Alhazmi[3] and D.N. Pandit[4]

[1] *Department of Computer Science, Veer Kunwar Singh University, Ara, India*

[2] *Al-Hafeez College, Ara, India*

[3] *College of Computing and Informatics, Saudi Electronic University, Riyadh, Kingdom of Saudi Arabia*

[4] *Department of Zoology, Veer Kunwar Singh University, Ara, India*

Abstract: An unprecedented outbreak of unknown aetiology pneumonia occurred in Wuhan of Hubei, China, in December 2019. The WHO reported a novel coronavirus causative agent outbreak with limited evidence of COVID-19. SARS-CoV-2 embodies the ssRNA genome containing 29891 nucleotides to encode 9860 amino acids and shows different types of mutations, such as D614G. The epidemic of this virus officially declared an emergency of International Concern by the WHO in January 2020. In the first week of April 2021, a new strain of coronavirus named N-440 was reported in Chandigarh, India. The number of cases of laboratory-confirmed coronavirus has risen at an unprecedented pace worldwide, with more than 132,573,231 cases currently confirmed, including 2,876,411 deaths as of April 06th 2021. The lack of funding to survive the epidemic of this virus, coupled with the concern of overloaded healthcare systems, has driven a lot of countries into a partial/total lockout situation. This epidemic has caused chaos, and a rapid therapy of the disease would be a therapeutic medication with experience of use in patients to overcome the current pandemic. In the recent global emergency, researchers, clinicians and public health care experts around the world continue to search for emerging technologies to help tackle the pandemic of this virus. In this chapter, we rely on numerous reputable sources to provide a detailed analysis of all the main pandemic relevant aspects. This research illustrates not only the immediate safety effects connected with the COVID-19 epidemic but also its impact on the global socio-economy, education, social life and employment. Artificial Intelligence (AI) plays a significant supporting capacity in countering COVID-19 and may prompt arrangements quicker than we can, in any case, achieve in different zones and applications. With technological developments in AI combined with improved computing capacity, the repurposing of AI-enhanced medications may be useful in the cases of this virus. Artificial intelligence has gotten one of those advances which can undoubtedly distin-

* **Corresponding author Md. Alimul Haque:** Department of Computer Science, Veer Kunwar Singh University, Ara, India; E-mail: shadvksu@gmail.com

guish the transmission of this virus; exceptionally hazardous victims are recognized and are significant for constant control of that contamination. Artificial intelligence could genuinely assist us in battling against this infection through network testing, clinical administrations and advice on controlling diseases. This chapter addresses recent applications of AI in fighting the pandemics of this virus, e.g., monitoring of the epidemic, forecast of hazards, screening and diagnosis, improvement of medical treatment, fake news breaks, strengthening lockdowns, preventing cyber-attacks and finally, effective online education. This chapter will provide a clear definition and general understanding of the field of this virus pandemic and the role of AI to readers and researchers.

Keywords: Artificial Intelligence, Coronavirus, Corona App, Contact tracing, COVID-19 Pandemic, Cyber Threats, Drugs and Vaccines, Global Economy, Social Life Impact, AI applications, Monitoring, Projection.

INTRODUCTION

COVID-19 or "Coronavirus Disease-2019" is one of the respiratory ailments caused by SARS-CoV-2 (Fig. **1**). SARS-CoV-2 is an encompassed infectious novel virus of order: Nidovirales, family: Coronaviridae of ss(+)RNA viruses and group: Betacorona virus. The shape of RNA is either helical or rounded in this virus. The virus may be L or S type with little contrasts at two spots. It is accounted that L type was more common in an early episode. Its non-segmented genome is comprised of 26-33.5kb encoded four structural (Nucleocapsid or N, membrane or M of ~25-30kDa, spike or S of ~150kDa and envelope or E of ~8.12kDa) proteins and few non-structural proteins. The club-like tip in the envelope gives the crown-like appearance of this virus. The protein groupings of the spike of ~80virus have been adjusted and taken a gander phylogenetically. The exact source of the virus, however, is unclear, and its gene sources are usually derived from bats and rodents [1]. It is reported that the spike of SARS-CoV-2 is stated to be 10-20 times bound to bind angiotensin-converting enzyme 2 (ACE2) in cells of human. ACE2 is produced by the gene SLC6A20 present on the 3rd chromosome of man. As indicated by one report, coronaviruses may be divided into four subgroups as α,, and . Six zoonotic coronaviruses, HCoV229E(α), Nl63(α), OC43(), HKU1(), SARS-CoV() and MERS-CoV(), are competent to cause either mild or severe and acute respiratory diseases. SARS-CoV-2 is also renowned for its D614G mutation in spike. In this mutation, D and G stand for aspartate and glycine, respectively. Therefore, the underlying D614 is now the G614 variant. Results indicated that patients tainted with G614 variants have a more viral load in comparison to D614. But S-G614 difficultly binds ACE2 more than S-D614. These findings derive more stability of S-G614 contrasted with S-D614. An average of 15 days is required for its mutation. SARS-CoV-2 multiplies with the help of its copy machine, sometimes known as coronavirus polymerase [2].

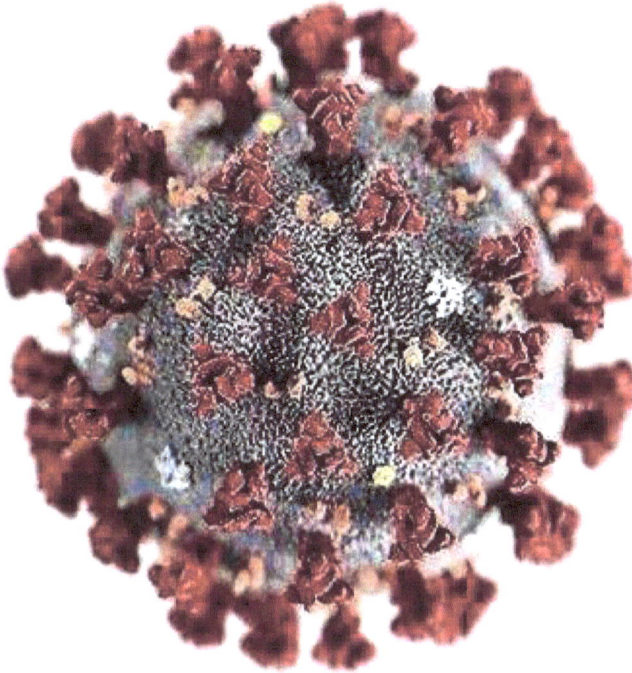

Fig. (1). SARS-CoV-2 version [3].

Like the flu infection, SARS-CoV-2 attacks respiratory frameworks and leads to burdens, for example, hack, fever, weariness and windedness. The virus was initially found to influence human existence in Wuhan of Hubei, China, in Dec. 2019. From that point forward, it has spread more stunning throughout the remainder of the world, signifying its essence in 213 countries and autonomous regions. As per the WHO, the current overall tally of affirmed Covid cases remains at 27,205,275, while the loss of life has arrived at 8,92,880 as on September 8 2020 [4]. The snappy in amount of these virus scenes on a global scale has actuated the necessity for sure-fire countermeasures to check the cataclysmic effects of the virus flare-up. To this end, the present chapter assesses the application of various advancements. Be that as it might, before exploring the possible inventive responses to the viral pandemic affect the executives, we give an exhaustive review of this virus, embracing its clinical symptoms, assurance, therapy, and its impact on its scene the overall economy.

The entire world is by and by under the most extreme threat inferable from COVID-19 spread by contamination of Covid. Most countries of the world have seen incalculable cases of this virus since December 2019 onwards. Dynamic instances of people with low opposition develop age, and clinical issues are uncommonly related to this virus and related lung diseases that are dynamically inclined.

Background

Coronaviruses are frequently round ss(+) RNA infections stretching out from 600-1400nm in diameter, with proteins. The SARS-CoV-2 episode started in the Guangdong area of China and later spread to over 37 nations around the planet, causing more than 8000 diseases and around 774 passing [5]. MERS-CoV was recognized in Saudi Arabia, which started a huge scope scene in the gulf nations prompting 871 fatalities [6].

The COVID-19 scene uncovered in December 2019 when 27 instances of pneumonia of unclear etiology were represented by WHO in Wuhan City of Hubei Province in China [4]. The focal point of the scene was connected to Wuhan's discount market for fish and other outlandish creatures, including snakes, bats and marmots [7]. Another strain of a significantly contagious coronavirus, SARS-CoV-2, has been viewed as a subject of the quick flare-up of this virus. Recognizing qualities of the infection join its amazingly infectious nature and moderately long hatching time of 1-14 days.

Clinical Features

Coronavirus shows clinical symptoms stretching out from an asymptomatic state to ARDS and MODS. As per the consequences of a progressing study driven by WHO *via* a joint effort with China, 55,924 labs insisted COVID-19 cases were analyzed, a larger part demonstrated clinical attributes, for example, fever, dry hack, weakness, weariness and sputum creation. Simply a little pack of patients displayed manifestations, for example, sore throat, cerebral pain, headache, myalgia and windedness. Simultaneously, Nausea, nasal clog, hemoptysis, loose bowels, and conjunctival blockage were discovered to be exceptionally uncommon side effects in the patients, as demonstrated in Table **1**. While the vast majority of patients of this virus built up a gentle to direct sickness, a couple of patients were determined to have an extreme (13.8%) and a basic (6.1%) type of the same. Patients with serious or basic illnesses frequently create somewhat blue lips and are slanted to an assortment of confusions, including ARDS, intense cardiac damage, and auxiliary contamination. As indicated by the US-CDCP, the people at the most noteworthy danger of serious ailment from this virus joined individuals (age >60 years) and individuals with existing ailments, for example, diabetes I and II, hypertension, asthma and CVD [8].

Table 1. COVID-19 Symptoms.

Common Symptoms		Less Common Symptoms		Rare Symptoms	
Fever	88%	Shortness of Breath	19%	Nausea	5.0%
Dry Cough	68%	Arthralgia	15%	Nasal Congestion	%
Fatigue	38%	Sore Throat	14%	Diarrhea	%
Sputum Production	33%	Headache	14%	Conjunctival Congestion	%

Transmission Mechanism

Even though there are a few investigations toward patho-physiological properties of COVID-19, its multiplication instrument remains somewhat slippery. Although the fundamental viral cases are related to the prompt openness of people to defiled creatures, the speedy scene of the disease has moved the point of convergence of the exploration to man-to-man transmission. An examination of 75,465 instances of this virus in Wuhan, China has uncovered that the viral infection mainly conveys individuals from the respiratory beads through sniffling and coughing [9]. These respiratory beads may cover a distance of about 1.8 meters. As such, an individual in very close contact with a contaminated individual is in danger of being presented with respiratory beads and infection. But indicative individuals have been recognized to be an essential wellspring of transmission of SARS-Co--2; there is likewise a chance of transmission using asymptomatic individuals. Immediate and roundabout contact with contaminated surfaces have been distinguished as another expected reason for the transmission of this virus [10].

Because of the presence of spikes on its surface, the SARS-CoV-2 breaks the biomembrane and powers the cell to make numerous duplicates of it. These recently produced duplicates burst cells and taint different cells of body. Following this, the infection dives into the bronchioles and arrives at the lungs, where it seriously weakens the host's alveoli.

Organization

The leftover piece of the chapter is formed in the following heads and sub-heads. In Section **2**, we have clarified the current works that have investigated the state of the pandemic due to COVID-19. Section **3** introduced the effect of the pandemic of this virus on the worldwide economy. Section **4**, inspects the current methodologies for this virus identification, treatment and antibody advancement. Section 5 explains the preventive estimates expected to insure oneself against the virus. In Section 6, the utilization of inventive advances, for example, Artificial Intelligence as an approach to managing the virus episodes adequately has been portrayed. Finally, Section 7 sums up the future extent of the investigation and inference.

The contributions of our chapters are:

1. This analysis presents the requirements of a more profound and important standard compared to other papers in the field of AI and COVID-19.
2. The review is to highlight its significance in reacting to and preventing the outbreak of COVID-19 severe effects of the flu epidemic of this virus.
3. Reviews the current safety guard and proposes the most recent applications of AI to overcome the COVID–19 pandemic. It will be helpful to the researchers, scientists and industrialists for further research in this field.
4. The challenges and future research direction of AI in concern of COVID–19 are finally summarized.

OTHER RELATED PAPERS

The enormous scene of COVID-19 has affected different researchers, scientists, labs, and associations around the planet to direct huge scope exploration to help arrange vaccinations and the progression of other treatment techniques. Following the viral episode, a few papers have uncovered different parts of COVID-19.

To decide the clinical credits of this virus, Dawei Wang *et al.*, supplemented some 138 patients in Wuhan of, China [10, 11].

Fang Jiang *et al.* saw the clinical credits of COVID-19 [12]. They have summed up these assessments in their work and given a compact framework of clinical highlights and drugs of this virus [13]. The specialists have checked the current composition on CT credits of this virus accessible on stages, for instance, Elsevier, Google Scholar and PubMed and so on [14]. To this end, the makers give a short study of this virus scene to the extent of its clinical highlights, countering, end, and treatment.

Despite the bounty of assessment in the locale of COVID-19 brand name examination and immunization movement, to the farthest degree that we could know, at the hour of the game plan, no outline provides a wide review of this virus erupt and its normal results. The paper presents the essential for an organized outline that offers both the occasion and the vertical point of view on this virus to the extent its clinical features, discovering, treatment, expectation methods, and imaginative courses of action being embraced to soothe the impact of this scene. In this paper, we are introducing a fundamental review of this virus pandemic that will help examine extending a more significant cognizance of the current overall situation because of the pandemic due to this virus. Prior to revealing an extraordinary assessment of the pandemic of this virus, we research a bit of the past pandemics in the portion.

EFFECT OF THE COVID-19 PANDEMIC ON THE GLOBAL ECONOMY

Because of non-attendance of strong therapy procedures, societal removing by and by has been distinguished as an ideal guard methodology against the pandemic of this virus. Nevertheless, the requirement for societal separation instigated Governments to force/power lockdowns, which has denoted a gigantic scratch in the economy. All insignificant and unnecessary administrations have been constrained to close down, causing all expectations and purposes of all the cutting edge fragments to face critical disturbances in the production network, placing more than millions of individuals at risk of losing their positions [15]. In this part, we research the impact of the pandemic of this virus on the overall economy by out and out examining its impact on various monetary territories.

Effects on the Lives of People

Coronavirus' effect on individuals' existences have been colossal than its impacts on work. Reports suggested extended homegrown friction, as demonstrated by higher reports of homegrown events around the world [16] and separate from fillings. The pressing factors made by COVID-19 on the existences of individuals are consequently a sincere game plan of issues to address. There are a few equals between the effects on occupations and effects on home life; thus; specialists are encouraged to think about such likely cover, some of which is trapped in the ways immediately.

Effects on Employment

The idea of business has likewise changed massively. The most unfavorable change is a work disaster. Another quick change, as indicated earlier, has been that most information labourers are working from home and may continue doing as such for quite a while. Disregarding the way that working from home isn't current, at no other time has it been the norm for extensive paces of whole associations to do as such, especially not for enhanced periods. Against these unprecedented and conceivably dependable changes, research on five arrangements of issues identified with livelihoods appears to be fundamental.

Employment Misfortune

Work hardship is anything but another subject. More than ever, the quantity of jobless individuals has reached hindering levels [17] and addresses perhaps the most genuine financial concerns, with expansive ramifications that consolidate a feeling of misery and ensuing unfavorable reactions. Thusly, the effect of business disaster is seriously clearing, and the ways for the jobless to search for work and for associations to fill openings might be radically unprecedented. For instance, there may be a dire need for working AI answers to measure the amazing number of business applications for each opening. Further, an advancing declaration by the US President has made it inconvenient for unfamiliar laborers to discover work [18], and this may additional presentation and stand-out difficulties. In this way, the bunch issues made by COVID, incorporating work difficulty, its effects, and possible recovery, are basic to consider.

TREATMENT AND VACCINE DEVELOPMENT

Coronavirus, brought about by SARS-CoV-2, has driven most parts of the world into a serious chaos. Till finish of the creation, no complete therapy or immunization exists for Covid. As the treatments are considered, the treatment of this virus is mostly suggestive, i.e., the sort of therapy based on the directed particular manifestations displayed by the victims.

Most occurrences of the Covid ailment have been assigned smoothly, with patients recovering isolated without the necessity for advancing consideration. Consequently, it is suggested that patients with smooth indications of this virus be regulated at hometoabstain, putting extra strain on the feasibly focused prosperity structures. In customarily, outrageous and essential occurrences of this virus will do, as a rule, require hospitalization. Patients experiencing hypoxemia may require the game-plan of additional Oxygen utilizing face veils or ventilators. Contamination due to a weak safe structure is treated with a key enemy of contamination specialists and antifungal solutions depending upon the situation [11]. Regardless, patients resolved to have the disease ought to be under serious withdrawal, free of the genuineness of appearances, to prevent future transmission.

While no total antiviral medication or vaccination for SARS-CoV-2 is accessible, different undertakings are being made to make one accessible for business use when the soonest opportunity. Inside the going with subsections, we address the try has a go at being made to create ground-breaking vaccination and medicines for the therapy of this virus.

Vaccine Development

Creating immunizations for viral illnesses is especially testing, attributable to their ability to change from one individual to the following. All things considered, the headway of solid and reliable immunizations is the solitary practical method of finishing the pandemic due to this virus. Following the scene, different clinical associations, research labs and scientists have been attempting to set up immunization for SARS-CoV-2 [19]. Likely the main endeavors being made toward immunization advancement for this virus are the accompanying:

MODERNA'S mRNA-1273

The approach of Moderna depends on the mixture of COVID-19 mRNA into cells to permit them to create proteins expected to battle the infection [20]. Dissimilar to the techniques received in traditional antibodies, this methodology doesn't have to grow huge quantities of the virus. Even though this antibody entered the main period of clinical preliminaries on 15th March 2020, its business discharge is dependent upon being longer than a year away [19, 21].

PittCoVacc

Not in the least like the mRNA immunizer contender made by Moderna, PittCoVacc acknowledges standard technique. The groundwork tests coordinated on mice uncovered that PittCoVacc set off the improvement of a gigantic number of antibodies against SARS-CoV-2 within a fortnight of being overseen [22]. Impending the FDA's underwriting, stage I of clinical primers for the neutralizer is to begin soon.

Vaccine from Johnson & Johnson

Johnson and Johnson and BARDA, a region of the US Department of HSS, have vowed to altogether offer some 1 billion US dollars COVID-19 immunizations and research. On 30th March 2020, Johnson and Johnson proclaimed a recognized lead up-and-comer immunization following three months of complete exploration on a few antibody applicants in a joint effort [23].

CEPI Multiple Efforts

The CEPI, set up to stimulate the improvement of vaccinations against emerging overwhelming ailments, has started joint endeavors with various affiliations and associations over the world to help inside the headway of convincing antibodies against the SARS-CoV-2. CEPI and GSK uncovered another relationship on February 3rd, 2020, which will see GSK make its present adjuvant advancement accessible to the CEPI [24]. In expansion to the association endeavors, the CEPI has vowed to begin financing for certain foundations, including the HKU, University of Oxford and the Pasteur Institute, to quiche the progression of reasonable vaccinations against SARS-CoV-2. Until this point, as expected, the CEPI has contributed a measure of 29.2 million dollars in the R&D of various inoculations of this virus [25].

Even though analysts around the planet are making decided undertakings to think about immunization for the extirpation of this virus, the fast-approaching appearance of a successful antibody appears ridiculous. Two essential purposes for the equivalent are referenced under.

i. In the last two Covid flare-ups, explicitly SARS and MERS, it was watched that once vaccination was sorted out some way to a person, it was an astonishing growth in his cytokine impacts. This impact routinely leads to ARDS that, as far as anyone knows, is the primary wellspring of death in patients of this virus. To keep an essential separation from such complexities and to ensure that the antibodies at present are not counter-convincing later, it is key to confirm that these inoculation has a fair prosperity report.

ii. Some of the time, a singular part of vaccination isn't good to make sufficient antibodies. Exactly when perceived, the requirement for very wide-scale making of the immune response of this virus to meet the world's necessities is seen to require a lot of time.

Potential Drugs

Various medication associations have considered potential meds courses of action to treat the Covid ailment. While no drug is thoroughly embraced as of, two or three of these prescriptions are being attempted, a few of them in various times of clinical fundamentals. Starting April 29, 2020, more than 1800 clinical fundamentals, in general, are recorded on the WHO's ICTRP [26]. Among the prescriptions being attempted, Remdesivir, Hydroxychloroquine and Arbidol have shown gigantic confirmation and are new experiencing clinical starters at a couple of crisis facilities over the world [27]. Before 2008, Arbidol seemed to have empowering results against the SARS-CoV disease in cell models. It was likewise demonstrated to be persuading against influenza type an and B contaminations, similarly to the Hepatitis type C disease.

It is crucial for note, notwithstanding, that right now, there is no evident verification sponsorship of the usage of SHL oral liquid as a therapy for this virus [28].

Yet, various endeavors are being made to make capable treatment strategies against this virus, a fiscally useful vaccination presumably will not be doable for in any occasion one more year [29].

PREVENTIVE MEASURES

As the world keeps to experiencing the COVID-19 well-being emergency, it is principal to take after compelling preventive estimates Fig. (**2**). To limit the likelihood of turning into another mishap. On the off chance that people and networks conform to the practices referenced beneath, the world may before long observer went to bend because of this virus. Leveling the bend construes, cutting down the spread of this virus to the degree where benefit-capable medical care offices can sufficiently deal with the impact of the sickness.

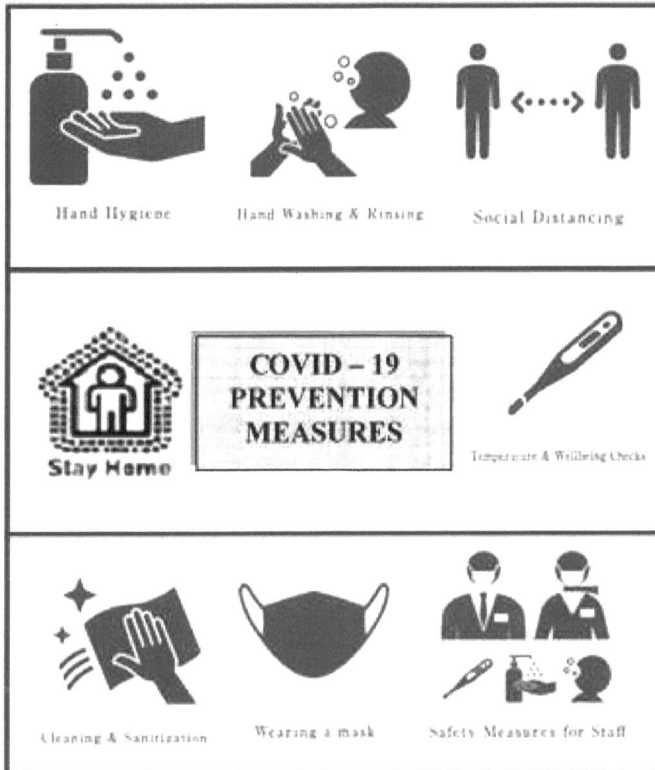

Fig. (2). COVID-19 Preventive Measures.

i. Cleaning hands as habitually as conceivable with liquor, sanitizer, cleanser, and water.

ii. Practice social separating – To maintain oneself to 2 meters (6 feet) from other persons.

iii. Stay home aside from, if fundamental, going out. Individuals over 60, individuals with concealed ailments and pregnant women are encouraged to avoid every social association.

iv. Avoid contacting eyes, nose or/and mouth in the absence of complete purging of their hands.

v. More frequently contacted surfaces, for example, entryway handles, work regions, phones/mobiles, fan/light switches and PC/PCs, might be regularly sterilized.

vi. Covering hacks and sneezing with a fabric, hanky or tissue paper. If these are not promptly accessible, hacking/wheezing into one's elbow pit is fitting.

EMERGING TECHNOLOGIES TO MITIGATE THE COVID-19 PANDEMIC EFFECT
Artificial Intelligence (AI) and COVID-19

AI is already being used in every field of life. Its economic impact can reach $15 trillion by 2030 [30]. The rapid emergence and evolution of AI and COVID-19 are two major factors contributing to the increasing demand for healthcare workers. The shortage of these workers is causing many regions to recall their retired health workers [31, 32].

The rapid emergence and evolution of AI and automation will not allow us to perform the most challenging tasks, such as providing an influenza shot. In the meantime, we are waiting to develop effective algorithms that can cure and prevent COVID-19. AI is also a crucial component in the race to develop a vaccine for COVID-19. It can help develop effective methods to break down the viral proteins that cause the disease. Usually, machine learning algorithms are used to identify the most effective way to kill the virus [33 - 36]. Convolutional Neural Networks (CNNs) are used to discover infection of COVID – 19 from chest X-rays [37].

Without such massive datasets, it would be impossible to get useful information about the disease outbreak. AI tools are also suitable for the prediction of the severity of the patients. The goal is to create a platform that can collect and store all the data related to an outbreak at all times. This way, researchers can immediately identify an antidote. The creation of such a platform would allow authorities to collect and store all the data related to an outbreak. Aside from being able to collect data, virtual agents could also function as chat bots that can answer various questions related to the coronavirus [38]. Aside from collecting data, virtual agents can also function as helpful assistants that can be used at a healthcare facility during a crisis. They can be localized to a certain geographical location and can provide updates to a certain group of people.

Due to the increasing number of AI experts needed in the fight against COVID-19, job opportunities in the tech industry are expected to increase significantly. One of the most critical factors in preventing the spread of the disease is to accelerate the testing of COVID-19 vaccines and other related technologies.

Various applications of AI are shown in Fig. (**3**).

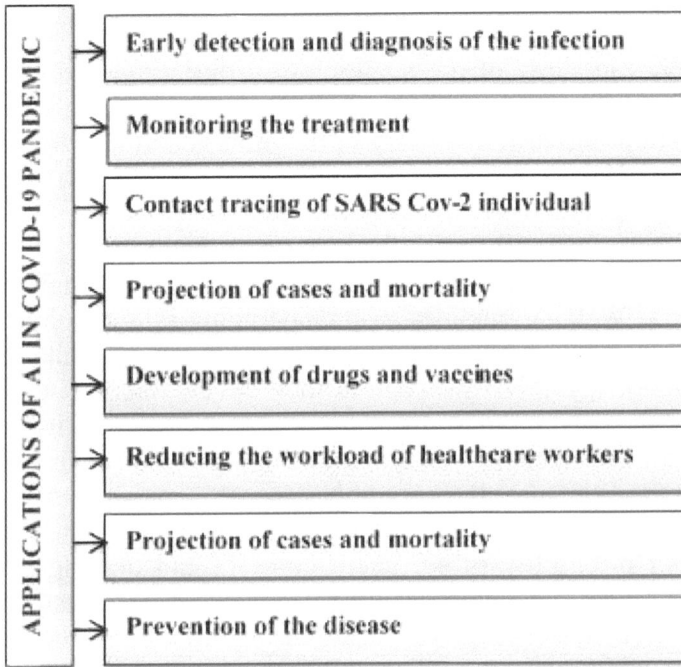

Fig. (3). Applications of AI to fight against COVID-19.

Applications of AI in COVID-19 Pandemic

Early Detection and Diagnosis of the Infection

AI will easily analyze multiple signs and other 'warning flags 'and therefore alert patients and, thus, health officials [38, 39]. It helps to provide decision-making that is easier and more cost-effective. It allows, by realistic algorithms, to create a whole new diagnostic and treatment framework for COVID-19 cases. With the help of medical imaging techniques such as computed tomography and magnetic resonance imaging scans of physical body components, AI is helpful in detecting infected patients [40].

Monitoring the Treatment

AI could develop an intelligent network for automated observation and prediction of this virus's propagation. In order to derive the visual choices of this condition, a neural network can also be built to promote effective monitoring and care of infected individuals [41]. It has the ability to provide patients with regular alerts and collectively provide options to be sought in the COVID-19 pandemic [35].

Contact Tracing of SARS Cov-2 Individual

AI will promote the study of the magnitude of this virus outbreak, identify the clusters and 'hot spots' and can effectively map people's connections and track them jointly. The long-term trajectory of this illness and its certain reappearance may be expected. If there is an individual diagnosis and COVID-19 is confirmed, Touch tracing interference of the larger disease unfolding is the corresponding critical step. The infection of COVID-19 spreads from person to person mostly through spittle, droplets or discharges from the nose through touch transfer, according to the WHO guidelines. Contact tracing is a required public health instrument to break the virus transmission chain in order to take care of SARS-COV-2 production [42]. To prevent further development, the contact tracing approach identifies and treats those recently exposed to an infected COVID-19 patient. Generally, the process detects the affected person with a follow-up for a fortnight after the exposure. If thoroughly used, this mechanism would sever the existing novel coronavirus dissemination chain and eliminate the irruption by giving a greater possibility of sufficient controls and helping to minimize the severity of the recent pandemic. Using various technologies such as Bluetooth, Global Positioning System (GPS), Social Graph, contact details, network-based API, mobile tracking records, card transaction data, and system physical address, many infected countries return to a digital contact tracking mechanism with the mobile application in this regard. In contrast to the non-digital device, the digital contact tracing process can work basically in real-time and much faster. All of these automated apps are meant to gather personal data that can be analyzed by ML and AI tools to track an individual who is vulnerable to the current virus because of its recent touch chain. Most of the countries were grouped in Articles with ML and AI-based touch tracing applications.

Development of Drugs and Vaccines

Through evaluating the available data on COVID-19, AI is employed for drug testing. It's useful for planning and developing medication distribution. This technology is used to speed up real-time drug monitoring, where regular testing takes a great deal. It may help classify effective medicines for treating patients with Covid-19. It has been a versatile instrument for designing assays and improving vaccinations. In the case of the vaccine, AI helps to produce vaccines and coverings at a much higher pace than normal and is also useful for clinical trials.

Reducing the Workload of Healthcare Workers

Healthcare workers have a high workload as a result of a rapid and unprecedented rise in the number of patients during the COVID-19 pandemic. AI will provide students and doctors with the most detailed instruction with respect to this new disease. AI will shape the future care of patients and address more possible problems that will minimize doctors' workload.

Prevention of the Disease

AI will provide updated information that is helpful in preventing this disease with the aid of real-time data processing. During this epidemic, it would be normal to forecast the likely locations of transmission and health services with professionals. With the benefit of prior mentored research on data prevalent at various times, AI is useful for long-term virus and disease prevention. It will provide a means of protection and combat many other diseases. AI will play a big role in providing both predictive and preventive healthcare in the future.

Summary of AI Applications for Covid-19

AI technologies can be used for COVID-19 outbreak identification and diagnosis, control and labeling, infodemiology and infoveillance, biomedicine and pharmacotherapy. The AI-based system is useful for testing the influence of the COVID-19 pandemic as a huge volume of COVID-19 data is much appreciated by different efforts. AI trials are not performed on a wide scale and scientifically validated in a wide-scale and tested clinic; they are also helpful as they provide medical personnel as well as politicians with immediate responses and secret meaningful knowledge. In designing AI algorithms, we face several difficulties, as the consistency and quantity of COVID-19 data sets should be further improved. That needs continuous researchers' efforts and monetary assistance with more accurate and high-quality data from official organizations.

FUTURE SCOPE OF THE STUDY AND CONCLUSION

The COVID-19 epidemic has critically impacted the health of individuals worldwide with a massive number of affected cases. COVID-19 has rapidly picked ground, andcountries, government agencies, and scholastics are attempting to address this global emergency. Various diagnostic methods are used in the identification of COVID-19. AI is expected to be the next generation of technology that can help track the status of infections and provide helpful recommendations for treating patients. This chapter started with an overhauled investigation of COVID-19. Following this, the steps in the transmission of the disease were discussed. To configure the devastating effects of COVID-19, a critical description presented the global economy's trend after its outbreak.

CONSENT FOR PUBLICATION

Not applicable.

CONFLICT OF INTEREST

The authors declare no conflict of interest, financial or otherwise.

ACKNOWLEDGEMENT

Declared none.

REFERENCES

[1]   M. Cascella, M. Rajnik, A. Cuomo, S. C. Dulebohn, and R. Di Napoli, *Features, Evaluation and Treatment Coronavirus (COVID-19).*, 2020.

[2]   S. Dey, Q. Cheng, and J. Tan, "All for one and one for all: Why a pandemic preparedness league of nations?", *Health Policy Technol.*, vol. 9, no. 2, pp. 179-184, 2020.
[http://dx.doi.org/10.1016/j.hlpt.2020.04.009] [PMID: 32427167]

[3]   WHO, "COVID-19", *WHO J. covid 19, Reg. Situational Updat. Africa,* 2020.

[4]   W. H. Organization, *Coronavirus disease (COVID-19),* 2020.

[5]   T. Singhal, "Review on COVID19 disease so far", *Indian J. Pediatr.*, vol. 87, no. 4, pp. 281-286, 2020.
[http://dx.doi.org/10.1007/s12098-020-03263-6] [PMID: 32166607]

[6]   P. Mehta, D.F. McAuley, M. Brown, E. Sanchez, R.S. Tattersall, and J.J. Manson, "COVID-19: consider cytokine storm syndromes and immunosuppression", *Lancet,* vol. 395, no. 10229, pp. 1033-1034, 2020.
[http://dx.doi.org/10.1016/S0140-6736(20)30628-0] [PMID: 32192578]

[7]   A. Bleibtreu, M. Bertine, C. Bertin, N. Houhou-Fidouh, and B. Visseaux, *Iconography: Focus on Middle East respiratory syndrome coronavirus.* MERS-CoV, 2019.

[8]   Z. A. CS M. K. N ON, and A. A. J. AK, "World Health Organization declares global emergency: A review of the 2019 novel", *Int. J. Surg.*, vol. 76, pp. 71-76, 2020.
[http://dx.doi.org/10.1016/j.ijsu.2020.02.034] [PMID: 32112977]

[9]   J. Wang, M. Zhou, and F. Liu, "Reasons for healthcare workers becoming infected with novel coronavirus disease 2019 (COVID-19) in China", *J. Hosp. Infect.*, vol. 105, no. 1, pp. 100-101, 2020.
[http://dx.doi.org/10.1016/j.jhin.2020.03.002] [PMID: 32147406]

[10]   G. Targher, A. Mantovani, X.B. Wang, H.D. Yan, Q.F. Sun, K.H. Pan, C.D. Byrne, K.I. Zheng, Y.P. Chen, M. Eslam, J. George, and M.H. Zheng, "Patients with diabetes are at higher risk for severe illness from COVID-19", *Diabetes Metab.*, vol. 46, no. 4, pp. 335-337, 2020.
[http://dx.doi.org/10.1016/j.diabet.2020.05.001] [PMID: 32416321]

[11]   Y. Bai, L. Yao, T. Wei, F. Tian, D.Y. Jin, L. Chen, and M. Wang, "Presumed asymptomatic carrier transmission of COVID-19", *JAMA,* vol. 323, no. 14, pp. 1406-1407, 2020.
[http://dx.doi.org/10.1001/jama.2020.2565] [PMID: 32083643]

[12]   N. Chen, M. Zhou, X. Dong, J. Qu, F. Gong, Y. Han, Y. Qiu, J. Wang, Y. Liu, Y. Wei, J. Xia, T. Yu, X. Zhang, and L. Zhang, "Epidemiological and clinical characteristics of 99 cases of 2019 novel coronavirus pneumonia in Wuhan, China: a descriptive study", *Lancet,* vol. 395, no. 10223, pp. 507-513, 2020.
[http://dx.doi.org/10.1016/S0140-6736(20)30211-7] [PMID: 32007143]

[13] F. Jiang, L. Deng, L. Zhang, Y. Cai, C.W. Cheung, and Z. Xia, "Review of the Clinical Characteristics of Coronavirus Disease 2019 (COVID-19)", *J. Gen. Intern. Med.,* vol. 35, no. 5, pp. 1545-1549, 2020.
[http://dx.doi.org/10.1007/s11606-020-05762-w] [PMID: 32133578]

[14] S. Salehi, *abedi a, Balakrishnan S, gholamrezanezhad a.* Coronavirus Dis, 2019.

[15] D. Goodman, *World economy faces $5 trillion hit that is like losing Japan.* Bloomberg, 2020.

[16] C. Bettinger-Lopez, and A. Bro, *A double pandemic: Domestic violence in the age of COVID-19, .*

[17] L. Levine, *The labor market during the Great Depression and the current recession, .*

[18] D. Trump, *Suspension of Entry of Immigrants and Nonimmigrants Who Present a Risk to the United States Labor Market During the Economic Recovery Following the 2019 Novel Coronavirus Outbreak: Proclamation 10052 by the President of the United States of America, June.* Office of the Federal Register: United States, 2020.

[19] D. van Riel, and E. de Wit, "Next-generation vaccine platforms for COVID-19", *Nat. Mater.,* vol. 19, no. 8, pp. 810-812, 2020.
[http://dx.doi.org/10.1038/s41563-020-0746-0] [PMID: 32704139]

[20] G.I. Perez Perez, and A. Talebi Bezmin Abadi, "Ongoing Challenges Faced in the Global Control of COVID-19 Pandemic", *Arch. Med. Res.,* vol. 51, no. 6, pp. 574-576, 2020.
[http://dx.doi.org/10.1016/j.arcmed.2020.04.016] [PMID: 32446538]

[21] A. Liu, *'China's CanSino Bio advances COVID-19 vaccine into phase 2 on preliminary safety data.'* *Fierce Pharma, .*

[22] L.D. Falo Jr, "Advances in skin science enable the development of a COVID-19 vaccine", *J. Am. Acad. Dermatol.,* vol. 83, no. 4, pp. 1226-1227, 2020.
[http://dx.doi.org/10.1016/j.jaad.2020.05.126] [PMID: 32485211]

[23] M.D. Shin, S. Shukla, Y.H. Chung, V. Beiss, S.K. Chan, O.A. Ortega-Rivera, D.M. Wirth, A. Chen, M. Sack, J.K. Pokorski, and N.F. Steinmetz, "COVID-19 vaccine development and a potential nanomaterial path forward", *Nat. Nanotechnol.,* vol. 15, no. 8, pp. 646-655, 2020.
[http://dx.doi.org/10.1038/s41565-020-0737-y] [PMID: 32669664]

[24] V. Chamola, V. Hassija, V. Gupta, and M. Guizani, "A Comprehensive Review of the COVID-19 Pandemic and the Role of IoT, Drones, AI, Blockchain, and 5G in Managing its Impact", *IEEE Access,* vol. 8, pp. 90225-90265, 2020.
[http://dx.doi.org/10.1109/ACCESS.2020.2992341]

[25] R. Mukherjee, "Global efforts on vaccines for COVID-19: Since, sooner or later, we all will catch the coronavirus", *J. Biosci.,* vol. 45, no. 1, p. 68, 2020.
[http://dx.doi.org/10.1007/s12038-020-00040-7] [PMID: 32385219]

[26] W.H. Organization, *WHO infectious disease report,* 2002.www. who. int/infectious

[27] M. Wang, R. Cao, and L. Zhang, "Remdesivir and chloroquine effectively inhibit the recently emerged novel coronavirus (2019 nCoV) in vitro [published online February 4", *Cell Res.,* vol. 30, 2020.

[28] W. Li, *The curative effect observation of shuanghuanglian and penicillin on acute tonsillitis.* Lin Chuang Er Bi Yan Hou Ke Za Zhi, 2002.

[29] H.J. Hutchins, B. Wolff, R. Leeb, J.Y. Ko, E. Odom, J. Willey, A. Friedman, and R.H. Bitsko, "COVID-19 mitigation behaviors by age group—United States, April–June 2020", *MMWR Morb. Mortal. Wkly. Rep.,* vol. 69, no. 43, pp. 1584-1590, 2020.
[http://dx.doi.org/10.15585/mmwr.mm6943e4] [PMID: 33119562]

[30] PwC, "Retrieved from The impact of automation", 2019.

[31] K. Wells, *MI-Radio . Retrieved from More Michi- gan healthcare workers are getting sick. What happens when there's a shortage?, .*

[32]   G.Z. Yang, B. J Nelson, R.R. Murphy, H. Choset, H. Christensen, S. H Collins, P. Dario, K. Goldberg, K. Ikuta, N. Jacobstein, D. Kragic, R.H. Taylor, and M. McNutt, "Combating COVID-19-The role of robotics in managing public health and infectious diseases", *Sci. Robot.,* vol. 5, no. 40, 2020.eabb5589 [http://dx.doi.org/10.1126/scirobotics.abb5589] [PMID: 33022599]

[33]   M.A. Haque, S. Haque, D. Sonal, K. Kumar, and E. Shakeb, "Security Enhancement for IoT Enabled Agriculture", *Mater. Today Proc.,* no. Feb, 2021. [http://dx.doi.org/10.1016/j.matpr.2020.12.452]

[34]   E.S. Md, "Alimul Haque, Shameemul Haque, Deepa Sonal, Kailash Kumar, Security Enhancement for IoT enabled Agriculture", *Mater. Today Proc.,* 2020.

[35]   D. Sonal, D.N. Pandit, and M.A. Haque, "An IoT Based Model to Defend Covid 19 Outbreak", *Int. J. Innov. Technol. Explor. Eng.,* vol. 10, no. 7, pp. 152-157, 2021. [http://dx.doi.org/10.35940/ijitee.G9052.0510721]

[36]   O. Etzioni, and N. Decario, *AI Can Help Scientists Find a Covid-19 Vaccine.* Wired, 2020.

[37]   L. Wang, and A. Wong, "COVID-Net: A Tailored Deep Convolutional Neural Network Design for Detection of COVID-19 Cases from Chest X-Ray Images", http://arxiv.org/abs/2003.09871 Online

[38]   M. Rahimzadeh, and A. Attar, "A modified deep convolutional neural network for detecting COVID-19 and pneumonia from chest X-ray images based on the concatenation of Xception and ResNet50V2", *Informatics in Medicine Unlocked,* vol. 19, 2020.100360 [http://dx.doi.org/10.1016/j.imu.2020.100360] [PMID: 32501424]

[39]   T. Ai, Z. Yang, H. Hou, C. Zhan, C. Chen, W. Lv, Q. Tao, Z. Sun, and L. Xia, "Correlation of Chest CT and RT-PCR Testing for Coronavirus Disease 2019 (COVID-19) in China: A Report of 1014 Cases", *Radiology,* vol. 296, no. 2, pp. E32-E40, 2020. [http://dx.doi.org/10.1148/radiol.2020200642] [PMID: 32101510]

[40]   H. Luo, Q. Tang, Y. Shang, S. Liang, M. Yang, N. Robinson, and J. Liu, "Can Chinese Medicine Be Used for Prevention of Corona Virus Disease 2019 (COVID-19)? A Review of Historical Classics, Research Evidence and Current Prevention Programs", *Chin. J. Integr. Med.,* vol. 26, no. 4, pp. 243-250, 2020. [http://dx.doi.org/10.1007/s11655-020-3192-6] [PMID: 32065348]

[41]   M.A. Haque, D. Sonal, S. Haque, M.M. Nezami, and K. Kumar, "An IoT-Based Model for Defending Against the Novel Coronavirus (COVID-19) Outbreak", *Solid State Technol.,* pp. 592-600, 2020.

[42]   W.H. Organization, "Statement on the second meeting of the International Health Regulations (2005) Emergency Committee regarding the outbreak of novel coronavirus (2019-nCoV)",

## CHAPTER 8

Intelligent Personalized E-Learning Platform using Machine Learning Algorithms

Makram Soui[1,*], **Karthik Srinivasan**[1,*] and **Abdulaziz Albesher**[1,*]

[1] *College of Computing and Informatics, Saudi Electronic University, Saudi Arabia*

Abstract: Personalized learning is a teaching method that allows the content and course of online training to be adapted according to the individual profile of learners. The main task of adaptability is the selection of the most appropriate content for the student in accordance with his digital footprint. In this work, we build a machine learning model to recommend the appropriate learning resources according to the student profile. To this end, we use Sequential forward selection (SFS) as a feature selection technique with AdaBoost as a classifier. The obtained results prove the efficiency of the proposed model with 91.33% of accuracy rate and 91.43% of precision rate.

Keywords: Boosting algorithm, Feature selection, Machine learning, Personalized e-learning.

INTRODUCTION

ONLINE education has become ubiquitous and important in our society. Hence, to improve the educational process, one of the most recommended solutions is E-learning personalization which considers individual's profile for adapting courses and learning scenarios. According to the National Academy of Engineering [1] institution, E-learning personalization is one of the most interesting challenges of the 21st Century. Personalized E-learning focuses on learners' differences in adapting learning scenarios and courses according to the learners' characteristics (such as learner's media preferences, level of knowledge, learning outcomes, learning resource type, *etc.*).

The scale of the eLearning industry was $176 billion in 2017 and is projected to hit $398 billion by 2026 [2]. Over the past 12 months, almost 50% of students have participated in at least one online course [3].

* **Corresponding authors Makram Soui, Karthik Srinivasan and Abdulaziz Albesher:** College of Computing and Informatics, Saudi Electronic University, Saudi Arabia; Tel: +966 55031038; E-mail: m.soui@seu.edu.sa

Prasad Lokulwar, Basant Verma, N. Thillaiarasu, Kailash Kumar, Mahip Bartere and Dharam Singh (Eds.)

As per a survey, 94% of students are satisfied with online learning and they suggest that it has or will have a positive return on investment (ROI) [4].

In the first quarter of 2020, the COVID-19 pandemic spread around the world fast. Because of this pandemic, all aspects of life, including education, were affected severely. The pandemic has led to the closure of schools and colleges, resulting in an alarming situation for institutions to provide education. To continue the learning process in a safe and secure manner, most of the countries have announced online classes. This major, sudden transition from conventional classroom learning to an entirely online learning framework has changed the way of delivering education and assessment activities to their students [5].

Due to the pandemic, most of the schools worldwide, started to conduct classes through e-learning tools and video telephony software. As of a recent study, around 89% of the world's student population is out of school due to the pandemic. This represents 1.5 billion students learning through online education platforms. This sudden change in the learning method leads to some challenges across countries. For example, 95% of students have a computer to do their homework in Switzerland, Austria and Norway, whereas 34% of students only have a computer in Indonesia. Also, schools use different software across the world to provide online education.

Nowadays, students want to gain maximum results in minimum time. To meet students' expectations, a personalized learning platform is most recommended. According to United States National Education Technology Plan 2017, adaptive e-learning recommendations, such as instructional approaches, learning objectives, and instructional contents, may all vary based on student's needs. Moreover, learning tasks should be more relevant and meaningful based on student interests [6].

Personalized learning is a learner-centric approach designed to meet the individual needs, desires, and goals of the learner. In terms of e-Learning, personalization is a technical approach that deals with the system to provide a learning experience for each user [7]. It is one of the wildly important techniques to improve the quality of teaching-learning methods by proposing an intelligent E-learning system that can confirm high-quality interaction for all learners [8]. In fact, the personalized course represents an efficient solution to increase the learner's motivation, and to reduce the time required to achieve his/her learning outcomes. In addition, customization of learning scenarios helps the learner to understand the learning objects efficiently.

However, it is difficult to consider all learners' preferences at the same time in the personalization process. First, the course may include many learning objects to match a set of learner's characteristics. Thus, an instructor may spend more effort and a lot of time preparing his/her course with different learning materials in various ways for learners having distinct characteristics. Second, collecting the learner's preferences manually is a tedious and time-consuming task. Also, there is no consent about the most interesting preference to use in the personalization process. To address this issue, we will study in this project how to use artificial intelligence methods to implement a new E-learning personalization process.

In this context, we propose an automatic E-learning personalization method based on the artificial intelligence algorithms on Learning Objective Metadata (LOM) standard defined in (IEEE 1484.12.1, 2002) and (IEEE 1484.12.3, 2020). The aim of this standard is to facilitate both learner and teacher to explore, assess and use learning objects by defining a common conceptual data schema. The idea is to use machine learning and evolutionary algorithms to personalize the course and the learning scenarios according to the learner's characteristics.

The objective of this work is to provide the learner with suitable learning resources (slides, narrative text, simulation, *etc.*) according to their user profile (age, level of study, motivation, *etc.*)

In summary, our main contributions are as follows:

• To review the recent development on E-learning personalization.

• To propose a model for course personalization.

RELATED WORK

Several approaches have been proposed in the literature about E-learning personalization. We classify existing personalized e-learning approaches into two broad categories 1) machine learning approaches, 2) rule-based classification approaches.

Machine Learning Approach

Several machine learning techniques have been used for E-learning personalization. Most of the work used information related to the learner, and/or an assessment of contextual information to discover the interests and preferences of the learners [9]. In particular, some authors in their study [10] exploited data mining techniques to group students into clusters based on the similarity of their behavior with respect to the Felder–Silverman learning styles model (FSLSM).

Murad and Yang [11] suggested a personalized content E-learning system based on a web mining technique to detect learner navigation patterns. The aim is to analyze the web content frequently visited by the learner to build a personalized content model. Shani and Shapira [12] proposed the EduRank algorithm for adapting educational content to learners based on a collaborative filtering algorithm. EduRank assigns a difficulty ranking for each student, the most common class among its similar students.

Shobana and Sathis Kumar [13] proposed a personalized e-Learning system using reinforcement learning. In this work, personalization is achieved by frequent interaction with the learner and analyzing the history of the learning activities. The authors used personalized document filtering system to learn users' behaviors and preferences to learn the information. Also, the system used implicit/explicit feedback management to evaluate user preferences. The implicit feedback automatically collects user preferences, whereas the explicit feedback collects the preferences from the learner explicitly, which helps to establish a customized and personalized learning path.

Rule-based Approach

The aim of a rules-based algorithm is to extract practical knowledge from a given data sets and transform it into usable and understandable information. Association rule is a popular method that aims to find relationships between contexts by a recommending E-learning system [14]. But, it seems an ineffective method when a large quantity of data is processed. Kolekar *et al.* [15] proposed the adaptive e-learning system, which is an expert rule tool based on Felder-Silverman Learning Style Model (FSLSM) to classify learners. This study suggests a common method to provide learning material with an adaptive learning interface.

Soui *et al.* [7] suggested an Adaptive tutoring application using fuzzy logic, which uses semantic patterns between learners' interests and data elements to extract an adaptive user interface appropriate to learners' characteristics. Rule-based algorithms are very helpful in extracting interesting patterns on E-learning personalization from large-scale data sets which complex data structures. The extracted patterns provide results which are easy to interpret. These classification rules are one of the widely used techniques since they represent a transparent model easily interpretable by human. In this context, we focus on the generation of adaptation rules to correctly personalize courses based on machine learning and evolutionary algorithms[16].

Laksitowening *et al.* [17] proposed a triple factor approach to achieve e-Learning personalization. This work adopts three factors such as learning style, motivation and knowledgeability, which affect the learning process. To achieve the goal, the study followed three steps: personalized e-Learning system, personalization rule, and intervention to improve learning type. The personalization rule proposed to implement dynamic personalization, which adapts users learning type and learning process in each stage. The rules are implemented in every topic that causes learners to access learning material and discussion forums more regularly, as well as increase their knowledge capability.

BACKGROUD

Feature Selection Techniques

SFS

Sequential Forward Selection (SFS) is a technique in which features are gradually inserted into an empty set until the insertion of remaining features does not minimize the criterion, such as misclassification rate. SFS is performed well when the optimal subset is small.

SBS

Sequential Backward Selection (SBS) is a technique in which features are gradually deleted from a full set until the deletion of remaining features does not boot up the criterion, such as misclassification rate. SBS is performed well when the optimal subset is large.

SFFS

Sequential Forward Floating Selection (SFFS) is a technique that consists of implementing, after each forward step, several backward steps performed until the obtained results perform better than previously obtained ones at that level. Therefore, backward steps not available suppose intermediate results of the current level cannot be improved.

Machine learning Algorithms

K-Nearest Neighbor (KNN)

The KNN is one of the supervised learning algorithms. It is very intuitive and simple. Given some data, it looks at the data around it (neighbors) and classifies it into categories that contain more data. The KNN algorithm is a method of classifying specific data with the largest number of classes of k neighboring data for a specific input data x. To find the nearest neighbor, calculate the distance between neighbors using Distance measures such as Euclidean distance, Manhattan distance *etc.* Next, search for as many as k neighbors with close distance. Finally, new data label prediction is based on the principle of majority voting on the found neighbors.

Support Vector Machine (SVM)

The SVM is a powerful machine learning supervised learning model that can be used for classification tasks. It is a model that provides a decision boundary, that is, a reference line for classification. So, when a

new point that has not been classified appears, it is possible to perform the classification task by checking which side of the boundary it belongs to. The range that we can perceive visually is only up to three dimensions. As the number of dimensions, that is, the number of attributes, increases, it will become more complex. The crystal boundary would also be a high-dimensional, not a simple plane, which is called a "hyperplane". Support Vectors refer to data points that are close to the decision boundary. These data play a crucial role in defining boundaries.

Random Forest (RF)

Random Forest is a representative algorithm of the bagging method that utilizes multiple decision trees. The random forest algorithm trains several decision tree classifiers and makes predictions based on the results. When training each decision tree, that is, bagging, data sampled by allowing redundancy in the entire training set. This is a method of training with the set as the training set of the individual decision tree classifier. Due to a large number of hyperparameters, it takes a lot of time for tuning.

AdaBoost

AdaBoost is adaptive which uses feedback to create the next tuned classifier based on a classifier error and is susceptible to noisy data and outliers. However, thanks to the adaptability of AdaBoost, when used properly, it has the characteristic of suppressing overfitting compared to other machine learning. AdaBoost applies weak classifiers to the training data in order from $t = 1$ to $t = T$, and determines whether each answer is correct. At this time, the weights for the wrongly classified samples are adjusted heavily, and conversely, the weights for the correctly answered samples are reduced.

Gradient Boosting

Gradient Boosting is an integrated learning algorithm in machine learning. In fact, it is the process of continuously improving the weak learner to become a strong learner. The name of Gradient Boosting consists of 2 parts: Gradient Descent + Boosting. Boosting means, just like "boosting" literally, obtaining a strong learner by improving a weak learner is the process of boosting. The process of training a strong learner through a weak learner continues with some of the advantages of a weak learner, so Gradient Boosting has good robustness and can effectively avoid overfitting. Overfitting is a trap that is easy to fall into in machine learning.

XGBoost

XGBoost is also known as Extreme gradient boosting. It has rapidly become one of the popular methods of machine learning classification. Typically, it is greedy in nature and has high performance than other methods. Due to its parallel computation, it performs better than gradient boosting. It is a more regularized model to control overfitting and give better performance. It is a tree-based algorithm for classification, regression and ranking with a custom loss function. It has the feature of sparse aware that means automatic handling of missing data values.

Motivation Example

In this section, a motivation example is given to illustrate our contribution. (Fig. **1**) shows an example of student X profile which consists of age=30, sex=male, program of study=IT, level=3, motivation=high, density=high. Student X prefers reading textbooks as a learning resource.

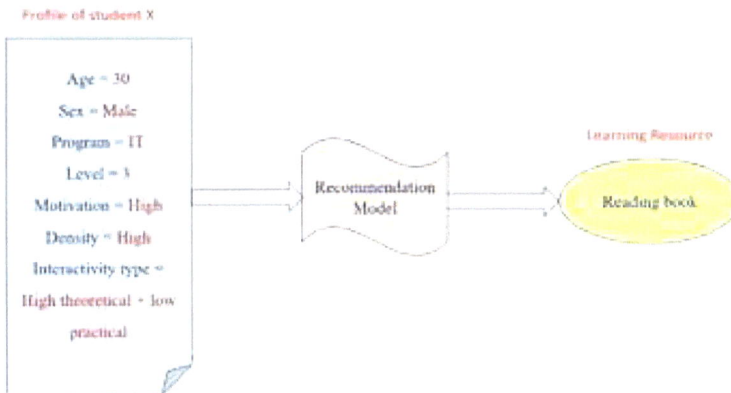

Fig. (1). Learning resource Recommendation for Student X

In this section, a motivation example is given to illustrate our contribution. (Fig. **2**) shows an example of student Y profile which consists of age=25, sex=female, program of study=Law, level=5, motivation=medium, density=low. Student Y prefers watching a video as a learning resource.

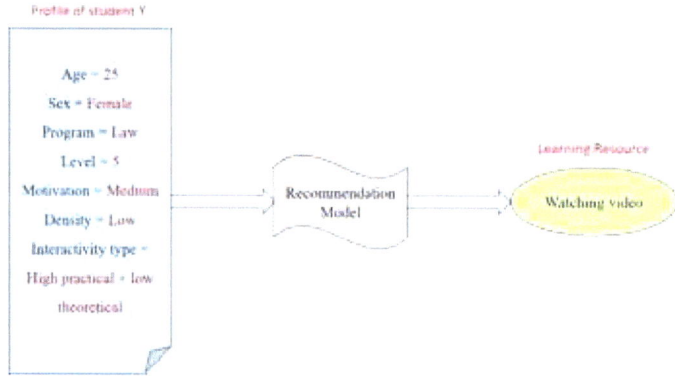

Fig. (2). Learning resource Recommendation for Student Y

PROPOSED APPROACH

In this section, we suggest a personalized model that relies on a feature selection phase and a classification phase to provide the learner with a personalized course. An overview of the proposed approach is illustrated in Fig. (**3**). It combines the preprocessing steps (Random oversampling, SFS feature selection) with the Adaboost classifier.

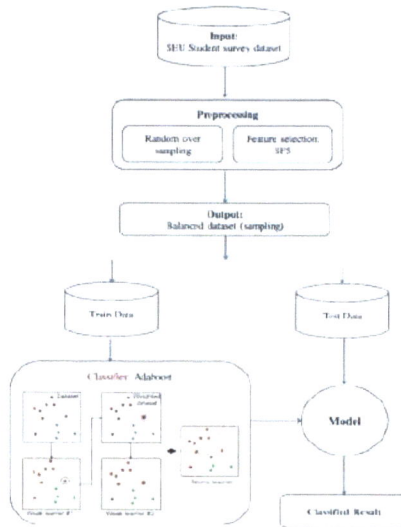

Fig. (3). Approach overview

Random oversampling is used in a standard normal distribution with a mean of zero and a standard deviation of one. SFS Feature selection technique is applied to remove the irrelevant features and keep only the relevant features in the training phase. The second phase is to train the model based on the Adaboost classifier to predict the personalized course for each learner profile. Last, a testing phase is conducted to assess the efficiency of the proposed model based on a test dataset.

Preprocessing

It is a data preparation that includes selecting, cleaning, constructing, formatting, and integrating data. These tasks can be very time-consuming but are critical for the success of the machine learning project.

In our work, we focus on two main data preprocessing techniques. Before conducting the feature selection process, two techniques such as standard scalar and random oversampling are used to perform standard distribution and handling imbalanced data, respectively. After standard distribution and balancing the data, the SFS algorithm is used for the feature selection purpose.

Standard scalar

This technique is used to transform attributes to a standard normal distribution with a mean of zero and a standard deviation of one. It is an estimator that normalizes features to have unit standard deviation and/or zero mean. It is most useful for techniques that assume the input features which represent a normal distribution.

Random oversamplng

This step aims to balance the dataset. Imbalanced dataset severely affects the performance of the model. To address the problem of class imbalance in dataset, a random oversampling method is used. As shown in algorithm 1, it duplicates samples from the minority class in the training dataset and can result in overfitting for some models.

The motivation is to balance the number of regular and unusual instances with the insertion of replicas of the most interesting and unusual instances in the bins containing instances with high importance. The number of created copies is automatically identified to guarantee: (1) a balance between unusual and regular instances and (2) the same frequency in the oversampled bins. The parameter 'o' permits the user to choose a particular ratio of oversampling to use in each bin with important values.

Algorithm 1

Algorithm: Random oversampling Algorithm
1: function RandOver(D, y,φ(y), tR, o)   2: // D - A data set   3: // y - The personalized course   4: // φ(y) – learner specified significance function   5: // tR - The threshold for significance on y values   6: // o - (parameter) Ratio of oversampling   7: Bins ← BinsConstructor(D, y, tR)   8: BinsO ← {Binsi: □(x, y)
Binsiφ(y) ≥ tR}   9: newData ← Bins   10: for each B □ BinsO do   11: if o then   12: tgtNr ← |B| × o   13: else   14: tgtNr ← Nr. instances in Bins\BinsO Nr of BinsO   15: end if   16: sel RareCases ← sample (tgtNr, B)   17: newData ← c(newData,sel RareCases)   18: end for   19: return newData   20: end function

SFS

It aims to reduce the data set size by deleting irrelevant redundant or attributes. The idea is to find a minimum set of dimensions that reflects the probability distribution of data classes like the original distribution gained by all features. As shown in algorithm 2, SFS algorithms are a version of greedy search algorithms that are applied to minimize an initial d-dimensional feature space to a k-dimensional feature subspace where k < d. It begins with a null model. Sequentially add features to the model one at a time. At each stage, this estimator chooses the best feature to add based on the cross-validation score of an estimator. If a feature is retained, it never drops from the model.

Algorithm 2

Algorithm: SFS algorithm
Input: -Y_0: Empty dataset   **Output**: The predefined number of selected features   **Initialize**: Empty set Y_0 = {φ}   1-Begin with the empty set Y0 = {φ}   2- Choose the next best feature x+ = x+=arg□max J (Yk+x) x□Yk□   3- Adjust Y_{k+1} = Y_k + x^+; k = k + 1   4- Go to step 2

Classification Phase

For binary classification, the most used boosting algorithm is AdaBoost. This algorithm was proposed by Freund and Schapire (Freund & Schapire, 1997). Algorithm 3 presents the behavior of this technique.

Algorithm 3

Algorithm: AdaBoost algorithm
Input: -A sequence of m instances S = {(x₁, y₁)...(x_m, y_m)} where x_i ∈ X_k with labels y_i ∈ Y={0,1} from SEU student dataset,   -Weak learner   -T (number of iterations)   **Output**: The final classifier with hypothesis Hx=sign(∑t=1Tát htx)**Initialize**: D_i(i)=1/m for all i =1,.....,m   1-For t = 1 to T   2- Call Weak learner using distribution D_t   3- Get Weak classifier and obtain hypothesis ht: X→{-1,+1}   4- Calculate the error rate e_t∑i=1mDti[ht (xi)≠yi] of h_t   5- If e_t > 0.5 then T=t-1 and abort loop   6- set át=12 ln☐(1-etet) 7- Update Dt+1(i)=Dt i exp☐(-át yt hti)Zt

As shown in algorithm 3, AdaBoost takes the training set of m examples from the SEU student dataset as input to perform a classification step. It initializes with a weight function Dt(x), which distributes the same weight to all training samples. In each iteration t, the weak learner is used to create a classifier with a hypothesis ht, which computes the error rate of the training samples.

The algorithm uses the error rate to adjust the probability distribution Dt(x). This adjustment puts more weight on the misclassified training examples and less weight on the ones that were classified correctly in the previous iteration. This process sequentially constructs several weak classifiers for T iterations.

The algorithms finally output a classifier with a hypothesis H, obtained using a weighted vote of the previous individual classifiers. The weight of each of these classifiers is obtained using the accuracy of the distribution Dt that they used.

VALIDATION

To better investigate our proposed model, we endeavored to answer the following two research questions:

Research Question 1. To what extent is the feature selection technique contributing to building high-performance models?

Description of the Experimental Database

To validate our work, we used a dataset that includes information about students having different profiles. Table **1** presents the profile attributes of our dataset.

Table 1. Dataset Description

ID	Feature	Description
1	Age	Age in Numeric value
2	Sex	Male or Female
3	Program	Student belongs to the program
4	College	Student belongs to the college
5	Level	Current level of the study
6	Branch	Student belongs to the branch (geographical location)
7	Job	Whether students have jobs or not
8	Attending method	What type of attending method do you prefer more?
9	Experience level	Experience level in handling e-Learning platform tools
10	No of lectures	Total number of lectures that students prefer to attend daily
11	Frequency of contact	Frequency of contact of students to their instructor to ask some inquiries
12	Motivation	Motivation level of students when using the interfaces of the e-Learning Platform
13	Recorded lectures	Interested level of students in revising the recorded lectures on the e-Learning platform
14	Interactivity type	Preferred level of interactivity type (theoretical and practical)
15	Assessment activity	Type of assessment activity that students prefer most
16	Semantic density	Preferred level of semantic density of students (amount of content) displayed in a single powerpoint slide
17	Preferred device	Electronic devices that students mostly prefer to access the course contents
18	Background color	Background color which students prefer for their e-Learning platform
19	Text color	Text color that students prefer for their course text contents

Evaluation Metrics

This step aims to assess the proposed model by classifying new customers. This step is based on a set of evaluation metrics such as accuracy, precision, AUC, *etc.* To this end, the predictive model tries to predict the class label of the tested dataset. In our work, we used the hold-out methods to assess the proposed model. 70% of the dataset for training and 30% for testing.

The accuracy refers to the ratio of the correctly predicted course personalization for a given learner profile:

$$Accuracy = \frac{TP+TN}{TP+FP+TN+FN} \qquad (1)$$

The area under the ROC curve (AUC) is an important performance indicator used to assess and compare the classifier's efficiency. It is mostly used for the binary classification problem. AUC determines the compromise between the sensitivity and specificity rate. It is calculated as follows:

$$AUC = \frac{Sensitivity + Specificity}{2} \qquad (2)$$

Where sensitivity is the percentage of positive examples that are correctly classified (*i.e.*, the true positive (recognition) rate). It is defined as:

$$Sensitivity = \frac{TP}{TP+FN} \qquad (3)$$

while specificity is the percentage of negative instances that are correctly classified (true negative rate). It is defined as:

$$Specificity = \frac{TN}{TN+FP} \qquad (4)$$

The precision represents the percentage of features that are correctly attributed to a specific class. As shown in equation 5, it is the ratio of true positives over the sum of false positives and true positives.

$$Precision = \frac{TP}{TP+FP} \qquad (5)$$

As shown in equation 6, recall is the ratio of TP over the sum of TP and FN. It represents the percentage of total relevant results correctly classified by the algorithm.

$$Recall = \frac{TP}{TP+FN} \qquad (6)$$

Finally, we used the F-score indicator, which measures the average between sensitivity and specificity.

$$F\text{-}score = \frac{2 \times Sensitivity \times Specificity}{Sensitivity + Specificity} \qquad (7)$$

Results for Research Question 1

Experimental Results With Full Dataset

We train the studied classifiers respectively using the full dataset. For both experiments, the dataset is divided into a training set (70%) and a testing set (30%). Six machine learning classifiers are applied: XGboost, Adaboost, Gradient Boosting, SVM, KNN, and Random Forest. The experimental results are shown in Table **2**, which compares our proposed model with the studied techniques. Adaboost outperforms all other used techniques. The proposed model provides 90.5% of accuracy, 91.08% of precision, 90.5% of recall and 90.63% of F1-score. It is closely followed by a gradient boosting algorithm which gives 87% of accuracy, 86.08% of precision, 87% of recall and 86.85% of F1-score. It is closely followed by KNN.

Table 2. Experimental results with full dataset

Classifier	Accuracy (%)	Precision (%)	Recall (%)	F1-Score (%)
XGboost	86	85.84	86	85.85
AdaBoost	90.5	91.08	90.5	90.63
Gradient Boosting	87	86.8	87	86.85
SVM	61.67	61.17	61.67	60.29
KNN	86.17	85.88	86.17	85.83
Random Forest	85.5	85.3	85.5	85.12

Experimental results with Filtered Dataset

We train the studied classifiers respectively using the full dataset, and filtered dataset. Three machine learning classifiers are applied: XGboost, Adaboost, Gradient Boosting, SVM, KNN, and Random Forest. The experimental results in Table **3** present the performance of the studied algorithms.

Table 3. Experimental results with filtered dataset

Feature selection	Classifier	Accuracy (%)	Precision (%)	Recall (%)	F1-Score (%)
	XGboost	89.5	89.53	88.89	88.8
SBS	AdaBoost	90.67	90.43	90.43	90.42
	Gradient Boosting	89	88.85	88.45	88.4

(Table 3) cont.....

Feature selection	Classifier	Accuracy (%)	Precision (%)	Recall (%)	F1-Score (%)
	SVM	77	76.96	77	75.6
	KNN	88.83	88.3	88.23	88.06
	Random Forest	85.5	85.51	84.69	84.44
SFS	XGboost	87.67	87.47	87.67	87.84
	AdaBoost	91.33	91.43	91.33	91.35
	Gradient Boosting	87.5	87.19	87.5	87.16
	SVM	77	76.96	77	75.6
	KNN	86.67	86.78	86.67	86.29
	Random Forest	86.17	86.02	86.17	85.83
SFFS	XGboost	86.67	86.6	87.04	86.65
	AdaBoost	90.5	90.95	90.82	90.85
	Gradient Boosting	88	88.04	88.36	88.11
	SVM	77	76.96	77	75.6
	KNN	86.83	87.19	87.17	86.85
	Random Forest	86.17	86.29	86.54	86.03

CONCLUSION

Personalized e-learning is an educational method that applies computer algorithms to interact with the learner and provide personalized resources to meet the preferences of each learner. Ultimately, the goal of personalized learning is to provide suitable learning resources according to the learner profile. To this end, we built a machine learning model recommendation system for course personalization. In our experiment, the combination of SFS and AdaBoost performs well and provides 91.33% of accuracy rate, 91.43% of precision rate, 91.33% of recall rate and 91.35% of F1-score. In our future work, we plan to study the efficiency of an evolutionary algorithm to build a model able to customize the course according to learners' preferences.

CONSENT FOR PUBLICATION

Not applicable.

CONFLICT OF INTEREST

The authors declare no conflict of interest, financial or otherwise.

ACKNOWLEDGMENTS

The authors extend their appreciation to the Deanship of Scientific Research-Saudi Electronic University, Ministry of Education in Saudi Arabia for funding this research work through project number ELI-CCI 20135.

REFERENCES

[1]   National Academy of Engineering, *NAE Annual Report 2014,* 2014.https://www.nae.edu/141629/NAE-Annual-Report-2014

[2]   Stratistics Market Research Consulting, *E-Learning - Global Market Outlook (2017-2026),* 2018.https://www.marketresearch.com/Stratistics-Market-Research-Consult-ng-v4058/Learning-Global-Outlook-11921584

[3]   E. Duffin, *E-learning and digital education - Statistics & Facts,* 2020.https://www.statista.com/topics/3115/e-learning-and-digital-education

[4]   M.A. Venable, *2021 Online Education Trends Report,* 2021.https://www.bestcolleges.com/research/annual-trends-in-online-education

[5]   A. Shahzad, R. Hassan, A.Y. Aremu, A. Hussain, and R.N. Lodhi, "Effects of COVID-19 in E-learning on higher education institution students: the group comparison between male and female", *Qual. Quant.,* vol. 55, no. 3, pp. 805-826, 2021.
[http://dx.doi.org/10.1007/s11135-020-01028-z] [PMID: 32836471]

[6]   P. Brusilovsky, S. Edwards, A. Kumar, L. Malmi, L. Benotti, D. Buck, and P. Ihantola, "Increasing adoption of smart learning content for computer science education", *Proceedings of the Working Group Reports of the 2014 on Innovation & Technology in Computer Science Education Conference.,* 2014pp. 31-57
[http://dx.doi.org/10.1145/2713609.2713611]

[7]   M. Soui, K. Ghedira, and M. Abed, "Evaluating User Interface Adaptation using the Context of Use", *Int. J. Adaptive Resilient Auton. Syst.,* vol. 6, no. 1, pp. 1-24, 2015. [IJARAS].
[http://dx.doi.org/10.4018/IJARAS.2015010101]

[8]   W. Mahdi, M. Soui, and M. Abed, "A new personalization approach by case-based reasoning and fuzzy logic", In: *2014 International Conference on Advanced Logistics and Transport (ICALT)* IEEE, 2014, pp. 103-108.
[http://dx.doi.org/10.1109/ICAdLT.2014.6864094]

[9]   S. Cakula, and M. Sedleniece, "Development of a personalized e-learning model using methods of ontology", *Procedia Comput. Sci.,* vol. 26, pp. 113-120, 2013.
[http://dx.doi.org/10.1016/j.procs.2013.12.011]

[10]   M. Despotović-Zrakić, A. Marković, Z. Bogdanović, D. Barać, and S. Krčo, "Providing adaptivity in Moodle LMS courses", *J. Educ. Technol. Soc.,* vol. 15, no. 1, pp. 26-338, 2012.

[11]   H. Murad, and L. Yang, "Personalized e-learning recommender system using multimedia data", *Int. J. Adv. Comput. Sci. Appl.,* vol. 9, no. 9, pp. 565-567, 2018.
[http://dx.doi.org/10.14569/IJACSA.2018.090971]

[12]   G. Shani, and B. Shapira, *Edurank: A collaborative filtering approach to personalization in e-learning.* Educational data mining, 2014, pp. 68-75.

[13]   B. Shobana, and G.A. Sathish Kumar, "A Personalised E-Learning System Using Reinforcement Learning technique", *Int. J. Pure Appl. Math.,* vol. 118, no. 18, pp. 4803-4813, 2018.

[14]   E. Lazcorreta, F. Botella, and A. Fernández-Caballero, "Towards personalized recommendation by two-step modified Apriori data mining algorithm", *Expert Syst. Appl.,* vol. 35, no. 3, pp. 1422-1429, 2008.

[http://dx.doi.org/10.1016/j.eswa.2007.08.048]

[15]   Sucheta V. Kolekar, and Radhika M. Pai, *Educ. Inf. Technol.,* vol. 24, no. 1, pp. 613-641, 2019.
[http://dx.doi.org/10.1007/s10639-018-9788-1]

CHAPTER 9

Automated Systems using AI in the Internet of Robotic Things: A New Paradigm for Robotics

T. Saravanan[1,*] and **P. Sasikumar**[2]

[1] *GITAM University, Bengaluru, India*

[2] *Malla Reddy Institute of Engineering & Technology, Secunderabad, India*

Abstract: The Internet of Things (IoT) allows a huge number of "things" with unique addresses to connect and exchange data through the current internet or suitable network protocols. This chapter proposes a new framework for controlling and monitoring activities at deployment sites and industrial automation systems, in which intelligent objects may follow peripheral occurrences, induce sensor data from a variety of sources, and apply ad hoc, local, and distributed "machine intelligence" to choose the optimal course of action, and then to act in a seamless manner to monitor or disseminate static or dynamic location conscious robotic things in the real world by giving the means to employ them as the Internet of robotic things (IoRT). While multi-robotic systems have progressed, and robots are continuously being enriched by vertical robotic service, and simpler developing functionalities. For the constant and seamless support for which they were created, centric divisions are insufficient. The important aspects of IoRT are highlighted in this article, which includes efficient Coordination Algorithms for Multi Robot Systems, optimization of multi robot task allocation, and modelling and simulation of robot manipulators. The purpose of this chapter is to obtain a better knowledge of IoRT architectural assimilation and to identify key research goals in this field.

Keywords: Geometric pattern, Internet of robotic-things, Multi-robot, Synchronization, Tardiness and coordination algorithms.

INTRODUCTION

During the last two decades, multirobot systems (MRS) that work together to complete a complex task have raised a great deal of interest. The technical community's curiosity in this path is justified due to MRS's numerous advantages. The key reason for using MRS is that they can improve the efficiency and effectiveness of a solution for a specific task, *i.e.*, a team of robots can perform a

* **Corresponding author T. Saravanan:** GITAM University, Bengaluru, India; Tel: +91- 9952871734; E-mail: tsaravcse@gmail.com

Prasad Lokulwar, Basant Verma, N. Thillaiarasu, Kailash Kumar, Mahip Bartere and Dharam Singh (Eds.)

task more efficiently and effectively by using distributed sensing and actuation. Multiple industrial manipulators, tactical aircraft, or autonomous networked transport vehicles, for example, can be divided into various groups depending on their implementations. The robot's agility has increased, allowing it to travel around the world and complete the different tasks assigned to it. Robots now have autonomous capabilities thanks to the tireless efforts of artificial intelligence researchers. Autonomous Robots are capable of completing tasks without the need for human interaction. Some tasks necessitate the use of multiple autonomous robots rather than a single robot [1]. When compared to a single robot, the use of multiple robots can provide more benefits.

Need for MRS

There are many reasons why researchers have begun to use multiple robots rather than single robots.

• When a large number of tasks need to be completed, deploying a team of robots outperforms deploying a single robot. The design of the task itself could be difficult for a single robot at times. As a result, task completion necessitates the use of several robots. Cooperative object handling, for example, necessitates the participation of several units in order to complete the task.

• Distributed jobs, such as cleaning a large house, can be performed more effectively and in less time using several robots. The use of multiple robots aid in the completion of such tasks in a parallel manner.

• Some dangerous activities, such as military applications, have a high chance of killing the robot. The presence of redundant units will help in the completion of the remaining tasks while a team of robots engages in such a dangerous mission.

• Since the deployed robots are in multiples, the mission can be completed in a variety of ways. Even if some robots fail, others can step in to finish the job. The system's fault tolerance provides a high level of robustness [2].

Major Gaps in MRS

Before launching MRS as a full-fledged operation, researchers must address a number of issues. The following are a few current areas that need further attention:

• Simultaneous Localization and Mapping for MRS addresses the issue of initialising the robot location in the region of interest, simultaneously creating a digitally shared map among the robots, and periodically updating the position of each robot on the map for active control and decision making.

• Multi-Robot Route Preparation and Obstacle Avoidance [3] is concerned with determining the shortest robot path to each robot's destination while preventing collisions with obstacles and other robots.

• Multi-Robot Task Allocation is the issue of determining the best possible allocation of robots to complete tasks in the shortest time possible.

• Workplace Fault-Tolerance Reallocation is concerned with disaster recovery and mitigation techniques for robots that malfunction during the mission. It also covers the procedures for task reallocation in order to complete the mission.

• MRS Communication Issues are related to task coordination between robot team members through inter-robot communication. For efficient monitoring, proper communication ensures that all robots and the base station receive timely data updates.

The word MRS is used in this chapter to refer to a group of mobile robots deployed in an indoor environment and must work together to solve complex real-world problems such as geometric pattern forming, simultaneous coverage of an unknown area, task allocation, and so on. The multi-objective optimization of MRS in a static environment for foraging and nonforaging tasks with or without precedence constraints is also addressed in this research. The number of tasks to be completed and the number of robots required to complete them are both known ahead of time. Furthermore, prior to assignment, the positions of tasks and robots were identified.

EFFECTUAL COORDINATION-ALGORITHMS FOR MRS

Theoretical algorithms for geometric pattern formation have been shown to be sound and complete under a set of overly simplistic assumptions. Robots, for example, are viewed as point objects that can feel and travel with infinite precision, among other things. When developing models or solutions for robotic systems, such assumptions are popular. It is known that in practise, these assumptions would not be strictly followed. Nonetheless, approximate solutions to these hypotheses can be found. As a result, such theoretical methods cannot be comparable to other empirical approaches until they are translated into practise. In this context, the uniform circle formation (UCF) problem with a group of autonomous mobile robots has gained a lot of interest. The circle has become a standard for studies since it is one of the most fundamental forms of all geometric forms. The following is an expression of a group of autonomous mobile robots, the uniform circular formation problem: Given a collection of N-autonomous mobile robots randomly distributed on a two-dimensional plane [4], they must first agree to organise themselves on the edge of a non-degenerated circle in limited time, then place themselves at regular intervals so that the angular distance between any two immediate neighbors's is 2/N.

Context of the Software Utilization

We proposed a software framework in this section to support the implementation of the two separate algorithms for solving the UCF problem. The framework's high-level architecture is summarised below:

Top-Level Design (TLD)

The proposed system employs two well-known software design patterns: onlooker and decorator. The robots are positioned in the environment at random. At first, it is impossible to tell if a robot is a leader or a follower. A robot may take on the role of leader or follower. There are two types of decorators: robot leader and robot follower. A leader election algorithm, such as the one proposed, is used to decide the robot that will be the leader. The elected leader robot is decked out with the duties of a leader. All other robots have been assigned the position of follower. For this, two concrete decorator classes, RobotLeader and RobotFollower, are used. The robot leader keeps track of all of the robot followers, does calculations, and sends out notifications to them of their required positions on the battlefield. The onlooker design pattern offers a framework for leaders and followers to share information. RobotLeader is a Subject, while RobotFollower is an Onlooker. The RobotSubject interface is used by RobotFollowers to become observers and to cancel their status as onlookers. This interface only contains one method that is named when the Subject's (*i.e.* , RobotLeader's) states change. RobotLeader is a concrete topic that implements the RobotSubject interface and includes methods for registering, removing, and notifying onlookers. Since it implements the RobotOnlooker interface, RobotFollower is a concrete onlooker. To receive updates, each RobotFollower registers with RobotLeader. With this TLD in place, we've proposed two algorithms for solving the UCF problem [5] in the following section. In simulation, the two algorithms are applied.

An UCF Central Algorithm

This theory proposes a centralised algorithm for solving the UCF problem. The proposed algorithm assumes that the leader robot, RobotLeader, has already been elected and decorated with the role of a leader, and that all other robots have already been elected and decorated with the role of a leader.

The position of the follower is decorated on the follower robots or RobotFollower. The following is the algorithm used by the leader robot to solve the UCF problem:

Step 1: Determine the SEC (Smallest Enclosing Circle) by following these steps: Assume that P = p1, p2, p3,..., pn points in the Euclidian plane 2 represent the location of all RobotFollowers. As illustrated in Fig. 3, SEC(P) is the smallest enclosing circle of P, which is the circle with the least radius that encloses all points in P. SEC(P) = SEC(H), where H is a suitable subset of P that consists of convex extreme points.

Step 2: Calculate Uniform Locations on the SEC Circumference: The RobotLeader is at the centre of the SEC circumference. It calculates the uniform locations of the RobotFollowers around the perimeter of SEC.

Step 3: In Fig. 1, the maroon colour dot represents Robot Leader, and the green colour dot represents Robot Followers, who were already on the perimeter and were picked at random as a reference point. It is named First Follower, and it is currently ranked top (will not move). The RobotLeader now discovers the coordinates of n-1 locations for n-1 remaining robots, starting with FirstFollower, so that all locations are separated by an angular distance of degrees: = 2/n-1, where n is the number of Robot Followers.

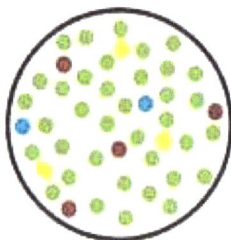

Fig. (1). Collection of points representing RobotFollowers

Step 4: The x and y coordinates of RobotLeader, as well as the angle of FirstFollower, are now known. It is necessary to obtain the x and y coordinates of the cross points on the circle of SEC as illustrated in Fig. (**1**).

Step 5: The following is how we measure two points, x and y: y = FirstFollower.y – RobotLeader.y x = FirstFollower.x – RobotLeader.x x = FirstFollower.y – RobotLeader.y We run a loop from I = 1 to n-1 and perform the following calculations to determine the x and y coordinates of cross points: RobotLeader = ai.x y*sin(i*) – x + x*cos(i*) RobotLeader.y + y*cos(i*) – x*sin(i*) = ai.y This allows us to identify all RobotFollower positions in a consistent manner finally positioned. The running time of this algorithm is O(n-1).

Step 6: RobotLeader keeps a list of uniform positions for RobotFollowers to choose from. After leaving the FirstFollower and its position alone, RobotLeader uses an optimal allocation algorithm to determine the position of each RobotFollower based on distance cost. Any RobotFollower is informed of their assigned location on the SEC's circumference. The Robot Followers take up their places. As a consequence, a circle is formed in the 2D plane by randomly scattering multiple mobile robots.

UCF Token Passing with a Weakly Centralized Approach

This section explains how to use token passing to place numerous mobile robots in a circular shape with a weakly centralised technique. This algorithm is a development of the centralised algorithm that was previously proposed. It's also a leader-following procedure, in which the leader robot calculates all of the follower robots' equally spread out places on the circular circumference. The difficulty of constructing a circle is broken into two parts: (a) leader selection and (b) finding positions for follower robots from the set of uniform positions computed by the leader robot. Both of these issues are solved using token passing to relieve the leader robot of the burden of assigning positions to all of the followers. It is now a weakly centralised algorithm due to the addition of token passing. This algorithm assumes that the leader robot has already been elected and that all of the positions for the follower robots on the SEC's circumference have been computed [6]. The follower robots are told of these positions. Only those follower robots outside the circle with the radius SEC radius 2 greedily choose their own location based on their distance from it and broadcast this information. It is likely that several robots would choose the same location to travel to. All of these robots form a virtual token ring between themselves based on their IDs, and then use token passing to bid for that role. The bid is simply the robot's distance from the location under consideration. The robot with the lowest bid is assigned to the location. The process is repeated until there are enough applicants for a particular role. Otherwise, if any robots are not assigned to a position and some positions are left vacant. All unoccupied positions are assigned to all unallocated robots by the leader robot. The leader robot is relieved of the task of assigning positions to all of the robots thanks to this algorithm. In this part, we've looked at two centralised algorithms. Furthermore, the second algorithm yields a less-than-ideal assignment.They also have little to do with the theoretical studies and algorithms discussed in the UCF literature. As a result, the discussion of these two algorithms will be restricted to this section. In the following section, we have systematically examined various properties and assumptions used in theoretical studies on geometric pattern formation with multi-robot systems, as well as various implementation options. The DK algorithm, which is one of the most representative state-of-the-art algorithms for solving the UCF problem, is then discussed.

OPTIMIZATION OF MULTI-ROBOT TASK PROVISION (MTRP)

MRTP problems can be solved in one of two ways: as single-objective or multi-objective problems. With a further classification of spatial, temporal, and utility-based objectives, some of the most widely considered minimization and maximisation objective functions are presented. (Fig. **2**) depicts the objectives-based classification of MRTP literature.

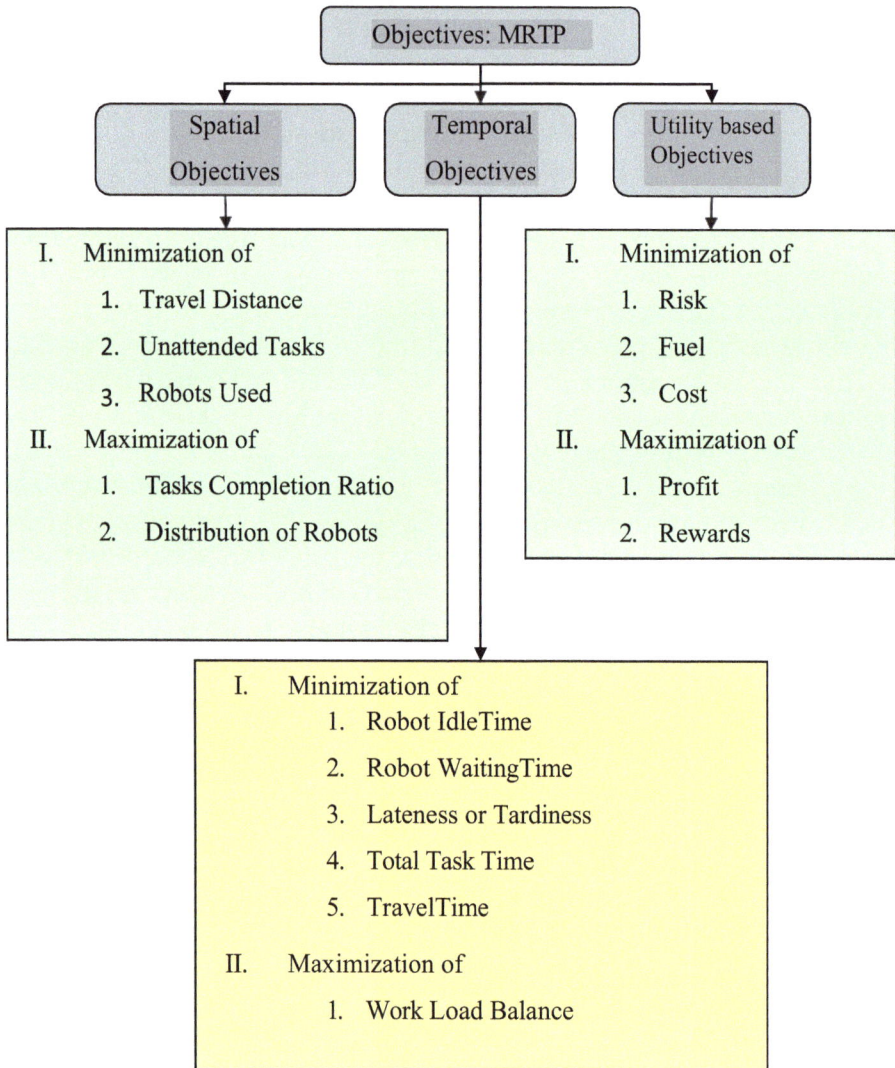

Fig. (2). Optimization Objective oriented clustering

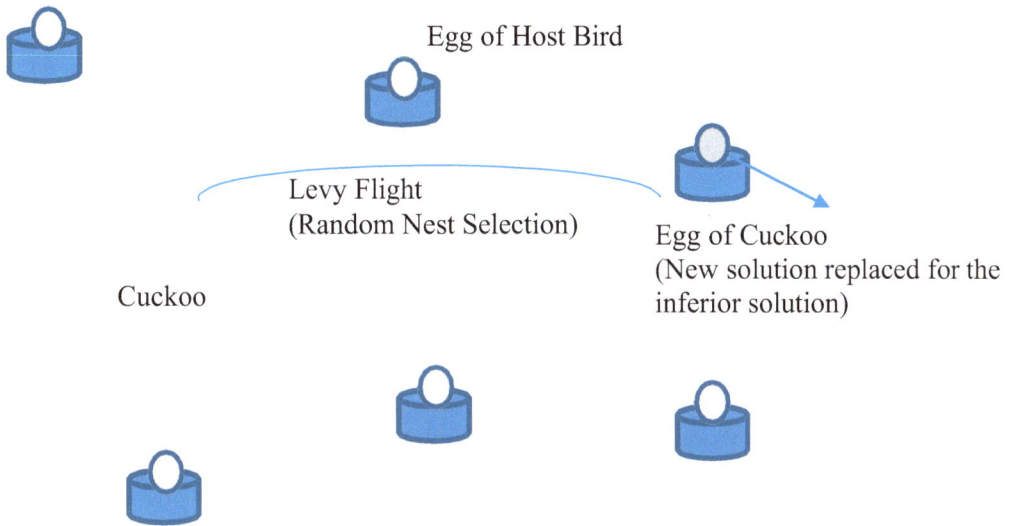

Fig. (3). CSA illustration

MRTP With Cuckoo-Search Rule

Genetic Algorithms (GA) and Search Algorithms (SA) rely heavily on solution improvement strategies such as experimentation, manipulation, and neighbourhood search. The Cuckoo-Search Algorithm (CSA) is a population-based algorithm that generates a random solution at each iteration.

Algorithm: Cuckoo-Search

It is a NatureInspired Algorithm. Cuckoos are obligate brood parasitic birds, which means they depend on other birds for reproduction. Cuckoos deposit their eggs in the nests of other host bird species [7]. If the host bird discovers that a particular egg belongs to another species, the cuckoo's egg will be destroyed, or the nest will be abandoned and a new one created. The metaphor used above is used to solve engineering problems for mobile robot navigation, route planning, and computer cell scheduling, which are some examples of cuckoo search algorithms used in robotic realms. Existing works have a discrete optimization of the travelling salesman problem, which is similar to ours, using the cuckoo search algorithm. However, no case of multi-robot task allocation using the cuckoo search algorithm has been published in the literature. This work introduces a multi-objective optimization of multi-robot task allocation using cuckoo search for foraging and non-foraging tasks.

Terminologies of CSA

The cuckoo search algorithm's terminologies are discussed here.

Egg: In the chromosomal GA signifies the answer to the problems. In CSA, the egg represents the solution to the problem, while in GA, the chromosome represents the problem.

There are two kinds of eggs:

• Egg of the Host

• Egg of the Cuckoo

Host Egg: The egg laid by the bird that is the host of the nest is known as a host egg. The initial population produced is referred to as the host egg.

Cuckoo's Egg: A cuckoo's egg is an egg laid by a cuckoo into another bird's nest. Cuckoo's egg is the solution that was created at random. The end goal of creating a new solution is to replace the existing one and strengthen it.

Parameter Optimizing in CSA

The output of most algorithms is determined by the parameters that are set when the algorithm is performed. The aim of this section is to determine the best parameters for running the cuckoo search algorithm. For cuckoo search optimization, the following criteria are taken into account.

• The number of times the cuckoo search operation is repeated (N-max) is the number of iterations. This has been set as a CSA stopping criterion [8 - 10].

• The size of the population chosen for the Cuckoo search algorithm is the number of nests (Nn).

• In each version, the Worst Solution Replacement Percentage (Rp) is the percentage of the population's worst solution that is eliminated and replaced with new solutions.

Three parameters with three levels each measured for the preparation are depicted in Table **1**.

To investigate the three parameters at three stages, the regular L9 Orthogonal array was chosen. Nmax, Nn, and Rp are assigned to the first, second, and third columns, respectively. Setting the parameters to the desired level for two replications results in nine experimental runs. The parameter effects are investigated using the 20 robots with 40 task problems. The ANOVA is presented based on the objective function value obtained in Table >2.

Table 1. CSA Parameters

Parameter	Level 1	Level 2	Level 3
N_{max}	300	500	700
N_n	10	20	30
R_p	0.2	0.3	0.4

Table 2. CSA with ANOVA parameters

Factor	Weight	DOF	L1	L2	L3	% Contribution	Significance (Yes/No)
N_{max}	0.0503	2	0.0252	6.4557	4.45	26.0747	Yes
N_n	0.1306	2	0.0653	16.7523	4.45	67.6626	Yes
R_p	0.0043	2	0.0021	0.5506	4.45	2.2237	No
Error	0.0078	2	0.0039	-	-	4.0390	-
Total	0.1930	8	-	-	-	100.00	-

Based on the response totals, the optimal levels for Nmax and Nn are level 2 (500) and level 3, respectively (30). Despite the fact that Rp is not a major factor, the response table suggests that level 3 (40 percent) is the best level.

CSA Algorithm

The following is the approach used to optimise the MultiRobot Task Allocation Problem using the Cuckoo search algorithm.
Step 1: Set the CSA parameters, including the size of the nest (Nn), the worst solution replacement percentage (Rp), and the maximum number of iterations (N-max). Step 2: Create a counter for the number of iterations n=1.
Step 3: Create a counter for the number of solutions x=1.Step 4: Create a new randomly generated solution Sx.Step 5: If x=Nn is true, go to the next step. Go to the website step 6 Else Increment 'm' by 1 and go to step 4.Step 6: Using Equation 3.1, evaluate each of the solutions using the multiobjective optimization function.Step 7: Snew (generate a new random solution).Step 8: Replace the old solution with the new one. If the new solution is better than the randomly chosen one, Snew for a randomly chosen solution from the nest (levy flight method).Step 9: Arrange the solutions according to their fitness value and save the best one.Step 10: NRep the number of worst solutions that need to be replaced. Nn x Rp = NRe pSet Counter Z to 1 (Step 11).
Step 11: Create a new solution to replace the previous one that corresponds to Nn.Step 12: Verify that Z = NRep. If the answer is yes, Continue to stage 14 Otherwise, Increment Z by 1 and go to Step 11.Step 13: Check n = Nmax. If yes Go to step 15. ElseIncrement 'n' by 1 and go to Step 3.Step 14: Print best results and stop.

ROBOT MANIPULATORS: MODELLING AND SIMULATION

An open loop kinematic and dynamic chain with multiple rigid links coupled in series by revolute or prismatic joints, as previously stated, can be used to describe a computer-based robotic manipulator. We are looking for a set of joint angles I to position the gripper because we already know the solution to the inverse kinematics problem Ti 0 that specifies a position and orientation with respect to the base coordinate. In robotic statics and dynamics, we deal with a collection of joint forces fi and joint torques I. Bond Graph Dynamic Modelling is used to achieve the gripper's necessary force and torque. As a result, we are interested in the inverse problem for manipulator dynamics: calculating the joint torques needed to produce given joint positions, velocities, and accelerations. There are basically three ways to get a set of governing connected [11 - 15] severely non-linear differential equations defining the dynamics of a robotic manipulator:

Bond Graph-Dynamic Modelling

• LagrangeEuler-Dynamic Modelling

• NewtonEuler-Dynamic Modelling

A bond graph is a graphical tool used in dynamic modelling to determine the energy structure of a system. The dynamic behaviour of systems is governed by the movement, storage, and exchange of energy across distinct subsystems, or constituents of the system. As a result, a complex system can be broken down into a number of basic elements that store, dissipate, transform, or supply energy. These basic elements, as well as their interactions, are graphically mapped when creating a dynamic model of a system in the bond graph language.Basic elements for storing kinetic and potential energy, dissipating energy, and transforming energy are provided by the bond graph language. Each of these elements has one or more power ports *via* which energy can flow. Electricity bonds are used to send power between these ports. The power modelling with variables is given in Fig. (**4**), and Table **3** shows the Tabulation of systems with its effort and flow metrics.

Table 3. Tabulation of systems with its effort and flow metrics.

Systems	Effort (Ef)	Flow (Fl)
Mechanical	Force (F)	Velocity (v)
	Torque ()	Angular velocity ()
Electrical	Voltage (V)	Current (i)
Hydraulic	Pressure (P)	Volume flow rate (dQ/dt)

(Table 3) cont.....

Systems	Effort (Ef)	Flow (Fl)
Thermal	Temperature (T)	Entropy change rate (ds/dt)
	Pressure (P)	Volume change rate (dV/dt)
Chemical	Chemical potential ()	Mass flow rate (dN/dt)
	Enthalpy (h)	Mass flow rate (dm/dt)
Magnetic	Magneto-motive force (e)M	Magneticfluxrate(d/dt)

Power Variables

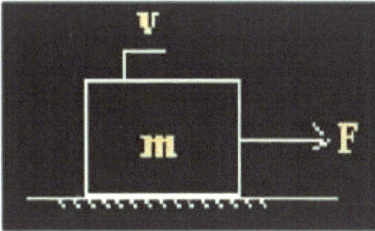

Power = F.v

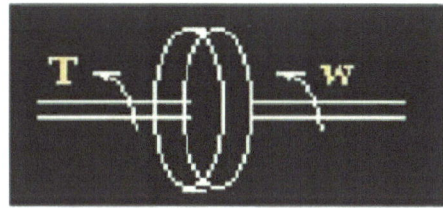

Power = T.w

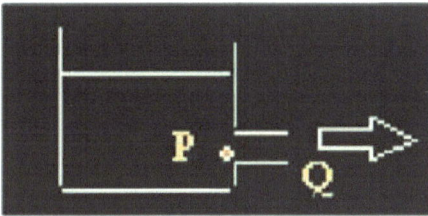

Power = P.Q

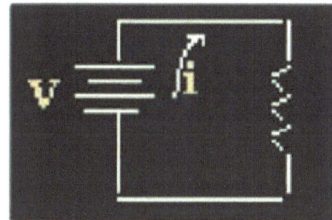

Power = V.i

Power = Effort (e) x Flow (f)

Fig. (4). Power variables while modelling

A device invariant is the direction of power flow at any given time. Its influences are force (effort) and velocity (flow).

$$\text{Power} = \text{Effort (e)} \times \text{Flow (f)} \tag{1}$$

The bond graph technique shown in Fig. (5) allows for more versatility in device equation modelling and formulation. Bond graphs may be used to model systems from a variety of engineering disciplines in a consistent manner. They depict the system's power exchange image. Multiplication of two variables, generalised effort and generalised flow, yields power. A modeller divides a structure into dynamic units consisting of compliances (C), inertances (I) and dissipations (D) in bond graph modelling (R). External source inputs to the system are represented by the source of effort (SE) or source of flow (SF) components. There are also two multiport components transformers (TF) and a Gyrator (GY). TF elements change the direction of flow or effort, whereas GY elements change the direction of flow or effort. Elements 1 (representing constant flow) and 0 (representing constraints) are used to represent constraints (representing constant effort). The elements are linked together by bonds [10], within the constraint structure and components, which indicate the direction of power exchange. The concept of causality can be used to formulate machine equations from eqn. 2 to eqn. 5.

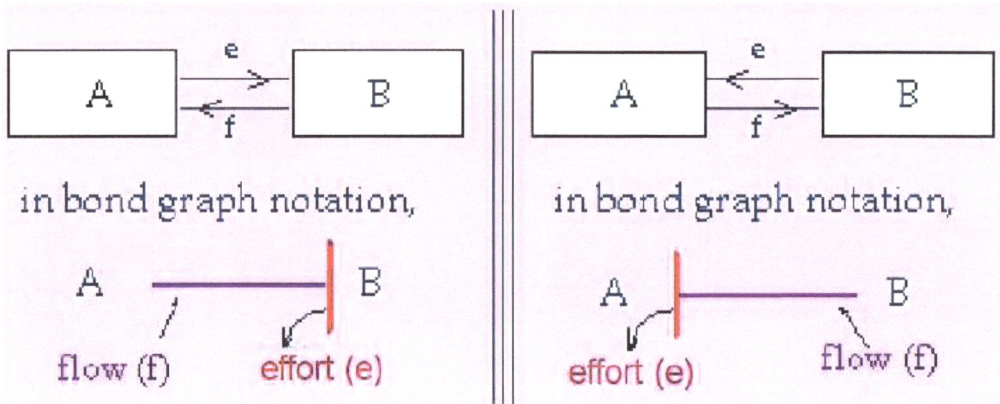

Fig. (5). Fl and Ef between A and B

It's a two-port component that alters the flow or effort magnitude. The transfer modulus connects one flow to another or one effort to another. The transfer modulus is denoted by the symbol b/a.

$$x_1 = l_1 \cos\theta_1, \tag{2}$$

$$y_1 = l_1 \sin\theta_1, \tag{3}$$

$$x_2 = l_1 \cos\theta_1 + l_2 \cos\theta_2 \tag{4}$$

$$y_2 = l_1 \sin\theta_1 + l_2 \sin\theta_2, \tag{5}$$

Bond Graph Modelling Simulation

The simulation lasts for 20 seconds. The robot's two joints are controlled by a PD controller. The joint control law is used to control the robot's joints.

(Fig. **6**) displays the variability of the robot tip in the X direction over time. (Fig. **7**) shows the variation of robot tip in the Y direction with respect to time. (Fig. **8**) shows the variation of the first joint angle with respect to time. (Fig. **9**) shows the variation of the second joint angle with respect to time. (Fig. **10**) shows the animation of the robot manipulator. From the animation of the robot, we see that the robot is achieved the given line tracking. In Fig. (**9**), second joint variation with time has severe late effects. The first joint variation with time (Fig. **8**) has fewer effects compared to (Fig. **9**), which is more important to the Internet of Robotic Things, and (Fig. **10**) shows the final robotic animation based on (Fig. **8**) and (Fig. **9**).

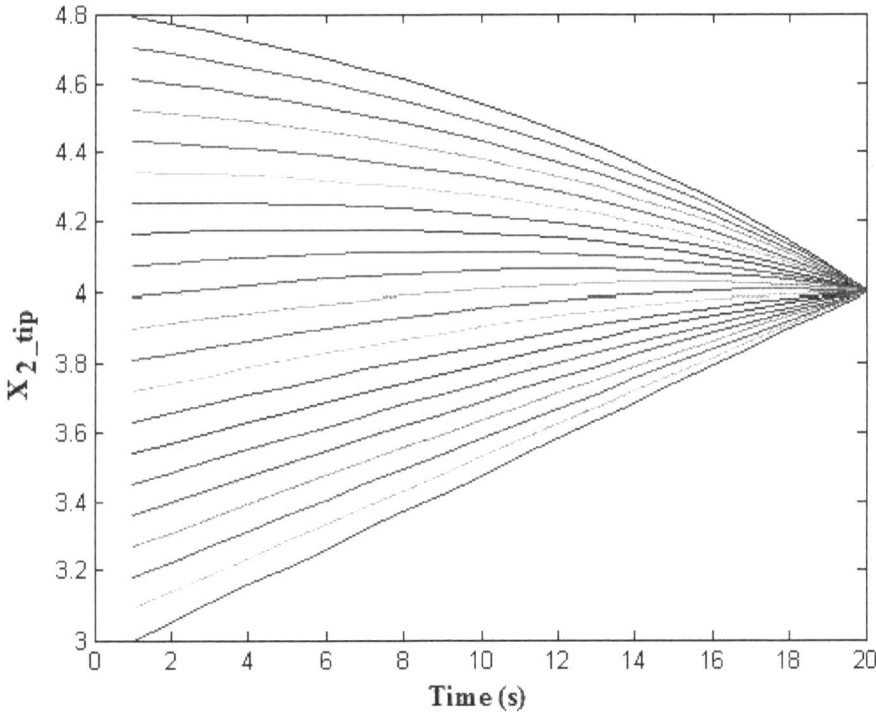

Fig. (6). X_2 Variation with time

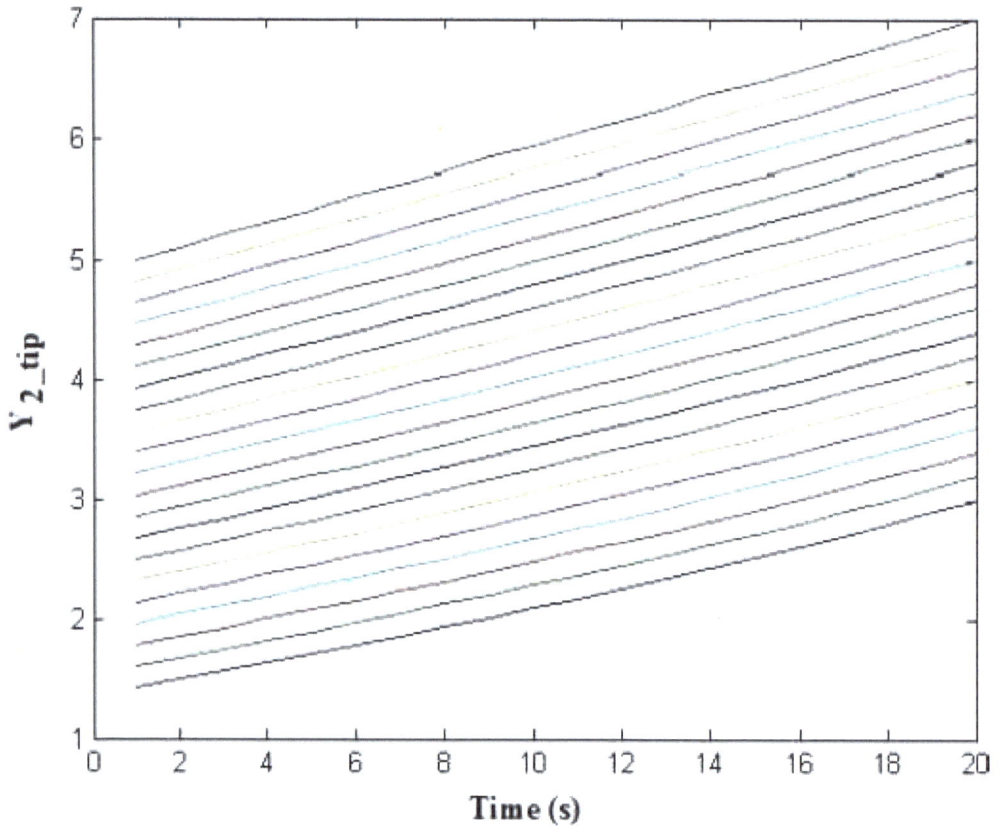

Fig. (7). Y_2 Variation with time

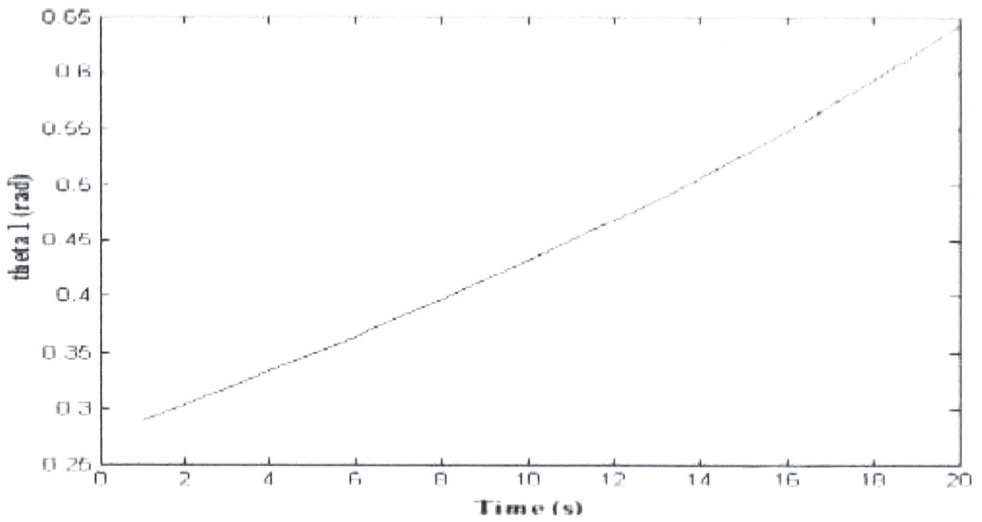

Fig. (8). First joint variation with time

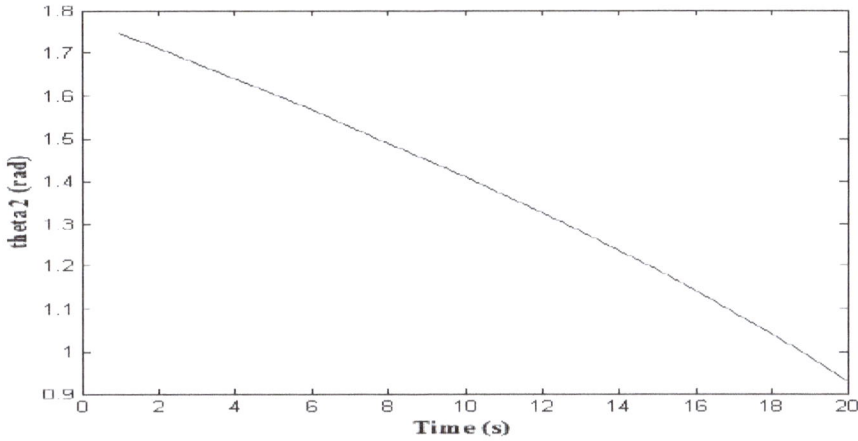

Fig. (9). Second joint variation with time

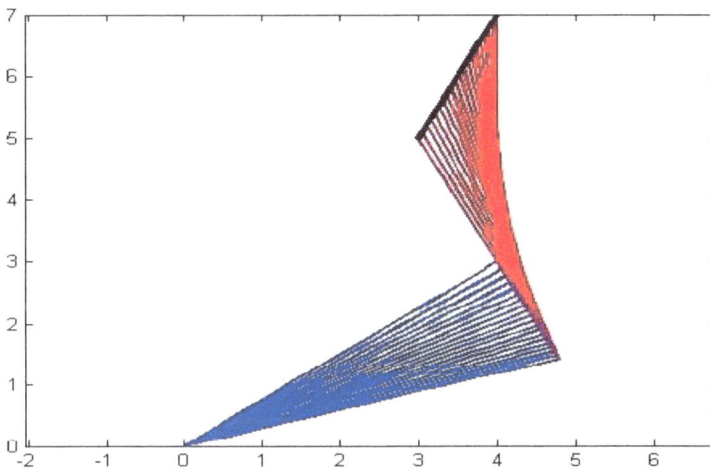

Fig. (10). Final robot animation

CONCLUSION

As an advancement of current cloud networked robots, this chapter proposes an Internet of Robotic Things (IoRT) based robotics architectural concept. The Internet of Robotic Things (IoRT) is a complex architectural structure that allows robots and robotic systems to interact, share, and disseminate distributed computing tools, business processes, background information, and environmental data with one another, as well as acquire innovative knowledge and specialised abilities that they could not learn on their own. This opens up a new frontier in linked robots, which we hope will lead to interesting new advances in the future. It does, in fact, allow for adaptation into a connected environment in which heterogeneous technologies, such as communications networks, processing units, various types of computers, and cloud services, are used to exploit resource-constrained deployment of inexpensive robots. The IoRT approach could lead to a slew of new technologies, including SLAM, grasping, navigation, and a slew of others that are outside the scope of this discussion. In this paper, a novel Internet of Robotic Things architecture is proposed that takes into account the marriage of recently developed IoT and robotics. Existing robotic systems, their peripheral devices, IoT processing units, and a cloud-based robotic platform have all been shown to exist or have the potential to arise, indicating the practicality of the suggested architecture. The importance of key characteristics is also discussed. The research problems are addressed in a clear and concise manner so that interested parties can participate in this innovative concept in the near future.

CONSENT FOR PUBLICATION

Not applicable.

CONFLICT OF INTEREST

The authors declare no conflict of interest, financial or otherwise.

ACKNOWLEDGEMENT

None declared.

REFERENCES

[1]   O. Vermesan, R. Bahr, M. Ottella, M. Serrano, T. Karlsen, T. Wahlstrøm, H.E. Sand, M. Ashwathnarayan, and M.T. Gamba, "Internet of robotic things intelligent connectivity and platforms", *Front. Robot. AI,* vol. 7, p. 104, 2020.
[http://dx.doi.org/10.3389/frobt.2020.00104] [PMID: 33501271]

[2]   L. Romeo, A. Petitti, R. Marani, and A. Milella, "Internet of robotic things in smart domains: applications and challenges", *Sensors (Basel),* vol. 20, no. 12, p. 3355, 2020.
[http://dx.doi.org/10.3390/s20123355] [PMID: 32545700]

[3]   A. Alamer, "A secure anonymous tracing fog-assisted method for the Internet of Robotic Things", *Libr. Hi Tech,* 2020.

[4]   Y. Liu, W. Zhang, S. Pan, Y. Li, and Y. Chen, "Analyzing the robotic behavior in a smart city with deep enforcement and imitation learning using IoRT", *Comput. Commun.,* vol. 150, pp. 346-356, 2020.
[http://dx.doi.org/10.1016/j.comcom.2019.11.031]

[5]   Z. Alsulaimawi, "A Privacy Filter Framework for Internet of Robotic Things Applications", *IEEE*

Security and Privacy Workshops (SPW)., pp. 262-267, 2020.
[http://dx.doi.org/10.1109/SPW50608.2020.00059]

[6]   T. Saravanan, "An Efficient Multi Channel Query Scheduling In Wireless Sensor Networks", *International Journal of Computer Science and Network Security,* vol. 14, no. 2, p. 71, 2014. [IJCSNS].

[7]   N. El Menbawy, H. Arafat, M. Saraya, and A.M. Ali-Eldin, "Studying and Analyzing the Fog-based Internet of Robotic Things", In: *International Arab Conference on Information Technology (ACIT).* IEEE, 2020, pp. 1-8.
[http://dx.doi.org/10.1109/ACIT50332.2020.9300093]

[8]   N. Thillaiarasu, "Enforcing security and privacy over multi-cloud framework using assessment techniques", *International Conference on Intelligent Systems and Control (ISCO), Coimbatore.*, pp. 1-5, 2016.
[http://dx.doi.org/10.1109/ISCO.2016.7727001]

[9]   T. Saravanan, and N.S. Nithya, "Modeling displacement and direction aware ad hoc on-demand distance vector routing standard for mobile ad hoc networks", *Mob. Netw. Appl.,* vol. 24, no. 6, pp. 1804-1813, 2019.
[http://dx.doi.org/10.1007/s11036-019-01390-9]

[10]   N. Thillaiarasu, S.C. Pandian, and V. Vijayakumar, "Designing a trivial information relaying scheme for assuring safety in mobile cloud computing environment", *Wirel. Netw.,* 2019.
[http://dx.doi.org/10.1007/s11276-019-02113-4]

[11]   T. Saravanan, and P. Sasikumar, "Assessment and Analysis of Action Degeneracy Due to Blackhole Attacks in Wireless Sensor Networks", In: *Proceedings of 6th International Conference on Recent Trends in Computing* Springer: Singapore, 2021, pp. 345-355.
[http://dx.doi.org/10.1007/978-981-33-4501-0_33]

[12]   A. Kamilaris, and N. Botteghi, "The penetration of Internet of Things in robotics: Towards a web of robotic things", *Journal of Ambient Intelligence and Smart Environments.*, vol. 1-22, pp. 1755-1762, 2020.

[13]   P. Preethi, R. Asokan, N. Thillaiarasu, and T. Saravanan, "An effective digit recognition model using enhanced convolutional neural network based chaotic grey wolf optimization", *Journal of Intelligent & Fuzzy Systems, (Preprint).*, pp. 1-11, .
[http://dx.doi.org/10.3233/JIFS-211242]

[14]   S. Ranjithkumar, and N. Thillaiarasu, *"A survey of secure routing protocols of mobile adhoc network." SSRG International Journal of Computer Science and Engineering.* vol. Vol. 2. SSRG-IJCSE, 2015.

[15]   T. Saravanan, and N.S. Nithya, "Mitigation of attack patterns based on routing reliance approach in MANETs", In: *International Conference on Advances in Computing, Communication Control and Networking (ICACCCN).* IEEE, 2020, 2020, pp. 387-392..
[http://dx.doi.org/10.1109/ICACCCN51052.2020.9362966]

## CHAPTER 10

Missing Value Imputation and Estimation Methods for Arrhythmia Feature Selection Classification Using Machine Learning Algorithms

Ritu Aggarwal[1,*] and **Suneet Kumar**[2]

[1] *Maharishi Markendeshwar Engineering College, Maharishi Markendeshwar Institute of Computer Technology and Business Management Mullana, Ambala, Haryana, India*

[2] *Maharishi Markendeshwar Engineering College, Mullana, Ambala, Haryana, India*

Abstract: Electrocardiogram signal analysis is very difficult to classify cardiac arrhythmia using machine learning methods. The ECG datasets normally come with multiple missing values. The reason for the missing values is the faults or distortion. When performing data mining, missing value imputation is the biggest task for data preprocessing. This problem could arise due to incomplete medical datasets if the incomplete missing values and cases were removed from the original database. To produce a good quality dataset for better analyzing the clinical trials, the suitable missing value imputation method is used. In this paper, we explore the different machine-learning techniques for the computed missing value in the electrocardiogram dataset. To estimate the missing imputation values, the collected data contains feature dimensions with their attributes. The experiments to compute the missing values in the dataset are carried out by using the four feature selection methods and imputation methods. The implemented results are shown by combined features using IG (information gain), GA (genetic algorithm) and the different machine learning classifiers such as NB (naïve bayes), KNN (K-nearest neighbor), MLP (Multilayer perception), and RF (Random forest). The GA (genetic algorithm) and IG (information gain) are the best suitable methods for obtaining the results on lower dimensional datasets with RMSE (Root mean square error. It efficiently calculates the best results for missing values. These four classifiers are used to analyze the impact of imputation methods. The best results for missing rate 10% to 40% are obtained by NB that is 0.657, 0.6541, 0.66, 0.657, and 0.657, as computed by RMSE (Root mean Square error). It means that error will efficiently reduced by naïve bayes classifier.

Keywords: Datasets, GA (genetic algorithm), Feature selection, IG (Information gain), Missing values imputation, RMSE (Root mean square error).

---

[*] **Corresponding author Ritu Aggarwal:** Maharishi Markendeshwar Engineering College, Maharishi Markendeshwar Institute of Computer Technology and Business Management Mullana, Ambala, Haryana, India; E-mail: errituaggarwal@gmail.com

Prasad Lokulwar, Basant Verma, N. Thillaiarasu, Kailash Kumar, Mahip Bartere and Dharam Singh (Eds.)

INTRODUCTION

In the medical field, many real-world problems could be detected. When data mining is employed on the dataset, it usually does not extract completely missing values and data for different kinds of diseases, such as metabolomics data, cardiovascular disease data [1], traffic data, kidney-related data, lung data, and other medical data . Many machine learning algorithms and techniques do not easily compute and analyze incomplete or missing value datasets. The different techniques and types for handling the missing values in the dataset [2].

Missing completely at random is based on the probability the responses are missing depends on the observed responses by the given dataset of missing values. The simplest solution of list-wise deletion is based on the missing values being deleted, but it could be problematic when the missing value and data are based on MNAR [3]. For the whole dataset, the missing rate is larger than a given certain value. The mean substitution is based on a variable that is used for that missing data value for the same variable. In this, no new information is added; only the size of a sample is increased [4]. In the regression imputation method, missing data is replaced with estimated values, it was not deleted dataset value, and it preserves all the missing data by replacing it. It computes the values as variables only for prediction. The model-based imputation methods were used to replace the missing values by training them and outperforming them by using statistical techniques [5]. The dataset contains the number of features that represent the data. Most of the features do not act as representatives. From the collected dataset, the irrelevant and redundant features must be filtered out [6]. The feature selection method is used for missing value imputation performed over the observed data. To filter the unrepresentative features, the feature imputation process was more efficient. In the domain of the medical field, two types of databases are available. The first dataset is for medical practitioners in which the special clinical trial data is generated. When imputation method needs a huge dataset and information, it could store it in their repository without considering for relevant research purposes. These records could be further used for the Clinical decision support system. Many records and missing values are incomplete and imbalanced regarding their corresponding label. In some of the patient's history, the medical report becomes blank because all the records that correspond to a particular disease and their test are missing or left blank [7].

When performing the feature selection over the imputation data, the main purpose of finding the missing value is to filter out the unreliable features that are not more efficient or not required for imputation. To understand the missing features for feature selection, the model should be trained for the lower-dimensional data and more efficiently estimates the values the selected features. In their research work, two types of datasets are used, *i.e.*, Cleveland and Hungarian heart disease datasets. Feature selection methods MICE [8] (Multivariate Imputation by Chained Equations), Model-based missing value imputation, Information gain and genetic algorithm, and mean mode imputation were employed by the machine learning techniques such as K-NN, MLP, and NB, Random forest. While performing the feature selection, the incomplete data and missing values are trained and tested accordingly in various domains, and then the best selected combined features are identified for the datasets using different lower and high dimensional datasets. In this paper, section 1, gives the introduction about the missing values and their method and techniques. The section 2 discusses the literature review, section 3 the Materials and methods for missing values and their imputation process, section 4 Machine learning classifier, section 5, the Experimental results, section 6 Conclusion and future scope and section 7 References.

Literature Review

Chia-HUI-HU- *et al.* [3] discussed that missing value in dataset is a very critical problem that affects the quality of data. In this study, the author used the main methods to find the missing values in the ECG data. It used the zero method, mean method, PCA method, and RPCA method. This method could successfully handle the missing value in the dataset, and it does not matter how many values are missing, it just indicates the higher classification accuracy when a large number of missing values are found in the dataset. It is used the MKDF-KNN classification algorithm to improve the performance and provide better parameters of MKDF-KNN. Fahd Saleh Alotaibi [6] researched the attributes of a clinical dataset utilizing a mix of highlight choice and order strategies to deal with missing qualities and comprehend the hidden measurable attributes of an ordinary clinical dataset. Ordinarily, when an enormous clinical dataset is introduced, it poses difficulties like missing qualities, high dimensionality, and unequal classes. This represents an inalienable issue when executing highlight choice and order calculations. With most clinical datasets, an underlying investigation of the dataset is done, and those credits with more than a specific level of missing qualities are killed from the dataset. Afterward, prognostic and analytic models are created with the assistance of missing worth attribution, including choice and order calculations. This paper has two principal ends: 1) Despite the idea of clinical datasets and their enormous size, strategies for missing worth ascription don't influence the last exhibition. What is pivotal is that the dataset is a precise portrayal of the clinical issue, and those techniques for attributing missing qualities are not basic for creating classifiers and prognostic/indicative models. 2) Supervised learning has been demonstrated to be more reasonable for mining clinical information than solo techniques. It is also shown that non-parametric classifiers, for example, choice trees, give better outcomes when contrasted with parametric classifiers, such as spiral premise work organizations (RBFNs).

Nilashi *et al*. [10] proposed a work in which the detection of heart disease is analyzed by using machine learning techniques. This study used two imputation approaches like, hot-deck and KNN, The experimental datasets are used to impute the missing values. Correlation is identified between the features of a dataset. SOM technique is applied to perform clustering. PCA approach was applied to each cluster to reduce and overcome the dimensionality of data and the multicollinearity issues according to data. To construct the classification model for heart disease diagnosis used, the fuzzy SVM. This method is implemented on the two datasets that are Statlog and Cleveland. Statlog dataset 279 instances, and the Cleveland dataset has 303 instances. Both of these are heart datasets. The slight difference is that statlog has 13 attributes, and Cleveland has a 14 attributes. Rahman *et al*. [14] proposed that authors can classify the data by using machine learning approaches to deteriorate the chances of heart disease. It used the fie ML algorithm and the rapid miner tool for better results in terms of accuracy. It used a small size dataset and a limited number of patient records.

Setiawan *et al*. [15] In this study, filtering rue is applied to investigate the missing value imputation. It used ANNRST imputation to know the impact of imputation. This method of missing value imputation is considered the best method in the case of UCI heart disease datasets.

Sitalakshmi *et al*. [16] The researchers used the classification or data mining methods on complete data to impute the missing values. This study used the dynamic clustering approach using the MV imputation algorithm. The health predictor variables are used for the prediction of CVD patients.

F. yang *et al*. [17] proposed work, stating that the researchers can propose an Imputation measure that requires a bunch of noticed information for ascription demonstrating whether or not factual or AI methods are utilized to create assessments to supplant the missing qualities, the nature of the noticed information is basic. In this paper, we center around the issue from the component choice viewpoint, accepting that a portion of the gathered highlights might be unrepresentative and influence the attribution results, driving thusly to the debasement of the last presentation of the classifiers when contrasted and the ones where include choice is performed. Five diverse clinical area datasets containing different quantities of highlight measurements are utilized for the examinations. What's more, three unique kinds of highlight determination strategies are analyzed, in particular, data acquisition (IG) as the channel strategy, the hereditary calculation (GA) as the covering technique, and choice tree (DT) as the implanted technique. For missing worth ascription, the multilayer perceptron (MLP) neural organization, k-closest neighbor (KNN), and backing vector machine (SVM) models are built exclusively. The trial results show that the mix of highlight choice and attribution can make the classifier (*i.e.*, SVM) perform better than the benchmark classifier without including determination for some datasets with various missing rates. For lower-dimensional datasets, utilizing GA and IG for include choice is suggested, though DT is a superior decision for higher-dimensional datasets. A few issues ought to be considered in future examination work. In the first place, other missingness instruments, including MAR and MNAR, can be researched for the component choice impact. Furthermore, some datasets normally have explicit quantities of missing information (*i.e.*, explicit missing rates) zcan be utilized. Then again, some different contrasts among the datasets that could impact the outcomes can likewise be utilized, for instance, twofold or numerous distinctions, or even the trouble in arrangement where the datasets contain a lot higher measurements or larger quantities of examples and classes. Second, in performing highlight choice and missing worth ascription, the significant impediment is that various noticed information (*i.e.*, D_complete) should be accommodated in the element determination techniques to choose some agent highlights and attribution models to create assessments to supplant the missing qualities. Subsequently, the impact of utilizing various quantities of noticed information on the component determination and ascription results ought to be researched. Then again, the over-inspecting methods used to make manufactured examples can be utilized for datasets that don't contain an adequate number of complete information tests. Ultimately, extremely high dimensional datasets in explicit space issues containing a few countless measurements, for example, text and sensor cluster information, ought to be explored to survey the degree of effect of performing highlight determination over exceptionally high dimensional fragmented datasets.

Z Hu., *et al*. [18] used the pattern recognition and classification method to solve the problem of missing values in real-life datasets. In this work, we inspected the presentation of ML strategies as missing worth attribution. The outcomes are contrasted by conventional mean/mode ascription. Test results show that all the ML strategies we investigated outflanked the factual strategy (Mean/Mode), because of sensitivity and a few cases' exactness. The way toward missing ascription with our proposed strategy can be computationally broad for huge quantities of quality having missing qualities in their characteristics. Notwithstanding, realize that information cleaning is essential for the information pre-preparing and undertaking of information mining which is anything but an ongoing errand and a nonstop cycle. Missing worth ascription is a one-time undertaking. It can be concluded that with the help of a machine learning classifier we could easily find the missing values in the dataset.

MATERIALS AND METHODS

The feature selection methods and their techniques are employed for estimating and calculating the missing values. Feature selection is the process of selecting the relevant features from the subset for a given dataset. It considers the public data and real-world datasets, usually, some of the features are duplicates and irrelevant; they were removed without losing the information. It could be used for the dimensionality reduction with the aim of obtaining the principal values to reduce the number of random variables. There are normally three types of feature selection methods filter method, wrapper method, and embedded method. In this research work, the main focus and implementation is sighting the following feature selection methods.

Feature selection methods MICE ((Multivariate Imputation by Chained Equations) and, Model-based missing value imputation, Information gain and genetic algorithm, and mean mode imputation by using the RMSE imputation method are analyzed. The method of missing value imputation was implemented to evaluate the percentage of the missing value. It was introduced randomly in the dataset imputation and then imputed with imputation methods. This data was classified by different machine learning by their classifiers and genetic algorithms. Information gain and RMSE classifiers were compared to find the best possible combination of the classifier with the imputation methods.

To implement this method, the various steps are to be used for performing:-

1. 10% data replace with null values 2. Apply the relevant imputation to impute the missing values. 3. The various machine learning classifiers, such as K-NN, MLP, and NB, and random forest classifiers to impute the data and calculate RMSE, IG, and GA of each classifier. 4. Put the value k=9 using KNN imputation to impute missing values 5. Repeat step3 6. This applies to mean imputation to impute missing values. 7. Repeat step 5 again.8. Repeat steps 2 to 8 by replacing 10%, 20%, 30%, 35% and 40% data in dataset with Null values.9. Find out the best classifier result and imputation method with the lowest value and highest value of RMSE, IG, and GAas shown in Fig. (1) proposed methodology for the missing value.

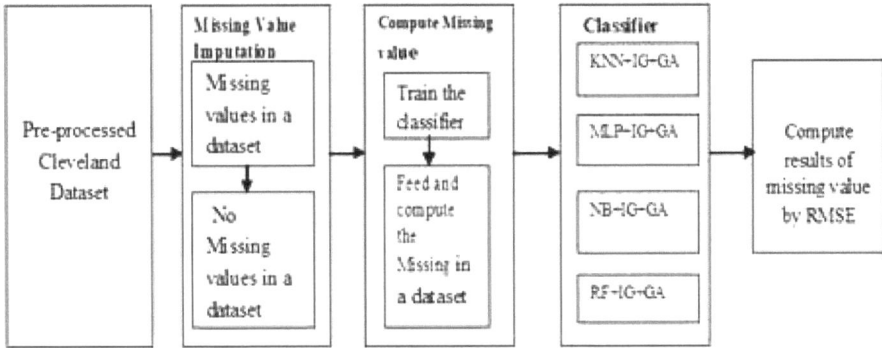

Fig. (1). Proposed Methodology for Missing value imputation.

MEAN/ MODE IMPUTATION

In the mean/Mode imputation, the available found data is frequently replaced by the attributes according to their observed value.

The following algorithm is as follows:

The method implies that is Mode Imputation, for input takes the missing values from the dataset. And the output is imputed the zero in the missing value according to the given dataset.

The following procedure is to be considered by which it's implemented:

1. select the first attribute and find out the missing value in a dataset
2. the most frequently occurring attribute and find out the value as its corresponding; say the value is X.
3. replace all the missing values in the attribute with the value X.
4. until the missing value is replaced, repeat steps 1 to 3 for all the attributes in the dataset.

K-NN IMPUTATION METHOD

In KNN missing value records are found, and correspondingmean values of attributes of these neighbors are replaced [9].

The following algorithm is as follows:

The method implies the KNN Imputation, for input takes the missing values from the dataset. And the output is imputed the zero in the missing value according to the given dataset.

The following procedure is to be considered by which it's implemented:

1. Find out the record of the attribute and find out the missing value in the dataset
2. Select the KNN imputation and the neighbors of the record corresponding to the remaining attributes from the record.
3. calculate the mean value X corresponding to the selected attributes of the record.
4. with the value X, replace all the missing values in the attribute.
5. until the missing value is replaced, repeat steps 1 to 4. For all the attributes in the dataset.

MICE

The multivariate imputation is done by chained equations in which the imputation is implemented multiple times. It takes the characteristics of MAR for missing data. In the MAR the data is selected randomly. It implements the regression model .in the regression, the prediction of missing value attributes from the remaining attributes from the dataset [10, 11].

Algorithm

The algorithm used MICE imputation.

1. Dataset with missing value is taken as an input.
2. For output, the imputed dataset with zero missing value.

Procedure:

1. For missing values of all attributes.
2. Replace one variable X with the mean imputation method with a missing value.
3. To predict the value for X, build a regression model and replace all the missing values with the predicted value X.
4. Repeat steps 2 to 3 for all the variables in the dataset.

GENETIC ALGORITHM

It is an algorithm that imitates different processes, such as natural selection, regeneration, and reproduction. It gives high-quality solutions for solving the missing values problem in a dataset. The main functions of GA are based on the three genetic operators that are as follows:-

The first procedure for handling the missing values by using GA is the selection method, and the next step is crossover, in which selected attributes for a particular gene are filled and replaced by the value of X. In the last step, the mutation is applied to produce the new individual set and filled the missing value of random gene with Value X.

MACHINE LEARNING CLASSIFIERS

To handle the impact of missing value for the heart disease dataset, the following machine learning classifiers are used, such as KNN, MLP, NB and Random forest.

KNN CLASSIFIER

KNN was introduced for pattern classification based on a nonparametric technique known as the neighborrule [12]. It is a very effective classification technique; by this classifier, no assumptions about the data mean there is very less prior knowledge of data for the data distribution. In this algorithm, the k- nearest data points are considered for the training set. According to the [13] data point, the target value is unavailable .To handle the missing values, KNN classifier is employed.

NAÏVE BAYES CLASSIFIER

It relies on the Bayes theorem with independence suppositions along with attributes. It used the features of the Bayesian theorem, and the output for that is not too hard to implement. The NB classifiers have no entrapped or repetitive parameters, which makes it supportive for large datasets. NB treats every variable independently, which is easy to predict that variables that don't have the proper dependency and relation with each other [14, 15]. It assumes the individual features of the data with their independence and calculated the probability of each class using their features. In the NB classifier, calculate the posterior probability of an occurring class x if the y occurs estimated by the given formula [16] as shown by equation 1.

$$P(\bar{x}|y) = P(y|x)P(x) \div P(y) \tag{1}$$

Where P(y|x) is a probability for occurring y corresponding to x known as the likelihood(y) is known as the probability of prior attribute that represents the probability of occurring x. so that the prior class probability is the P(x) that is a probability of occurring class x.

4.3. RANDOM FOREST

In random forest, based method that ensemble in the random forest to make classification, the multiple decision trees are used. Its structure in the form of a tree. The tree has a root node, internal node, and termination node. In the classification process, each tree node participates, but the node's final prediction is based on the voting classifier. The majority of final decision trees are called vote-based classifiers [17].

In the decision tree, there is a problem with fitting means that is when the data is to e train, then the model gives accuracy. From the training data, the samples for construction, their decision trees will be chosen randomly. In every step when constructing a tree, a subset of features is chosen randomly. There are many steps for considering making this algorithm as shown in Fig. (**2**) labelled as Random forest using a vote classifier.

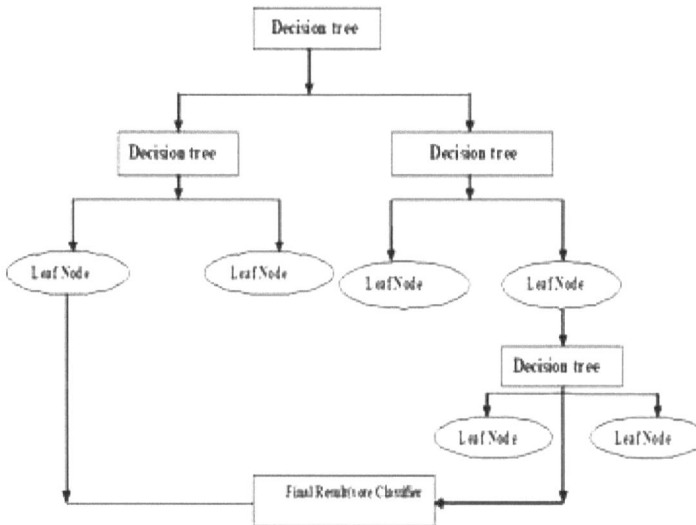

Fig. (2). Random forest using Vote classifier.

1. Select the random samples from the dataset.
2. from the selected samples, construct multiple decision trees.
3. for each decision tree, perform prediction.
4. use a voting classifier or mechanism for the final predicted results.

MLP (MULTILAYER PERCEPTRON)

It is based on a supervised machine learning algorithm in which we learns the function f(.): RM implies Ro. This function is used for training on a dataset.

M represents the input dimensions in the the form of numbers, and O represents the number of dimensions for output.

Consider a given set of features A=a1, a2...............am. MLP learns from nonlinear functions and it is used for classification and regression. It has more hidden layers except the input and output layers [18].

EXPERIMENTS AND RESULTS

With the help of feature selection, the different combinations of imputation methods such as K-NN, MLP, and NB, and Random forest are developed for lower dimensional datasets with their different missing values. The combinations formed are GA+MLP, IG+MLP, RF+KNN, GA+KNN, NB+IG, GA+NB, NM+KNN. For each dataset, the accuracy is obtained by training the KNN and testing it on the original dataset as shown by Fig. (**3**).

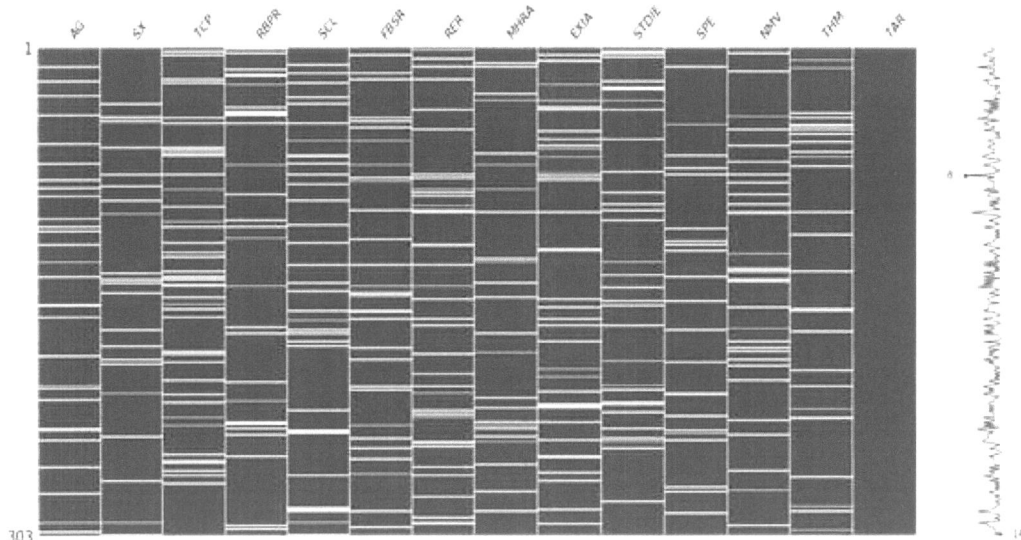

Fig. (3). Missing values Results.

The experiments are based on the UCI machine learning repository. This Cleveland dataset has 303 instances, and 14 features have been selected for the 2 classes. From this dataset, choose that values have a different dimensional lead for features to make the final result shown. The Fig. (**3**) shows the missing values for the dataset, and Fig. (**4**) shows ROC curve for Naive Bayes

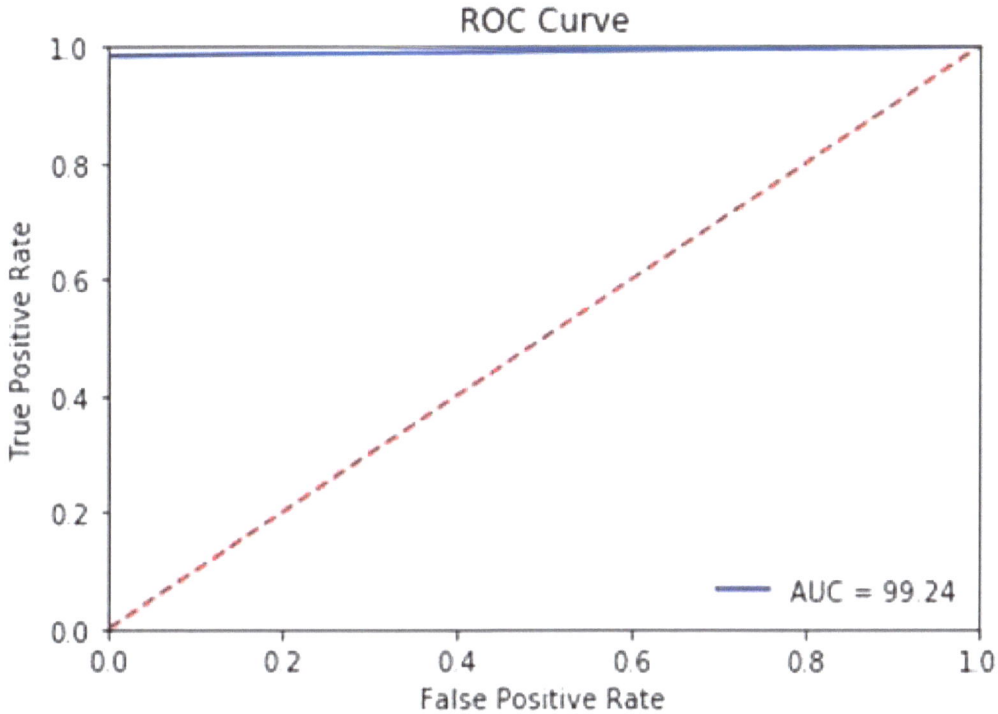

Fig. (4). ROC curve for Naive Bayes.

The different missing value imputation methods were analyzed for the Cleveland heart disease dataset. The missing rate of 10% to 40% is calculated.

Different imputation methods were imputed after introducing the missing values and checking them by using different classifiers for machine learning. These classifiers are K-NN, MLP, and NB. Random forest machine classifiers also check the performance and accuracy of imputation methods.

The lower-dimensional dataset value is implemented by the combination of information gain (IG), and genetic algorithm (GA), and the results were implemented and checked by performance measure RMSE. The result is shown in Table **1** in which the performance of the MLP classifier is implemented by the combination of IG and GA imputation methods.

In our experiments, the lower-dimensional dataset value (Random forest+ multilayer perception, RF+MLP, GA(Genetic algorithm)+MLP, (information gain) IG+MLP, MLP imputation method is analyzed as shown in Fig. (**5**) labelled as Results for Classification method MLP.

Table 1. Classification Performance of imputation method using MLP.

Sr.No	Missing Rate	RF+MLP	GA+MLP	IG+MLP	MLP	Calculate RMSE
1	10%	0.7662	0.7699	0.7895	0.5652	0.4033
2	20%	0.7502	0.7594	0.7769	0.5645	0.4313
3	30%	0.7568	0.7479	0.775	0.5653	0.4349
4	35%	0.739	0.7464	0.7466	0.5667	0.4436
5	40%	0.7358	0.735	0.7598	0.5653	0.4126

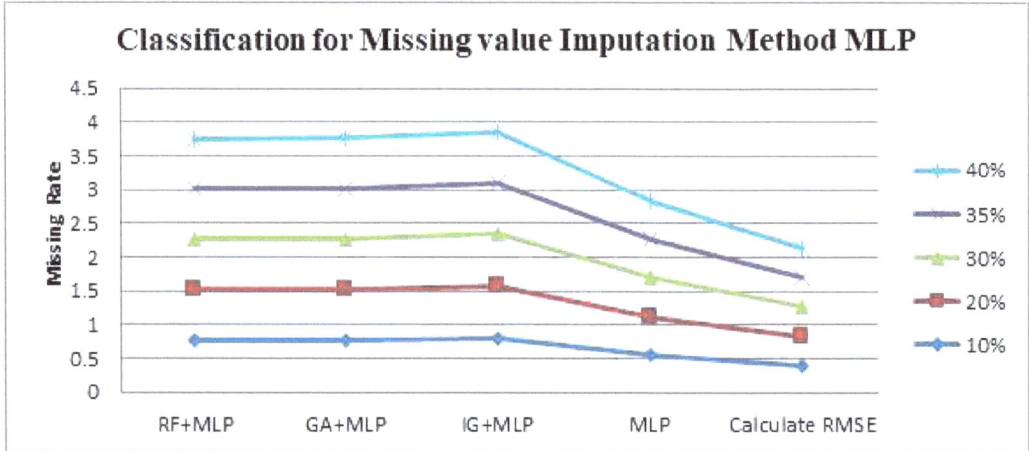

Fig. (5). Results for Classification method MLP.

Different combined approaches were used to show the average classification accuracy, such as RF+KNN/IG/GA, RF+SVM/IG/GA, RF+NB/IG/GA, RF+MLP/IG/GA, *etc*. The missing imputations models are NB, SVM, KNN, MLP; RF do not include the feature selection. With the help of IG and GA, the feature selection is performed effectively. The numbers of features were to be filtered out. The filtration of features could degrade the performance of the imputation model. Fig. (**6**) shows the Feature selection and missing value imputation combined result process for KNN, Fig. (**7**) Feature selection and missing value imputation combined result process for Naïve Bayes and Fig. (**8**) and Feature selection and missing value imputation combined result process for Naïve Bayes, KNN, ML and Table **3**.

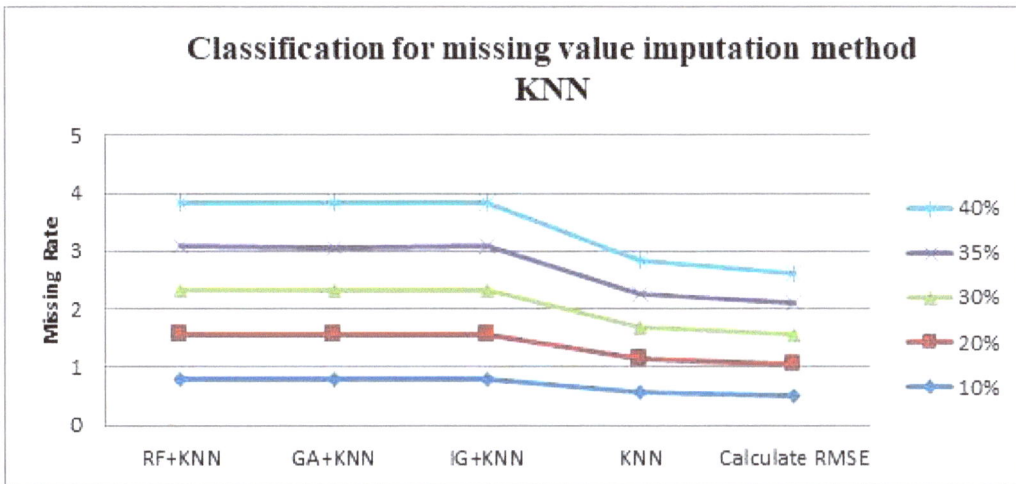

Fig. (6). Feature selection and missing value imputation combined result process for KNN.

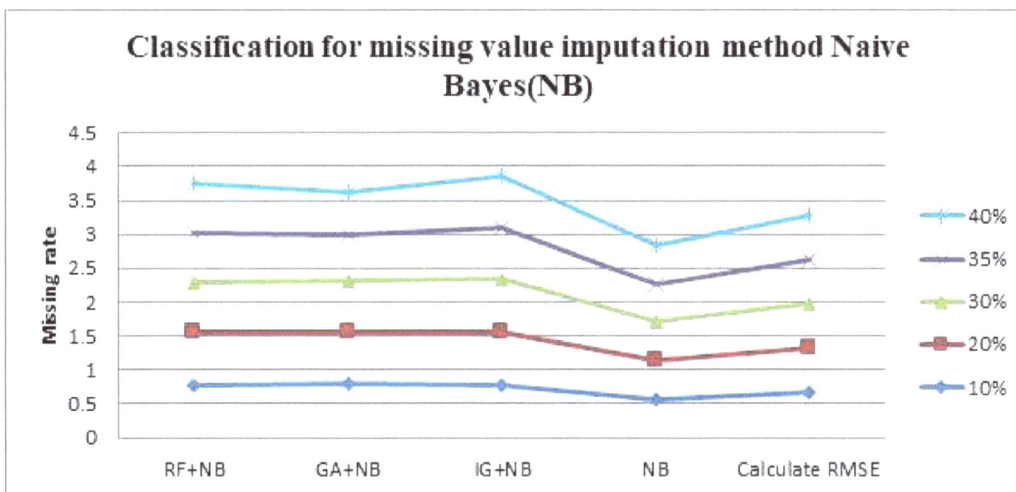

Fig. (7). Featureselectionandmissingvalueimputation combined result processfor Naïve Bayes.

Table 2. Classification of feature selection using KNN and calculates result using RMSE.

Sr.No	Missing Rate	RF+KNN	GA+KNN	IG+KNN	KNN	Calculate RMSE
1	10%	0.7895	0.7799	0.7754	0.5658	0.5033
2	20%	0.767	0.7657	0.7776	0.5658	0.5313
3	30%	0.7634	0.7694	0.77	0.5658	0.5349
4	35%	0.768	0.7538	0.7649	0.57	0.5436
5	40%	0.75	0.7443	0.7517	0.568	0.5126

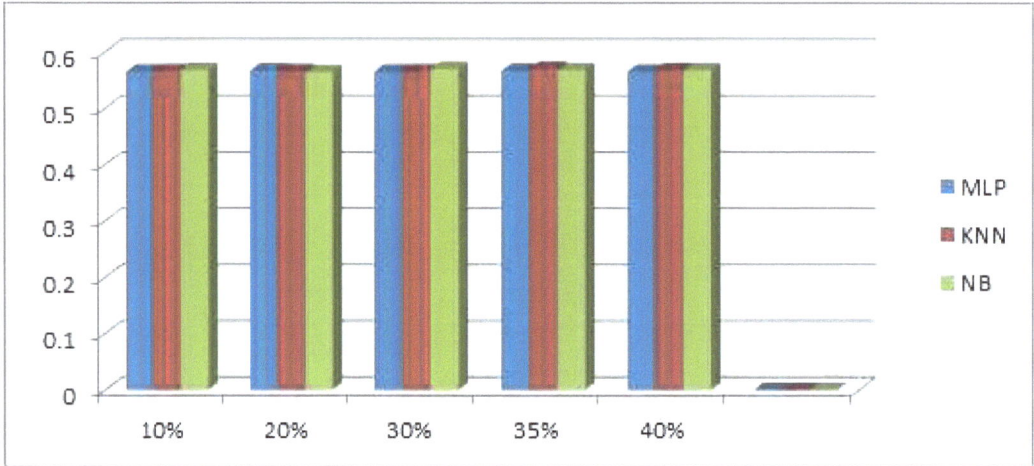

Fig. (8). Feature selection and missing value imputation combined result process for Naïve Bayes, KNN, ML.

Table 3. Classification for missing value imputation method NB and calculates result using RMSE.

Sr.No	Missing Rate	RF+NB	GA+NB	IG+NB	NB	Calculate RMSE
1	10%	0.7768	0.788	0.7812	0.568	0.657
2	20%	0.7696	0.7797	0.7812	0.5644	0.6541
3	30%	0.7412	0.7427	0.7716	0.57	0.66
4	35%	0.7397	0.6844	0.7606	0.568	0.657
5	40%	0.7197	0.6244	0.7597	0.568	0.657

For every classifier and approach used in this chapter, computed results according to the missing rate.

Table 4. performance of imputation model for missing value using classifiers

Sr.No	Missing Rate	MLP	KNN	NB
1	10%	0.5652	0.5658	0.568
2	20%	0.5667	0.5658	0.5644
3	30%	0.5653	0.5658	0.57
4	35%	0.5667	0.57	0.568
5	40%	0.5653	0.568	0.568

In the above Table **4**, the best imputation method is analyzed, which is Naïve Bayes.

Table 5. Missing value Performance by RMSE.

Sr.No	Missing Rate	Calculate RMSE(MLP)	Calculate RMSE(KNN)	Calculate RMSE(NB)
1	10%	0.4033	0.5658	0.657
2	20%	0.4313	0.5658	0.6541
3	30%	0.4349	0.5658	0.66
4	35%	0.4436	0.57	0.657
5	40%	0.4126	0.568	0.657

In the above-mentioned table, the RMSE provides the best results for classifier Naïve Bayes Shown in Fig. (**9**). Results of best classifier NB for missing value imputation using RMSE

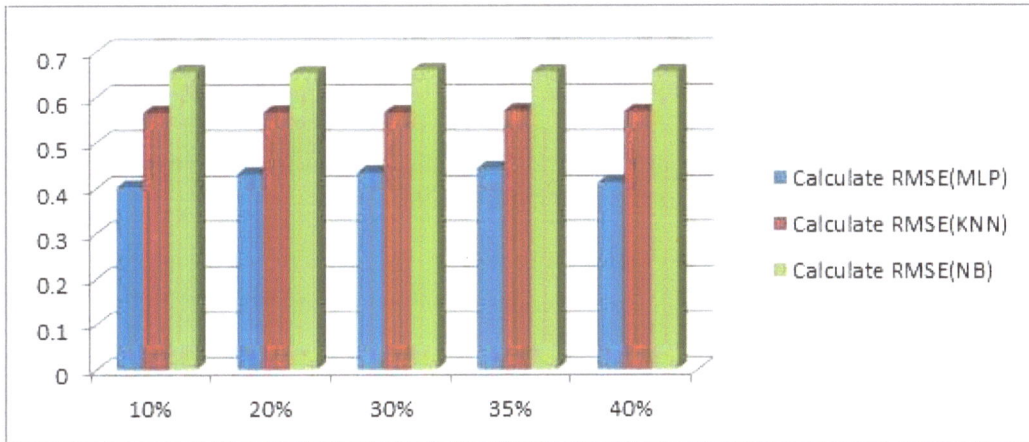

Fig. (9). Results of best classifier NB for missing value imputation using RMSE.

The comparative results and their analysis for all the missing value imputation is shown in above Fig. (**7**). The RMSE and lower dimensional imputation methods are used. The combined approach with RMSE and lower and high dimensional datasets provided the results. The increased value does not mean that it provides an error for each. The missing value imputation method handled the missing values for heart disease and could provide suitable performance.

IMPLEMENTATION RESULTS IN HIGHER DIMENSIONAL VALUE

Table **6** shows the classification results for high dimensional datasets with a 40% missing rate with the different combinations of imputation and feature selection methods. The comparison is shown by: RF+MLP, GA+MLP, IG+MLP, MLP, RF+KNN, GA+KNN, IG+KNN, KNN, RF+NB, GA+NB, IG+NB, NB, the random forest allow this imputation model for better imputation results as shown in Table **6**.

Table 6. Results for higher dimensional value for Arrhythmia.

Comparison Results	RF+MLP	GA+MLP	IG+MLP	MLP
Arrhythmia	28.28	29.17	29.14	29.16
-	-	-	-	-
Arrhythmia	RF+KNN	GA+KNN	IG+KNN	KNN
-	43.28	39.17	39.12	39.12
Arrhythmia	RF+NB	GA+NB	IG+NB	NB
-	48.28	49.17	49.12	49.12

CONCLUSIONS AND FUTURE SCOPE

This study aims to compute the missing values in the dataset according to percentage rate with information gain, genetic algorithm. RMSE.MICE and mean mode imputations methods are used to calculate the value applying to ML and other approaches discussed in the proposed study.

In this chapter, the missing value imputation method is implemented on the Cleveland heart disease dataset. The, computed missing value is a solution for finding out the incomplete values for a given dataset. This chapter focuses on the feature selection method, and imputation methods. The results are obtained by implementing it on machine learning classifier such as KNN, NB, MLP, RF, *etc*. The best results for missing rate 10% is 0.657,20% is 0.6541,30% is0.66, 35% is 0.657to 40% is 0.657 obtained by NB (naïve bayes classifier) and. in future used this model by other imputation methods, and different dataset could be employed for better performance and reduced error rate.

CONSENT FOR PUBLICATION

Not applicable.

CONFLICT OF INTEREST

The authors declare no conflict of interest, financial or otherwise.

ACKNOWLEDGEMENT

Declared none.

REFERENCES

[1]   R. Aggarwal, and S. Kumar, An automated perception and prediction of heart disease based on machine learning.
[http://dx.doi.org/10.1063/5.0076788]

[2]   R. Aggarwal, and P. Thakral, Meticulous Presaging Arrhythmia Fibrillation for Heart Disease Classification Using Oversampling Method for Multiple Classifiers Based on Machine Learning.*Advances in Data Computing, Communication and Security. Lecture Notes on Data Engineering and Communications Technologies.,* P. Verma, C. Charan, X. Fernando, S. Ganesan, Eds., vol. Vol. 106. Springer: Singapore, 2022.
[http://dx.doi.org/10.1007/978-981-16-8403-6_9]

[3]   C.H. Liu, C-F. Tsai, K-L. Sue, and M-W. Huang, "The Feature Selection Effect on Missing Value Imputation of Medical Datasets", *Appl. Sci. (Basel),* vol. 10, no. 7, p. 2344, 2020.
[http://dx.doi.org/10.3390/app10072344]

[4]   R. El-Bialy, M.A. Salamay, O.H. Karam, and M.E. Khalifa, "Feature analysis of coronary artery heart disease data sets", *Procedia Comput. Sci.,* vol. 65, pp. 459-468, 2015.
[http://dx.doi.org/10.1016/j.procs.2015.09.132]

[5]   F Yang, J Du, J Lang, W Lu, L Liu, and C Jin, *commissioning Value Estimation Methods Research for Arrhythmia Classification Using the Modified Kernel Difference-Weighted KNN Algorithms, .*

[6]   F.S. Alotaibi, "Implementation of Machine Learning Model to Predict Heart Failure Disease", *Int. J. Adv. Comput. Sci. Appl.,* vol. 10, no. 6, 2019.
[http://dx.doi.org/10.14569/IJACSA.2019.0100637]

[7]   R. Luengo-Fernandez, J. Leal, and A.M. Gray, "UK research expenditure on dementia, heart disease, stroke and cancer: are levels of spending related to disease burden?", *Eur. J. Neurol.,* vol. 19, no. 1, pp. 149-154, 2012.
[http://dx.doi.org/10.1111/j.1468-1331.2011.03500.x] [PMID: 21951976]

[8]   C.J. McAloon, L.M. Boylan, T. Hamborg, N. Stallard, F. Osman, P.B. Lim, and S.A. Hayat, "The changing face of cardiovascular disease 2000–2012: An analysis of the world health organisation global health estimates data", *Int. J. Cardiol.,* vol. 224, pp. 256-264, 2016.
[http://dx.doi.org/10.1016/j.ijcard.2016.09.026] [PMID: 27664572]

[9]   S. Mendis, *Global atlas on cardiovascular disease prevention and control.* World Health Organization: Geneva, 2011.

[10]   M. Nilashi, H. Ahmadi, A.A. Manaf, T.A. Rashid, S. Samad, L. Shahmoradi, N. Aljojo, and E. Akbari, "Coronary Heart Disease Diagnosis Through Self-Organizing Map and Fuzzy Support Vector Machine with Incremental Updates", *Int. J. Fuzzy Syst.,* vol. 22, no. 4, pp. 1376-1388, 2020.
[http://dx.doi.org/10.1007/s40815-020-00828-7]

[11]   N. Poolsawad, L. Moore, C. Kambhampati, and J.G.F. Cleland, "Issues in the Mining of Heart Failure Datasets", *International Journal of Automation and Computing,* vol. 11, no. 2, pp. 162-179, 2014.
[http://dx.doi.org/10.1007/s11633-014-0778-5]

[12]   A.K. Paul, P.C. Shill, M.R.I. Rabin, and K. Murase, "Adaptive weighted fuzzy rule-based system for the risk level assessment of heart disease", *Appl. Intell.,* vol. 48, no. 7, pp. 1739-1756, 2018.
[http://dx.doi.org/10.1007/s10489-017-1037-6]

[13]   R. Aggarwal, and S. Kumar, "An Enhanced Fusion Approach for Meticulous Presaging of HD Detection Using Deep Learning", *2022 IEEE International Conference on Distributed Computing and Electrical Circuits and Electronics (ICDCECE),* 2022pp. 1-4
[http://dx.doi.org/10.1109/ICDCECE53908.2022.9793141]

[14]   M.M. Rahman, and D.N. Davis, "Machine Learning-Based Missing Value Imputation Method for Clinical Dataset",

[15]   Setiawan, Noor Akhmad & Venkatachalam, P. & Mohd Hani, Ahmad Fadzil, "A Comparative Study of Imputation Methods to Predict Missing Attribute Values in Coronary Heart Disease Data Set", [http://dx.doi.org/10.1007/978-3-540-69139-6_69]

[16]   S. Venkatraman, "Missing Data Imputation for Individualised CVD Diagnostic and Treatment, Computing in Cardiology", [http://dx.doi.org/10.22489/CinC.2016.100-179]

[17]   G.C. Yang, S. Ao, L. Gelman, Ed., *IAENG Transactions on Engineering Technologies'. Lecture Notes in Electrical Engineering.* vol. Vol. 229. Springer: Dordrecht. [http://dx.doi.org/10.1007/978-94-007-6190-2_19]

[18]   Z Hu, and D Du, *A new analytical framework for missing data imputation and classification with uncertainty: Missing data imputation and heart failure readmission prediction,* . [http://dx.doi.org/10.1371/journal.pone.0237724]

## CHAPTER 11

Analysis of Abstractive Text Summarization with Deep Learning Technique

Shruti J. Sapra Thakur[1,2] and **Avinash S. Kapse**[3,*]

[1] *Department of Computer Science and Engineering, Amravati University*

[2] *Department of Computer Science and Engineering, G H Raisoni College of Engineering, Nagpur*

[3] *Department of Information Technology, Anuradha College of Engineering, Chikhli, Amravati University*

Abstract: In today's era, data in textual format has got great importance and is used to extract useful information from this data to design various kinds of information systems such as Document Generation, Prediction systems, Report Generation, Recommendation Systems, and Language modeling, and many more. That is why such techniques are very important, which will reduce the amount of data while saving the information and various parameters concerning this information. One such technique is text summarization which retains essential and useful information. This technique is very simple and convenient as compared to other techniques of summarization. For processing data, the Apache tool of Kafka is used. This platform is useful for real-time streaming data pipelines and many applications related to it. With this, one can use APIs of native Apache Kafka to populate data lakes, stream variants to and from databases, and power machine learning and analytically carry out. The input portion in this situation is a spark base platform for analytics. For the fast development of workflows for complex machine learning systems, Tensorflow is evolved as a significant library of machine learning.

Keywords: Abstractive Summarization, Apache Kafka, Azure ML, Extractive Summarization, MemSQL, Tensorflow, Text Summarization.

INTRODUCTION

Historical Development

Researchers in the initial days designed a faultless system contingent on the neural networks of intelligence based on human analogy.

---
[*] **Corresponding author Avinash S. Kapse:**Department of Information Technology, Anuradha College of Engineering, Chikhli, Amravati University, Amravati; E-mail: askapse@gmail.com

They grouped and mixed most of the mathematics and algorithms to create the below process (Fig. **1**).

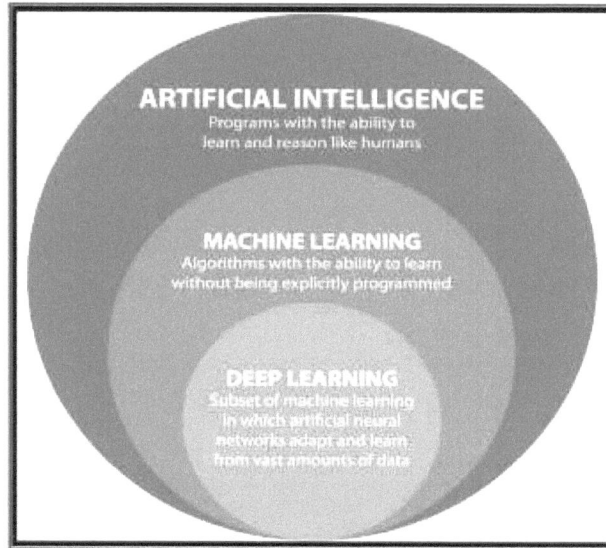

Fig. (1). History of Deep Learning.

After that, there was a great development in this process with the advent of deep learning methods. With this improvement in the techniques, there is an advancement of the Back Propagation model discovered by researchers. The first discovery in AI concentrated on the design of the neural network. They are based on the human thinking analogy in which we take input and give some output after thinking or after processing some operations on those inputs and hence machine learning becomes popular.

This process can find the different patterns in data and can go through all the data; in this way, the machine can learn information and can apply that information to the process of solving the problems or in other words, it can apply that learned information for problem-solving. Such type of AI has a great number of applications in the fields like detection of malware and can predict the future in economic software of the share market and may suggest favourable stock and trades [1].

In this way, we can say that machine learning is a very modern technique of deep learning that is very advanced, which may complete many more expectations as it is a more innovative technique. This technique is very advanced and useful in many sectors like entertainment, weather predictions, stock market and has become very popular in computational sciences too.

Area of Research and its Contribution

What is deep learning?

Deep learning is a subgroup of machine learning in artificial intelligence (AI) that has networks accomplished of learning unsupervised starting data that is unstructured or unlabeled. It is also identified as a deep neural network or learning.

A branch of machine learning that is the subfield of learning representation of data is very useful in pattern learning; such systems are very useful though the system is provided with a very large amount of information.

What is Machine Learning?

Machine learning is one such area of computer science that provides systems the capability to learn without being programmed explicitly (Fig. **2**) [2].

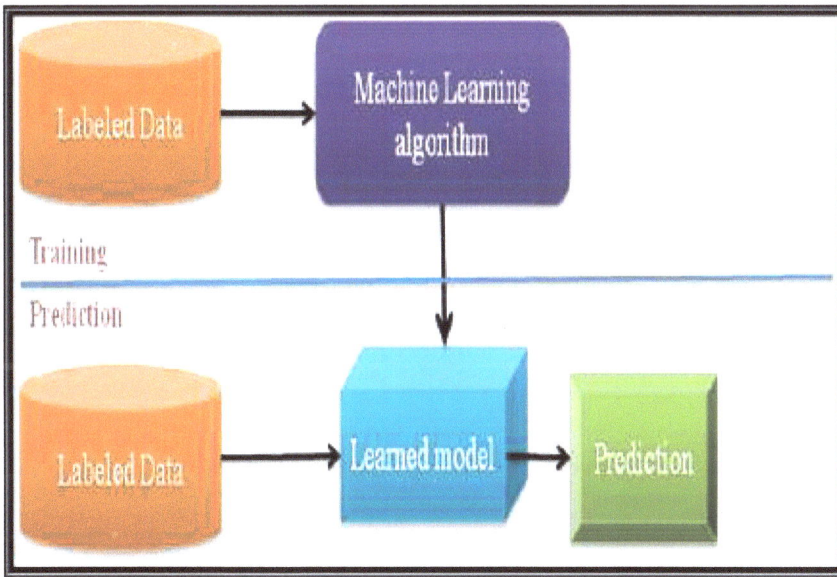

Fig. (2). Techniques of Machine Learning.

Techniques which will learn from and will make predictions on data:

Supervised: Supervised Learning can be possible using a training set that is labeled.

Example: *Classification of emails* with the help of labeled emails.

Unsupervised: In Unsupervised learning, patterns are discovered using patterns in unlabeled data.

Example documents similar in the *cluster are grouped* based on text.

Reinforcement learning: This system will learn to act depending on feedback/reward.

Example: The game will play go and in reward, it will win or lose Characteristics	Machine Learning	Deep Learning
Amount of labeled Data	Large	Huge
Features	As per Pick	Learns Automatically
Time to Results	Short	Long
Accuracy	Good	Best
Debugging	Easy	Hard
Computational Cost	Lowest	Highest
Decision Path	Known	Not Easy to Identify

Fig. (3). Characteristics and properties of Deep Learning.

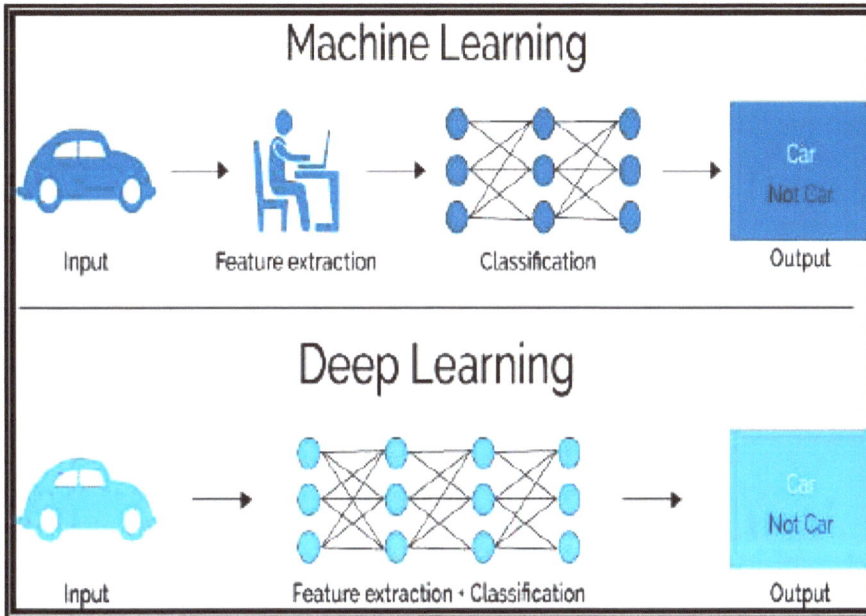

Fig. (4). Machine Learning *Vs* Deep Learning.

Trends in Area of Research

Nowadays, a large amount of data is being generated, maybe millions of gigabytes per day and hence mankind cannot process such a large amount of data and draw some useful inferences from such large data.

One can also see that machine learning will be replaced soon in all areas of neural networks and deep learning as it has a great number of applications in time series analysis and weather forecasting, and it is also believed that deep learning will come to an end (Fig. **3**).

Current Challenges in the Area of Research

Deep learning has architectural variations for validation and is also proved in different experiments, and someone may require an attempt at how deep learning achieved such good results and a great performance.

Although many different kinds of mathematical units for computation have been proposed depending on their characteristics, the latest studies on their characteristics are only for the time being and not permanent in performance and results. Consequently, some of the good parameters are required to assess the different techniques in this field to achieve a great performance (Fig. **4**).

KEY CHALLENGES IN DEEP LEARNING

Deep Learning Needs Enough Quality Data

Deep learning will give better results as it has plenty of quality data and becomes available to obtain from it, and it circulates as the available data increases. But if the quality data is not available, this may result in the loss of data which may be severe or may create damage to the whole system due to loss of useful data.

There is another great example where researchers make the deep learning system of Google fooled by introducing errors and by changing the useful data and adding noise. Such errors are forcefully introduced by the researchers on a trial basis in the case of image recognition algorithms. And it is found that the performance is greatly hampered because of the changes in the quality and quantity of data that was introduced with the system.

Though there are very small data changes, it is found that the results are greatly changed, and no change in the input data is allowed in such cases, hence it is suggested not to alter the input data, therefore it is has become essential to add some constraints to deep learning algorithms that will improve the accuracy of such systems which will lead to great efficiency of the system performance.

AI and Expectations

There is a great difference between the workers and how the AI methodologies work, and the techniques and super-smart system will lead to replacing most jobs that humans do in the industry today.

As system and data science give great performance in all the work in the industry and with all kinds of available data, all such expectations are not fulfilled only by such techniques, and such techniques cannot fully replace the human brains; hence there is a great need of model which can enhance the performance to a great level, which is now very essential and is the necessity of the time.

Becoming Production-Ready

Recent statistics show that 80% of industries are investing in these new techniques of AI; hence there is great pressure on the production of new inventions in AI solutions because AI solutions are solving real-life problems with great efficiency, thus increasing the popularity of these techniques.

The researcher's main interest will be on "operationalizing" AI facilities through innovation of technology structure, and resolving security issues such as informational integrity and the security of the AI platforms, and ensuring the high availability of AI solutions so they can deliver results, predictions, etc. when needed. The main issue of AI in industries is for machines to assist specialists and others involved in making crucial decisions.

Deep Learning Does not Understand Context Very Well

There is a great scope of advancement in the structure and architecture of the deep learning algorithm as these algorithms must understand how to defeat the human player in any intellectual game, so algorithms must behave smartly and achieve the task in a specified time and create a competitive environment so that the human player enjoy that competitive environment. But these advancements in architecture are not so easy and cannot be achieved in simple steps; hence requires great proficiency in algorithm design and modification; then this achievement is possible.

There is a great increase in demand for real-time local analysis of data, for example, devices with IoT services, deep learning models to be quickly quantified, and innovative information may be useful to increase the speed of data entry.

Deep Learning Security

Deep learning networks are very useful in the case of cyber security. And these networks are modified after the input is provided to the system, as these systems are more prone to cyber-attacks. In other words, one can say that these systems are always subject to modifications or alterations, which cause severe changes in the system leading to malicious output from the system. Hence security is the prime concern for such systems and such systems should be modified to achieve good output.

Closing Thoughts

While much has been inscribed about the irresistible array of applications and practices for intelligence to be introduced artificially and learning things deeply, it is important to accept in mind that the acceptance of such technologies presents many challenges in addition to all the buzz and anticipation.

These challenges are by no means insurmountable, and both talented data scientists and developers work tirelessly to enhance and refine the underlying models. However, a more informed perspective can only be a good thing if you are to get the most from AI and deep learning [3].

TensorFlow

Tensorflow is very useful for computational and logical frameworks for various applications in the case of different algorithms such as linear regression, neural networks and deep knowledge, and many more algorithms like these. Though the base is objective-oriented languages like C++ or low level but mostly designed using python.

Tensorflow is a complex system that involves some complex logical and mathematical operations, and hence it is not easy to implement in the system. It is not very compatible with deep learning and machine learning applications.

A real-life application of the stock market gets worse; suppose one has to create a stock market application for data regarding the various situations in the stock market must be fed to the system. Then the system must interpret and understand various situations for the stock market and should act accordingly. The whole task is very time-consuming and does not need continuous training of the system. The system should behave correctly concerning the situations of the future predictable trends and this training process is very tedious, and one must carefully insert all the datasets into the system. System working must be understood properly for the proper functioning of the system. While the feeding or training process, various parameters of the system must be taken into consideration for the effective and efficient working of the system.

The first 40 days are used to train the system and later 20 days are used for the testing of the system, which is again an essential factor for the system to predict the future trends of the market. The whole process of training and testing needs to be done with great care and by proficient persons to meet the actual requirement of the desired system [4].

What is a Text Summarization?

The textual data has got great importance, as its demand is ever increasing as it may consist of valuable information for the proper functioning of all sorts of systems. This type of data is again useful for the production of the various kinds of systems, which plays a crucial role in the information industry. While preserving the data, it is again essential to preserve the proper and useful meaning and integrity of the data so that whenever required, data can be used for designing and implementing the vital systems which are very useful for information generation which is specific to the domain required and which can solve the problem in less amount of time. The summarization of text is essential and useful for the production of languages which are natural and collect important information from the given data which is essential for the designing and development of new required systems which are very useful for fast operations and produce the desired output within the specified amount of time. The main concern while designing such a system is the speed of operation, because if the speed of operation is slow in such cases, it may produce a delay in the production of useful information, which cannot be tolerated.

There are various issues regarding the process of summarization which are mainly the availability of different tokens at the time of testing, and the presence of proper words and sentences. Accuracy of the facts is again the very important parameter or issue regarding the reproduction of useful information, and this step of summarization is very important in the whole system development and implementation and any small changes in the process may change the output considerably.

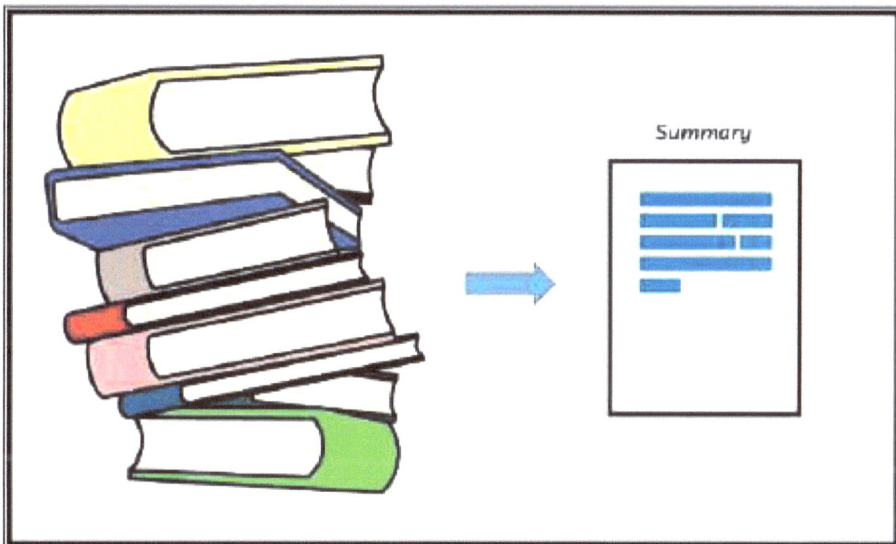

Fig. (5). Text Summarization.

There are two prominent types of summarization algorithms.

I. Extractive summarization: This method copies some of the parts of the given text by selecting the importance of the data and may combine the selected parts of the data or sentences to make the summary for proper use. This method uses the mathematical and computational method for the selection of the part or part of sentences (Fig. **5**) [5]

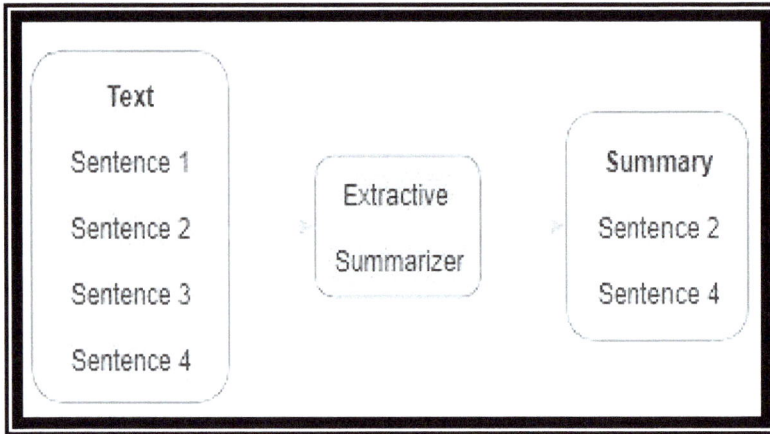

Fig. (6). Extractive Summarization.

II. Abstractive summarization: This method is very hard to implement as this method is based on the production of the phrases based on the text available, which is very difficult to design and implement. This system would probably read the whole text and then create the abstract for the text read and which may depend on the consideration of the system itself and may give different meanings to the text; hence it requires a very proficient tool to develop such a system. It is again important to note that the system must know the real world to produce such abstract meaning for a large number of text available as input (Fig. **6**) [6].

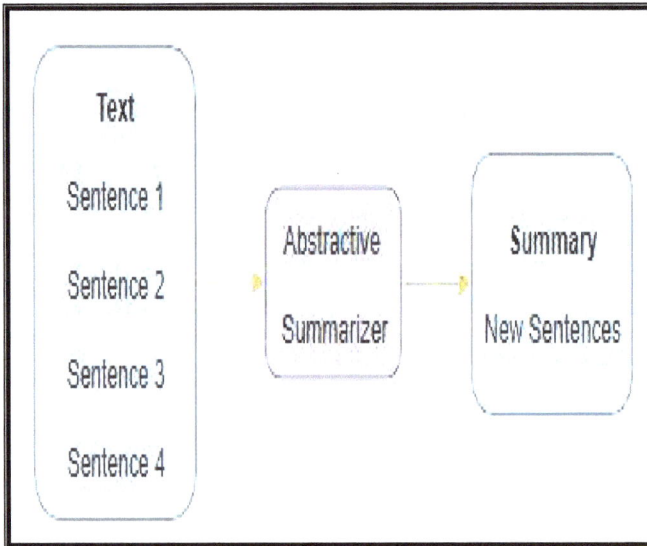

Fig. (7). Abstractive Summarization.

Challenges in Abstractive summarization

• Acceptance of duplicate content

• Rearrangement of specific words

• Various meanings for the same word

• Repetition of the content available

• Interest may be different for different context

• Errors in the available text

• A large amount of information

Importance of Text Summarization

There is a large amount of information available in the form of textual data, and it is again increasing each second. The internet is full of web pages and blogs, and various kinds of information is changing day by day, or in other words, each of the information on the internet is getting updated with a great amount of speed. One can just type and can get all the data over the internet within a second or if one just typed some specific title, it would generate a large number of sources for the same information within a fraction of a second.

But there is a great need for the system to be developed for the information which is to be available in a short period as the whole information on the internet is very detailed and elaborative. Hence getting more abstract information to be developed in a short amount of time is essential as one does not have time to read the whole information available on the internet though it is available at a less cost [7].

Textual information available on the internet is very large and is in an unorganized format. Most of the time the user is not aware of the flow of the information as it is not available in the specific structure. So, it is very important to define a specific structure for the information as per the constraints of the user or make the information so short that the user can read the whole information and get the meaning in less amount of time; in short, this may increase the readability of the user for the particular information and this may also save the user crucial time which may be used for another useful task [8]

One cannot generate or make the whole information available in the abstract form. There is a great need for some automatic system or some method that will do these things and make the task of abstraction easier. The process of creation of a summary has to be automatic and should be done by following some specific flow. If the process of summary creation is done by humans, then it may lead to lots of biasing, or human experience or intervention would create different meanings to the text, and the summary would not be of the actual requirement after creation. Hence it is an automated process. This automatic process will save human time considerably, making the proper use of every resource available for the complete system design, development, and implementation.

The mechanism for the automatic creation of summaries will be very useful in all aspects as compared to the summaries created by humans (Fig. **7**).

The summary is considered the perfect document, which will be one of the new and individual documents in all aspects and is very useful for the user [9]

Examples of Text Summaries

There are several reasons and usages for a summary of a larger document.

Several examples can be given for the text summarization, but the most useful or understandable for all users is the example of shortening of news which is from the current news article which is very long to read, and users get bored by reading the whole article, or the user has to invest a large amount of time in reading the whole news article. In this case, the summary is greatly useful, saving the user time considerably and with the proper meaning of the news.

In a book published in1999 on the topic of high-minded "*Advances in Automatic Text Summarization*" the authors presented a valuable list of everyday examples of text summarization [10].

Types of Masses Benefited

• News from the whole the world

• Internet (studies for students)

• Topics (of a meeting)

• Reviews (of films)

• Opinion about (a book, CD, etc.)

Aim

• Make use of Deep Learning in Abstract Summarization to yield good results than previous technologies.

• Make use of deep learning to develop various kinds of systems, which will be very useful in all areas of information systems.

• Make use of Tensorflow which has emerged as one of the tools for the development of essential components for the system development as a whole.

• Make use of Apache Kafka streaming and tf. Keras & tf. data responsible for streaming data in & out. So, the TensorFlow-io package can include support for a very extensive range of data formats and frameworks.

Objectives

• To study Literature Survey and analysis of different abstractive summarization techniques.

• To study and compare the proposed abstractive summarization with the traditional and extractive methods of Text Summarization.

• To study current techniques, methodologies, mathematical models, datasets, algorithms, finding out effective systems.

• To propose a deep learning model and an algorithm using deep learning techniques for Abstractive text summarization.

• To evaluate the matches which are suggested by machines for the different persons in different constraints.

• To state and formulate the improvements, result analysis, and performance evaluation of the proposed system with the existing system.

LITERATURE REVIEW

V. Sukriti et al. (2019) [5], proposed a text summarization method for realistic reports using a deep learning model. This method has three parts, first is feature extraction, second is feature enhancement, and third is summary generation. All these parts combine to form core information, thus resulting in a single summary that is comprehensive. This method finds various features to develop an effective summary; this method also uses a Restricted Boltzmann Machine to improve the accuracy of the summary without losing any essential information. Experimentation carried out on numerous articles determines the effectiveness of the proposed approach. Several accurate reports from various domains of health, technology, news, sports, etc., with changing numbers of sentences, were used for experimentation and assessment. The proposed algorithm was run on each of those, and system-generated summaries were associated with the summaries produced by humans.

A. Mehdi et al. (2017) [6] said that due to the increasing growth of the internet, there is a large amount of data or information available on various sources in the form of blogs, websites, web pages, that is why the information is also available very easily as compared to older times. This leads to an explosion of the data available through the number of sources. Thus, there is a great need for summarization of information or rather, an automatic summarization of information is essential in this context. In this research, the important methods to automate the procedure for the summarization of text are explained and pros and cons of different methods are also described.

S. Bhumika et al. (2020) [7] defined summarization is used to reduce the high-volume data into short meaningful volume data. It can be extractive and abstractive. As each person has a different interest, data may be in any form, such as judgments, ideas, opinions, news, etc. In Extractive Summarization, the summarized content lacks original content. Abstractive summarization is the extraction of knowledge using proper modification in data. This research first compares different algorithms for different summarizations, and based on their pros and cons, various parameters are discussed, then proposes a new algorithm for abstractive summarization with the help of NLP to generate shortcuts from the content that make it easier to memorize the content.

M. Inderjeet et al. (2018) [10] explained a growing demand for text summarization as there is a huge amount of information generated or available on the internet with the use of technology. This availability of information is due to the developments in technology, such as online information sources and the advancement in the devices such as phones or mobiles. Many industries are progressively starting to provide summarization in text, often using tools for information retrieval. In this research, the significance of some latest improvements in this technology is described. Summarization is very useful in all these contexts. But there is again more scope for improvement in this research.

According to *L. Abualigah et al.* (2020) [11], Text Summarization is useful for making short notes for anything which is in detail and is very useful for taking more information in less amount of time. Due to the great amount of data these days, the significance of this mechanism has increased drastically. This research provides the latest information on the process of text summarization. This will provide a new dimension to the advancement of this research.

F. Marcelo et al. (2004) [12] discussed a semantic abstraction approach summarization to be automated in the domain of biomedical sciences. This aspect is useful on a semantic processor, which acts as the interpreter for the source, and a list of assumptions is generated. A transformation step then summarizes and simplifies this list, and generates a disorder input topic. The final input can be shown in graphical form. Also, the application of this method is described in this research. This research also discusses the various merits and demerits of this procedure of summarization in view of different parameters. There is a great scope for the improvement of the modification in the process of summarization and advancement can be achieved using the advancement in the algorithms for text summarization

RESEARCH ISSUES

• Some of the recent works concentrate on how to convert or code big and complex sentences and words; hence there is a great need for a tool or automated tool which can efficiently convert these complex sentences [11].

• Some of the works also focus on the issues in abstractive summarization, considering the quality of the generated summary, evaluation measures, and dataset [12].

• The parsing, alignment of parse trees, and generalized framework are difficult for abstractive summarization which are the important research issues to be considered [13].

• Another issue involved in the summarization is the use of the ROUGH for the process of evolution. In some cases, it is found that it is an excellent method for summarization [14]

Gaps in Research Issue

• In the area of Natural Language Processing (NLP), Text summarization is a great challenge because of this reason, it requires specific designing of text, such as semantic designing and lexical designing, to produce an excellent summary. An excellent summary must have important information and must have short notes and also consider properties such as coherence, readability, non-redundancy, relevance, and attention. The summary which includes all these properties is known as an excellent summary [15]. Modern research on summarizing has been inspired by the framework known as encoder-decoder format. Further, this model is smoother as compared to most of the models defined earlier, as the encoder-decoder framework is also suitable for controlling the number of parameters easily [16]

Motivation

• In most of the research, Paraphrase detection can be used for extractive summaries.

• Most of the research in this area is also trying to work on this aspect of extract generation with the help of data-driven policy for most of the Indian languages [17].

• It is also discussed in the method of Tensorflow, which is also one of the most popular deep learning methodologies which are very useful for the process of summarization.

• Tensorflow has been used extensively in production across a broad spectrum of industries [18].

• The future Tensorflow 2.0, which announces recently, will be present at huge this year with many changes. The high-level tf. Keras API, willing execution, and tf. data importantly make the practice simpler.

However, the data input processing module tf. data in Tensorflow specifically covers a small set of file formats. Users from different industries frequently come across challenges assimilating Tensorflow with data sources not generally seen in the machine learning community. One example is the accumulation of Tensorflow with Apache Kafka. Apache Kafka is extensively used for stream handing out and carries by most of the big data frameworks such as Spark and Flink. For an extensive time, though, there was certainly no Kafka streaming provision in Tensorflow. The data formats, such as TFRecords and tf. in Tensorflow, are also hardly seen in big data or data science communities. Many users are required to combine these two frameworks in a very uneasy way: set up another infrastructure, read messages from Kafka, convert the messages into TFRecords format, invoke Tensorflow to read the TFRecords from a file system, run the working out or interpretation, and including the models or results back to the file system. This method is error-prone and hard to keep up from an infrastructure viewpoint. In addition to Apache Kafka streaming, TensorFlow-io also consists of support for a very extensive range of data formats and frameworks. It supports Apache Ignite for memory and caching, Apache Parquet and Arrow for serialization, AWS Kinesis and Google Cloud Pub for streaming, and various video, audio, and image file formats. Python and R languages could be used, which are especially convenient to the data science community. It is meant to mention that TensorFlow-io is affecting as a part of the tf. data pipeline and natural extension lead of Tensorflow 2.0 API. In additional words, users are capable of reading the data from Kafka and tf. Keras [19].

Scope

The deep learning approach will work efficiently in abstractive text summarization, linguistically meaning probably English and Hindi datasets, such as DUC2002 and DUC2004, designed for challenging the way of summarizing for the time being before existence verified into a private dataset [20]. The impost of the proposed scheme is performed using the most significant properties or characteristics to generate a set of words to form a summary, regularity correspondence, interval between sentences, and semantics. The projected system will associate with the dissimilar, existing systems [21].

Current Technologies Used

Python, Jupyter Notebook

Jupyter is an existent advanced program that is open source and uses the facilities for computing collaborative work done by many methods across dozens of languages used for programming. So, it is a great method to form distinct models using the framework of Python [22].

However, designing a plan becomes more difficult, and practical design in a Jupyter notebook with the features of Python is a great difficulty than designing a portable, scalable, and giving performance for machine learning models is also a challenging task. (Fig. **8**) [23]

One must think about use cases before the huge production. Consider an example of global web applications with a large number of people joined to car infrastructures. One more example is payment and fraud detection systems. This is where the proposed system plays a role.

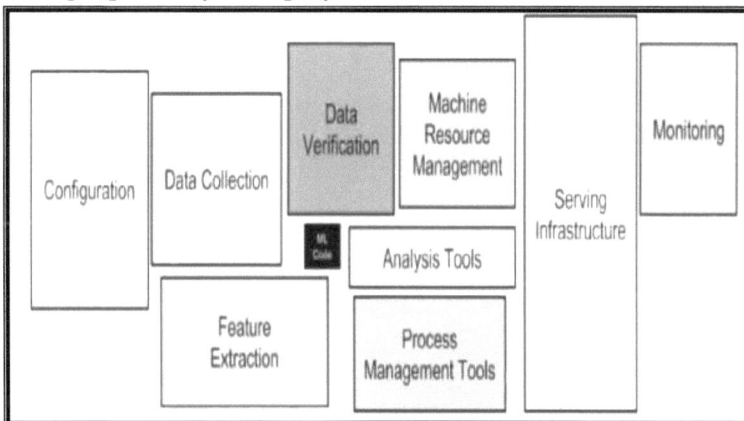

Fig. (8). Jupyter Notebook.

Apache Kafka and KSQL

This is software which is a stream processing and also an open-source also it is designed by LinkedIn [24].

This is an engine for SQL which allows different types of input data and their easy processing as compared to the other different types of software available. Thus, it also produces a good output considering the different parameters in this situation, it is very useful for the system managers to allow the use of such software in the system development and implementation. This system also allows data streaming, aggregation, and filtering, which are also useful characteristics of this approach [25].

Kafka and Python and Jupyter to resolve the abstract Technical Dept. in the proposed model:

To resolve the abstract analytical dept. in organizations, one may associate the reimbursements of Machine learning related applications with the proposed system:

Applications of Python such as stack scikit-learn and Jupyter can also be used.

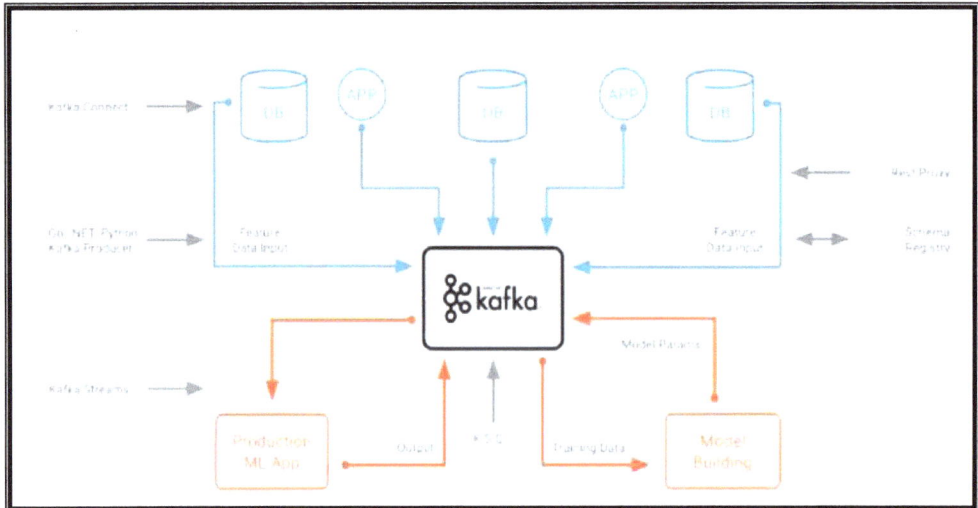

Fig. (9). Apache Kafka.

Tools

1. Hardware requirements

Sr. No.	Details	Options if available
1	System configuration: system with 800 GB hard-disk and 5GB primary memory	It is not useful

2. System qualifications

Sr. No.	Details	Options if available
1	Windows XP or 10/8 with MS-excel	Ubuntu 64-bit with open Office/Linux OS 7.4/Fedora 7.0/
2	Apache Kafka 2.7.0	Apache Kafka 3.4.0
3	Tensorflow Core 3.3.0	-
4	Data streaming	-
5	Python 2.0	-

Database

The present database, platform streaming, enables different data from different sources, and in the same direction, it will be applicable. For instance:

Astronomical measurements

IoT sensor data [26]

Web traffic logs [27].

```
curl -sSCL https://archive.ics.uci.edu/ml/machine-learning-databases/00279/SUSY.csv.gz
```

The first column in Fig. (**9**) is the label of class (0 for signal, 1 for background), characterized by the 18 properties (9 high-level properties and 9 low-level properties). The first 9 properties are non-kinematic and counted in the accelerator. The last 11 structures are actions of the second 9 properties. These are low-level properties obtained by physicists to demonstrate and find the difference between the two classes.

```
COLUMNS = [
            # labels
            class ,
            # low-level features
            lepton_1_pT ,
            lepton_1_eta ,
            lepton_1_phi ,
            lepton_2_pT ,
            lepton_2_eta ,
            lepton_2_phi ,
            missing_energy_magnitude ,
            missing_energy_phi ,
            # high-level derived features
            MET_rel ,
            axial_MET ,
            M_R ,
            M_TR_2 ,
            R ,
            MT2 ,
            S_R ,
            M_Delta_R ,
            dPhi_r_b ,
            cos(theta_r1)
            ]
```

The complete database may have thousands of rows. However, for the application of this instance, let's imagine that there is only a small amount of data (100,000 rows), so less amount of time will be required on the traveling of the data, and extra time will be used for the API.

	class	lepton_1_pT	lepton_1_eta	lepton_1_phi	lepton_2_pT	lepton_2_eta	lepton_2_phi	missing_ene
0	0.0	0.072861	0.653855	1.176225	1.157156	1.739873	0.874309	3.567765
1	1.0	1.667973	0.064191	-1.225171	0.506102	-0.338939	1.672543	3.475464
2	1.0	0.444840	-0.134298	-0.709972	0.451719	-1.613871	-0.768661	1.219918
3	1.0	0.381256	-0.976145	0.693152	0.448959	0.891753	-0.677328	2.033060
4	1.0	1.309996	-0.690089	-0.676259	1.589283	-0.693326	0.622907	1.087562

```
train_df, test_df = train_test_split(susy_df, test_size=0.4, shuffle=True)
print('Number of training samples: ',len(train_df))
print("Number of testing sample: ",len(test_df))


x_train_df = train_df.drop(['class'], axis=1)
y_train_df = train_df["class"]

x_test_df = test_df.drop(['class'], axis=1)
y_test_df = test_df['class']

# The labels are set as the kafka message keys so as to store data
# in multiple-partitions. Thus, enabling efficient data retrieval
# using the consumer groups.
x_train = list(filter(None, x_train_df.to_csv(index=False).split('\n')[1:]))
y_train = list(filter(None, y_train_df.to_csv(index=False).split('\n')[1:]))

x_test = list(filter(None, x_test_df.to_csv(index=False).split('\n')[1:]))
y_test = list(filter(None, y_test_df.to_csv(index=False).split('\n')[1:]))
```

Define the tfio train dataset

The `IODataset` class is utilized for streaming data from kafka into tensorflow. The class inherits from `tf.data.Dataset` and thus has all the useful functionalities of `tf.data.Dataset` out of the box.

```
def decode_kafka_item(item):
    message = tf.io.decode_csv(item.message, [[0.0] for i in range(NUM_COLUMNS)])
    key = tf.strings.to_number(item.key)
    return (message, key)

BATCH_SIZE=64
SHUFFLE_BUFFER_SIZE=64
train_ds = tfio.IODataset.from_kafka('susy-train', partition=0, offset=0)
train_ds = train_ds.shuffle(buffer_size=SHUFFLE_BUFFER_SIZE)
train_ds = train_ds.map(decode_kafka_item)
train_ds = train_ds.batch(BATCH_SIZE)
```

Since only a slight portion of the database is being examined, their efficiency is characterized to ~68% in training. However, there are additional data stored in the system to improve the performance of the model. Also, there is a good deal to determine the characteristics of the system, and given the database, a very small network with less complexity was applied. However, one may resolve the problem of the system by a small change in the learning plan [28].

EXISTING METHODOLOGY/TECHNOLOGIES AND ANALYSIS

In the whole process, many challenges are discovered as the web pages are developed using various sources, and again, the web pages have information that has different structures. But the most important characteristic of this process is it gives an efficient output in a very less amount of time, and another important thing to note is that it produces these outputs with very little redundancy. These two important characteristics made this process of summarization a very significant process.

This method is proven to be beneficial as the information produced by this method is very rich and significant. But, on the other hand, following this process of summarization is a very challenging task as it involves some of the difficult parameters to achieve. The first and most important parameter is the output, which should be correct, concerning the semantics, and this parameter must follow the correct grammar or the correct sequence of the words to get the useful meaning. The information produced after the summarization process has to be correct in all aspects of the language and should convey the right information in an abstract form in a short time. Due to these reasons, this process of summarization has got rating in the proposed research work. Hence most of the research works use the summarization process involving the abstractive method [29].

This summarization process can also be divided into two different kinds, which are as follows. The first is a process based on structure, and the second is a process based on the semantics of the language used.

Structure-based Abstractive Summarization Methods

This method is also useful and contains various kinds of methods like graph-based method, Ontology method, tree-based method lead, body phrase method, rule-based method, etc.

Semantic-based Abstractive Summarization Methods

It also has different kinds of methods which involve a method based on information items, semantic text representation modeling, a method based on semantic graph and multimodal semantic modeling, etc. The most simple and easy form is a method of subject-verb-object which involves the sentences to be measured and used for the abstractive summarization method [30].

Methods for Abstractive Summarization are Written Below

1. Earlier, following methods were used: Sequence, as sequence is a very important Attention Model [31], Encoder-Decoder model, RNNs, and Beyond Method for text summarization using the abstractive method. Currently, advanced summarization techniques are used. The summary produced by the Rule-based technique is of high information density but it is very tedious work since all the rules and patterns are written manually.

2. In Ontology, the use of the uncertain information is one of the parameters and is not acceptable in the simple domain of ontology. An issue with this method is that an individual domain person may describe. The necessary field is a very time-consuming process.

3. In the Tree-based technique, the superiority of summary gets better quality because of the use of a language generator. The individual issue with this kind of method is that the important sentences with context may get excluded during the catching process and coming process while gathering phrases.

4. In the Information item-based technique, the selection of important information can be done. Based on particular information items, the sentences and summaries are produced. This method may produce a very small, intelligible output, and the summary may become rich in information. Occasionally important information such as vital items gets disallowed, and this can be considered as the main issue regarding this method while the construction of meaningful and grammatically accurate sentences diminishes using linguistic excellence of summary.

5. Multimodal semantic model method produces an abstract summary in which it comprises textual data as well as graphical data and hence, gives exceptional results. The problem with this method is that assessment is to be done by any [32].

6. In this semantic-based technique of graph, sentences produced are very meaningful and correct concerning the grammar of the language. But this method may be used and limited to only a single-page document.

6.1. Here is a technique that is accessible, using semantic graph reduction technique for the process of summarization of text using the abstractive method. This distinct technique for encapsulation of single-page document input by using a semantic method is called Rich Semantic Graph (RSG) [33].

a. This technique based on semantics and uses detail with the syntactic method of analysis in which the text input is used, which then produces some sort of dependency and typed associations which are in the form of grammatical or mathematical relations, which is a very great concept related to the process of the summarization and may be useful.

The Rich Semantic Graph Creation Phase: This phase starts with the deep syntactic analysis of the input text, then produces typed dependency associations (grammatical relations) and syntactic and morphological identifiers for each word. Subsequently, for each sentence, the model interconnects the right sequence of the sentences to form a meaningful and useful summary which can be very useful for the process of summarization. This process is widely accepted by many researchers in the process of summarization as it consumes less amount of time, and modeling is very easy as compared to the other methods of summarization. The most important thing about this method is that it produces the output very consistently throughout the process of summarization, which produces a great impact on the use of this method in different models.

Pre-processing of the module: It involves four important procedures which are as follows, pronominal resolve processes, cross-reference purpose, morphological and syntactic exploration and entity appreciation.

b. The Rich Semantic Graph Reduction Phase: In this phase, traditional heuristic rules are truthful on the produced rich semantic graph to reduce it by inclusion, eliminating or merging the graph nodes. The experimental rule of each sentence is composed of three nodes: Subject Noun (SN) node, Main Verb (MV) node, and Object Noun (ON) node.

c. The method of summarization is useful as this process produces the shortest text. The production of the shortest text has great significance during the process of summarization and is an essential part of the summarization process. This process includes all the essentials required for the summarization and hence got great importance.

6.2. In a study [34], Rich planned the semantic process of illustration and discovered a technique for the generation of text which may be considered the latest model to generate textual English from RSG.

a. **The Text Planning Level:** This procedure includes the produced must be in the form of the text generated.

b. **The Sentence Planning Level:** This process produces the semi-paragraph output based on the various grammatical components of the sentences.

The process of planning a sentence may comprise the following procedures:

Lexicalization Process: In this process, the synonym is used, which is very useful for generating a text.

During this process, nouns and verbs are used to collect the sentences, and the verb connected to that noun is also used to generate a meaningful and useful short sentence.

c. **Aggregation Process:** This process decides how pseudo sentences should be joined into semi-paragraphs.

d. **Referring Expression Process:** This process involves the use of pronouns for the generation of short sentences and uses the process of summarization and is very useful for the generation of meaningful sentences.

e. **Surface of Realization Level:** This method generates paragraphs with a higher level of grammar and punctuation concerning the language used for summarization.

f. **Writing of Styles with Selected Essay Generation Level:** Here, the end-user decides the writing method, and the final output is also decided by the user concerning the requirement.

g. **Evaluation Level:** This method or level uses the paragraph which is used most frequently, and words are replaced by alternative sentences or words which have the same meaning as that of the previous words or sentence. This factor is also called the factor of supplementary.

6.3. A new method is described for the process of summarization in which the various rules are set by the user and according to the different rules set, the output is defined. This output scarifies all the requirements of the user as all the rules are defined and described according to the user. This approach is one of the efficient approaches for the process of summarization

a. This method describes the input documents using the graph of semantic method and produces a good output ;hence it is used here for the process of removing the unwanted information from the text, and all the essential components are used or remain in the text, and this will make the text rich or in other words, the information produced in the text is valuable and useful. After the process of summarization, the output is very fine and understood by the user very clearly. It comprises three different modules:

• The Pre-processing Module: This module is a combination of different modules which concentrate on the different aspects of the summarization. This module concentrates on the relation between the various documents involved in the process of summarization, and the words which are coherent and have the same meaning are removed to make the paragraph short and easy to read. The whole input text is scanned for the words which are the same. Such same words may have also meant and may be removed according to the need of the document or may be kept as it is required, keeping in view the shortening of the paragraph. Thus, the paragraph is shortened using fewer words and sentences.

• Rich Semantic Sub-Graphs Generation: The main aim of this method is to generate the validation process for the summarization. In this process, words form like nouns and verbs are produced for the input text, and new text is generated on the process of validation of the grammar, and subgraphs are produced based on the grammatical components like verbs and nouns. The new sentences or short sentences are created using these collected grammatical components and the produced sub-graphs play a vital role. Hence this process is a very creative process for the shortening of the sentences and paragraphs. Thus, this process helps to produce the final rich document, which uses fewer words and sentences to express the same information. This increases the readability of the information and requires less amount of space to store tie information on web pages or web servers.

b. This process produces the different rules for the summarization or graph creation based on which the whole summarization process is carried out to produce the shortened paragraph or, in other words, information is shortened. This process may include or exclude the information by the creation of graphs. And may add or delete some of the information based on the graphs of information produced, which will reduce the time for the process of summarization.

c. The Text Generation Stage: This process aims to create the summary based on the input information [35]

Text Planning: It removes the elongated information from the input text.

7. The process of summarization is a very typical task and difficult challenge in the domain of Processing Natural Language [36]. This process involves lexical and semantic analysis for the process of summarization. This process creates a

great summary that involves the text, which has all the features, and after removing the repeatable words, increasing the readability and reliability of the text, the text will become very short and precise. In other words, this information, after all processing, becomes rich in content with the specific words and has a meaning which is of great use [37].

So, the different data sources which are used in this examination of summarization of different types of text are papers available on the sciencedirect.com site, ieeexplore.ieee.org and dl.acm.org. This text summarization process is very famous and studied by the latest research articles available on the web pages and different sites available on the internet. One must enter the specific keywords to get the specific information about the process of summarization of the text, and all the valuable information is available on the different sources of the internet [38].

To encounter each precise necessity, information regarding the process of summarization of the text is considered in the various research articles, and research papers which are published in journals, and the latest conferences describe the importance of the summarization of the text. All such articles are studied carefully to generate short, rich, and meaningful text, and a strong database is created to understand and analyse the meaning behind each term mentioned in the different aspects of the research. The study of the latest articles is essential to learn all the insights of the summarization of the text and finally to generate a good quality of text, which is helpful for all the end-users. This is very crucial to understand how summarization is done in the latest methods and how it is applied and implemented using different techniques, and algorithms used in summarization are also studied.

Once the research article phase is recognized, it will be filtered out for various articles that fix the measures during the generation of the adjustment process. The main issue of the research article criteria involved in the observation to initiate the inclusion in place of exclusion procedure is shown in Table **1** In addition, to produce limited research articles, for next generation review, an important technique is described in Fig. **10** [39].

The important research article which was designed while observing the main research by automatically considering keywords, abstracts, and titles, was found in 1338 studies. After that, the matching of the contents of the complete information with all the research articles was found in around 85 research articles. Lastly, the results of the 85 research articles will be short, and their analysis will be done later.

Different software is used to improve three final results, and it is observed that the software Mendeley's is the best to generate good results, and it is very easy to use and group the information depending on the topic.

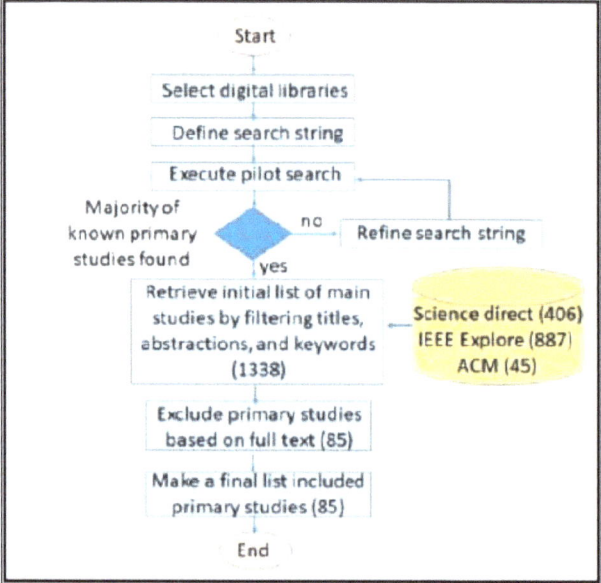

Fig. (10). Problem Statement for researchTopic.

Table	Inclusion and Exclusion Criteria.
Inclusion criteria	Studies that summarize texts include topics, problems, datasets, techniques and methods used
	This research consisted of journals and papers from the conference that specifically discussed the summation of texts
	The publications taken were studies from 2008 to 2019
Exclusion criteria	Studies that do not have experimental results and use a dataset are unclear
	Studies that discuss topics beyond summarizing texts
	Studies not written in English

Table 1: Inclusion and Exclusion Criteria.

At the final stage, the research article is analyzed, checked and filtered using certain criteria and various matches are done. Also, the search modifications process is followed, accepting the research criteria involved in the important study, as defined in Table **3**. Also, advanced observation on the latest research article is made as shown in Fig. (**10**). The starting research articles are observed for the different parameters such as the keywords, different abstracts, and titles found in 1338 studies. After this process, the important article is studied, accordingly, 85 articles are tied together with the same criteria Finally, a complete analysis is done using the 85 research articles based on the different criteria set, and different parameters are also observed accordingly. The main software used to group the contents all together is Mendeley's software. This software is found to be of great convenience while grouping the contents [40].

IMPLICATIONS

This outstanding remembrance is the major consequence of highlighting the information experience of the computer commended summary. The aim is to qualify reviewers to invent as much of the needed information in summary as likely and to reduce the need for showing a manual full-text review for lost data. The assessment conducted by Wallace *et al.* is concentrated on the correctness of the maximum rank sentences, a general measure in information retrieval, and question-answering systems. However, a suggestion is the most important metric in trying the superiority of an automatic text summarization system, the viewpoint of regular evaluation development.

After that, assembled composed the assessment of the sample size and group size. The sample size might not continuously be stated explicitly in the text, but it can be incidental by summation of all group size values. To account for true positive sample size or group size, there is a binary rule: true if the sentence comprises a sample size value or all of group size values, and false else.

Tested a proposal that text summaries produced by the machine learning classifier maintain additional information for organized reviews than titles and abstracts. Title and abstract, in human-written summary, are overall and popular information sources in SR advancement. But those sources might not have sufficient information needed for gathering SR data. This hypothesis estimates the computer-generated summary next to the title and abstract to serve as a possible alternative information source for SR citation also showing data-mining practices.

It is certain that ML/AI applications need a bunch of data, sometimes large amounts when having video data sources, to train and assess their algorithms. Predictably, ML/AI data is initiated at data stores and huge files, which makes it difficult the sharing between users and applications. As per an outcome, in maximum cases, users and developers have a local copy of the dataset (let us suppose the impression of this for a medium-big company) or use public infrastructures to process and access datasets. On the other hand, identical datasets might be compulsory to compute different algorithms and methods, which will be insufficient in systems not measured for forwarding data. With the broadcast of the IoT, data is spinning from static sources to data streams. The Internet is a supplementary enormous substance of information and data streams.

However, most of the current ML frameworks have not been planned to work with data streams, i.e., they directly do not support them or they just make available a connector but have not been appropriately included with ML/AI pipelines. This does not only include inference tasks where data streams can be used to make expectations for incoming data but also the incorporation of data streams for the training and assessment phases of ML/AI pipelines. Working and having data streams along network links can sustain a data loss, which might not be present in local file systems and should also be measured. Additionally, the aim is to make ML and AI open and available for everyone. In this logic, AutoML initiatives such as Google Cloud AutoML have contributed to bringing high-quality models and solutions, modified to multiple business needs, to developers with limited experience.

However, these innovations have not yet been appropriately combined with data stream pipelines. Another way to cover the method of users into ML and AI provided a missing ecosystem where they can share trained models and metrics (e.g., loss and accuracy) that can also be used to calculate different models and configurations. ML/AI descriptions classically need requirements that are difficult to be proficient in personal computers, and developers are likely to adopt public infrastructures to deploy their applications. Additionally, highavailability, load balancing in accumulation to fault-tolerance may be required in ML/AI mission critical applications and must be provided in a visible way to users.

This would license users and developers to motivation on ML models and the commercial logic, enabling the life cycle of ML/AI applications in development systems. To sum up, imagine a system that reduces the gap between data streams and ML frameworks, adopting AutoML features and enabling the sharing of ML models, metrics, and results in high performance in addition to high availability infrastructures.

CONCLUSION

This study shows various methods of abstractive summarization. Abstractive summarization methods produce highly adhesive, consistent, less superfluous and information-rich summaries. The cognitive content is to provide a large survey and comparison of various techniques and approaches of abstractive summarization. This chapter shows some of the challenges, and forthcoming research directions are also detailed. Also, the literature in abstractive summarization describes major progress in various prospects. However, these works still have not addressed the various challenges of abstractive summarization to its full stage in terms of space and time complexity.

CONSENT FOR PUBLICATION

Not applicable.

CONFLICT OF INTEREST

The authors declare no conflict of interest, financial or otherwise.

ACKNOWLEDGEMENT

Declared none.

REFERENCES

[1]   Stuart Jonathan Rusell, "Artificial Intelligence, A Modern Approach", *Prentice-Hall Publisher.* Third Edition. Prentice-Hall Publisher,

[2]   M. Tom, "Machine learning", *Indian edition. Tata Mc Graw Hill Publications.,* 2017.

[3]   Ian Goodfellow, Yoshua Bengio, Aaaron Courville, and Francis Bach, *Deep Learning (Adaptive Computation and Machine Learning Series),* 2017.

[4]   Bharath Ramsundar, and Reza Bosagh Zadeh, *TensorFlow for Deep Learning, O'Reilly Media.,* 2018.

[5]   Sukriti Verma, and Vagisha Nidhi, "Extractive Summarization using DeepLearning", cs. CL]

[6]   M. Allahyari, S. Pouriyeh, M. Assefi, S. Safaei, E.D. Trippe, and J.B Gutierrez, "KrysKochut, Text Summarization Techniques: A Brief Survey",

[7]   V. Bhumika, "Abstractive Summarization with NLP Makes Easier to Memorize", *International Journal of Recent Technology and Engineering (IJRTE).,* vol. 8, no. 5, 2020.

[8]   S. Singhal, and B. Arnab, "Abstractive Text Summarization", In: *ACM Journals*, 2018.

[9]   D. Sahoo, A. Bhoi, and R.C. Balabantaray, "Hybrid Approach To abstractive Summarization", In: *International Conference on Computational Intelligence and Data Science.* Elsevier, 2018.

[10]   I. Mani, *Recent Developments in Text Summarization.* ACM Journals, 2018.

[11]   L. Abualigah, M.Q. Bashabsheh, H. Alabool, and M. Shehab, "Text summarization: A brief review", *Studies in Computational Intelligence,* vol. 874, pp. 1-15, 2020.
[http://dx.doi.org/10.1007/978-3-030-34614-0_1]

[12]   M. Fiszman, T.C. Rindflesch, and H. Kilicoglu, "Abstraction summarization for managing the biomedical research literature", In: *Proceedings of the HLT-NAACL Workshop on Computational Lexical Semantics.*Boston, Massachusetts, 2004, pp. 76-83.
[http://dx.doi.org/10.3115/1596431.1596442]

[13]   P.B. Baxendale, "Machine-made index for technical literature – An experiment", *IBM J. Res. Develop.,* vol. 2, no. 4, pp. 354-361, 1958.

[http://dx.doi.org/10.1147/rd.24.0354]

[14]   R. Levy, and G. Andrew, "Tregex and Tsurgeon: Tools for Querying and Manipulating Tree Data Structures", In: *Proceedings of the fifth international conference on Language Resources and Evaluation.* Citeseer, 2006.

[15]   Y. Lu, "Artificial intelligence: a survey on evolution, models, applications and future trends", *Journal of Management Analytics.,* vol. 6, no. 1, pp. 1-29, 2019.
[http://dx.doi.org/10.1080/23270012.2019.1570365]

[16]   M. Gambhir, and V. Gupta, "Recent automatic text summarization techniques: a survey", *Artif. Intell. Rev.,* vol. 47, no. 1, pp. 1-66, 2017.
[http://dx.doi.org/10.1007/s10462-016-9475-9]

[17]   R. Barzilay, K.R. McKeon, and M. Elhadad, "Information fusion in the context of multi-document summarization", In: *Proc. 37th Annual Meet. Assoc. Computer. Linguist*, 1999, pp. 550-557.
[http://dx.doi.org/10.3115/1034678.1034760]

[18]   P-E. Genest, and G. Lapalme, "Fully abstractive approach to guided summarization", In: *50th Annul. Meet. Assoc. Computer. Linguist*, 2012, pp. 354-358.

[19]   M. Abadi, P. Barham, J. Chen, Z. Chen, A. Davis, J. Dean, M. Devin, S. Ghemawat, G. Irving, and M. Isard, "TensorFlow: A system for large-scale machine learning", In: *Symposium on Operating Systems Design and Implementation*, 2016, pp. 265-283.

[20]   Neelima Bhatia, "Literature Review on Automatic Text Summarization Single and Multiple Summarizations", *IEEE,* vol. 117, 2017.

[21]   Dipanjan Das, "A Survey on Automatic Text Summarization", *ACM Journals,* 2007.

[22]   R. Bhargava, Y. Sharma, and G. Sharma, "ATSSI: Abstractive text summarization using sentiment Infusion", *Procedia Comput. Sci.,* vol. 89, pp. 404-411, 2016.
[http://dx.doi.org/10.1016/j.procs.2016.06.088]

[23]   Dima Suleiman, "Generating abstract using abstractive summarization methods is a difficult task since it requires more semantic and linguistic analysis", *Hindawi Mathematical Problems in Engineering.,* 2020.

[24]   L. Yeager, J. Bernauer, A. Gray, and M. Houston, *Digits: the deep learning GPU training system.* ICML-France, 2015.

[25]   R. Bhargava, "Yashvardhan Sharma, Deep Extractive Text Summarization", In: *International Conference on Computational Intelligence and Data Science ICCIDS-2019.* ELSEVIER, 2019.

[26]   H Mi, "Baskaran Sankaran, Zhiguo Wang, and Abe Ittycheriah,Coverage embedding models for neural machine translation",

[27]   M. Díaz, C. Martín, and B. Rubio, "State-of-the-art, challenges, and open issues in the integration of Internet of things and cloud computing", *J. Netw. Comput. Appl.,* vol. 67, pp. 99-117, 2016.
[http://dx.doi.org/10.1016/j.jnca.2016.01.010]

[28]   C. Martin, P. Langendoerfer, P.S. Zarrin, M. Diaz, and B Rubio, "Kafka-ML: connecting the data stream with ML/AI frameworks",

[29]   S. Yeasmin, "A Survey of Abstractive Text Summarization", In: *IEEE International Conference on Circuit, Power and Computing Technologies.*India, 2017.

[30]   N.R. Kasture, "A Survey on Methods of Abstractive Text Summarization", *International Journal for Research in Emerging Science and Technology.,* vol. 1, no. 6, 2014.

[31]   T. Siddiqui, "Jawad Ahmed Shamshi, Generating Abstractive Summaries using Sequence to Sequence Attention Models", In: *International Conference on Frontiers of Information Technology (FIT).* IEEE, 2018.
[http://dx.doi.org/10.1109/FIT.2018.00044]

[32] K. Cho, B. Van Merrienboer, Ç. Gulcehre, D. Bahdanau, F. Bougares, H. Schwenk, and Y. Bengio, "Learning phrase representations using rnn encoder- decoder for statistical machine translation", *preprintarXiv*, p. 1406.1078, 2014.
[http://dx.doi.org/10.3115/v1/D14-1179]

[33] R. Nallapati, B. Zhou, C. dos Santos, Ç. Gulcehre, and B Xiang, "Abstractive Text Summarization *via* Sequence to-sequence RNNs as well as Beyond".,

[34] I. Fathy, D. Fadl, and M. Aref, "Rich Semantic Representation based Approach for Text Generation", 8th International Conference on informatics and Systems (INFOS).

[35] Bidoki Mohmmad, "A Semantic-Based Approach for Abstractive Multi-Document Text Summarization", *International Journal of Advanced Research in Computer to Communication Engineering, India.*, 2020.

[36] Jun Suzuki and Masaaki Nagata, *Cutting-off redundant repeating generations for neural abstractive summarization.* EACL, 2017, p. 291.

[37] J. Qiang, P. Chen, W. Ding, F. Xie, and X. Wu, *Multi-document summarization using closed patterns.* Knowledge-Based Syst, 2016, pp. 28-38.

[38] X.W. Han, H.T. Zheng, J.Y. Chen, and C.Z. Zhao, "Diverse Decoding for Abstractive Document Summarization", *Appl. Sci. (Basel)*, vol. 9, no. 3, p. 386, 2019.
[http://dx.doi.org/10.3390/app9030386]

[39] A . P. Widyassari, S. Rustad, G. F. Shidik, E. Noersasongko, A. Syukur, A. Affandy, and R. De, "Review of automatic text summarization techniques & methods", *Journal of King Saud University.*, 2020.

[40] Deepa Anand, "Effective deep learning approaches for summarization of legal texts", *Journal of King Saud University.*, 2019.

CHAPTER 12

Advanced Topics in Machine Learning

Sana Zeba[1,*], Md. Alimul Haque[2], Samah Alhazmi[3] and Shameemul Haque[4]

[1] *Department of Computer Engineering, Jamia Millia Islamia University, New Delhi, India*

[2] *Department of Computer Science, Veer Kunwar Singh University, Ara, India*

[3] *College of Computing and Informatics, Saudi Electronic University, Riyadh, Kingdom of Saudi Arabia*

[4] *Al-Hafeez College, Ara, India*

Abstract: This chapter reveals the infancy of the striking experience near the "Internet of Things (IoT)". Machine learning technology is a part of Artificial Intelligence that grew from the training of computational learning approaches and pattern recognition of artificial intelligence. Over the last few years, Machine Learning approaches have been advanced inquisitively for various sectors such as smart city, finance, banking, education, *etc*. Today machine learning is not similar to the previous machine learning because of various new advanced computing techniques. Machine learning technique is defined as data analysis that automates the building of analytical models. The iterative factor of learning algorithms is significant as models are uncovered to new datasets; they are skilled in autonomously adjusting. The study from earlier computations generates reliable, efficient, repeatable decisions and experiment results. Therefore, Machine Learning measures have been used to protect various smart applications from any illegal activities, threats, and various attacks. Furthermore, Machine Learning provided suitable solutions for preserving the security of various advanced applications. The patent growth rate is 34% in the machine learning field from the year 2013 to 2017, according to Patent Service IFI Claims. Also, in the world, 60% of companies are using various learning algorithms for numerous purposes. In this chapter, we have discussed efficient, advanced, and revolutionary machine learning algorithms in detail.

Keywords: Algorithm of Machine Learning, KNN, Linear Regression, Machine Learning, SVM, PCA.

* **Corresponding author Sana Zeba:** Department of Computer Engineering, Jamia Millia Islamia University, New Delhi, India; E-mail: sanazeba.mau@gmail.com

Prasad Lokulwar, Basant Verma, N. Thillaiarasu, Kailash Kumar, Mahip Bartere and Dharam Singh (Eds.)
All rights reserved-© 2022 Bentham Science Publishers

INTRODUCTION

The subpart of Artificial Intelligence is Machine Learning (ML) which has been proficient in learning without code or programs. According to Arthur Samuel, the term machine learning is "a study that stretches the skill to computers to learn without any programming." While, Tom M. Mitchell gave an extensively quoted and extra formal explanation: "A computer code is called as learn that belongs from experience E corresponding to performance P and few classes' tasks T, in such a manner performance P at task T improves on behalf of experience E." This explanation is prominent for its crucial machine learning in essence working rather than cognitive. Machine learning is not a novel method, although it is strictly related to AI. Computers are able to perform numerous procedures around Machine Learning, like prediction, extraction of features, classification, regression, sorting, pattern recognition, clustering, *etc*. Such advanced machine algorithms function by structuring a model on the basis of past example inputs to make data-driven decisions or predictions. Machine learning is one of the most common applications of artificial intelligence. Through cognition of various machine learning, hardware, devices, and software have worked similarly to human beings. The various machine learning applications for computing techniques contain:

- Bioinformatics
- Computational advertising
- Affective computing
- Cheminformatics
- Information retrieval
- Recommender systems
- Speech and handwriting recognition
- Machine perception
- Sequence mining
- Structural health monitoring
- Optimization and metaheuristic
- Robot locomotion
- Computational finance
- Brain-machine interfaces
- Software engineering
- Adaptive websites
- Internet fraud detection
- Medical diagnosis
- Game playing
- Classifying DNA sequences

LITERATURE REVIEW

In the zone of Artificial intelligence, several AI-based machine learning techniques have been established to gain efficient and sustainable trades. The aim of the researcher is to analyse scientific and systematic literature reviews related to machine learning approaches, applications of machine learning and artificial intelligence in industry [1].

The comparative study of various machine learning has been performed, such as artificial neural networks (ANN), extreme learning machine (ELM), group method of data handling (GMDH), classification and regression trees (CART), *etc.*, at various depths for soil temperature. The various climate variables have been considered for developing the model [2].

In the paper, the author [3] has presented a literature survey related to machine learning algorithms and various machine learning techniques for the processing of big data analytics. Firstly, the author reviewed the machine learning approaches and considered several auspicious learning approaches in their recent studies, like active learning, deep learning, transfer learning, representation learning, parallel and distributed learning, *etc.*, and then performed analysis of the issues as well as probable solutions through machine learning for processing of big data [3].

For the health care system, the author [4] has proposed a deep learning-based solution that focuses on the detection of foods according to the patient's diseases. The deep learning-based datasets have also considered various features such as calories, age, weight, fat, gender, protein, *etc.*

The paper provided a summary of the machine learning application for networking and communications. The author has also classified relevant reviews dealing with the topics related to machine learning and also tried to find new possible research directions [5].

Erwin Adi1 *et al.* [6] presented a serious review study to produce data for machine learning-based IoT and the issues of IoT environment. However, the author has projected a framework to allow learning approaches with IoT applications and give a case study in real-time applications.

Tahsien *et al.* [7] presented a comparative study of IoT systems with the machine learning approach and also conferred about the probable attacks of IoT systems. In the paper, an inclusive comparison of threats and security in IoT and Machine learning-based safe IoT systems up to 2019 is discussed.

Sherali Zeadally *et al.* [8] discovered how to recover threats and security of IoT system with a machine learning approach at the host level and network level. They have been discussed on numerous types of machine learning techniques for both host and network levels.

Yasser Alsouda *et al.* [9] discovered numerous constraints of SVM learning and KNN algorithms to compute optimum classification of the sound example in the dataset. The proposed technique used both KNN, SVM algorithm and MFCC algorithm for feature extraction. For implementation, this proposed technique used Raspberry Pi Zero W and performed experimentations with several environments that sound similar, like a car horn, *etc*.

The author [10] of the paper has proposed an open-ended recurrent learning framework based on machine learning techniques by retaining transfer learning for feature extraction on deep models, Relief F for feature selection, and incremental kernel learning for classification. The ARCIKELM novel classier vigorously alters network architecture to decrease disastrous forgetting.

TYPES OF MACHINE LEARNING ALGORITHM

Machine learning techniques of Artificial Intelligence have been comprised of numerous approaches like supervised, unsupervised learning, semi-supervised, and reinforcement learning that can be practically applied to avoid any fraud and also detect threats or attacks of the various applications.

Machine learning is classically categorized into various broad types, depending on the learning "feedback" or "signal" obtainable to a learning system. Fig. (**1**) shows various types of machine learning approaches below:

Supervised Learning

The most common learning approach is supervised learning in machine learning that is based on labelled examples like output is identified based on an input. In various applications, a supervised algorithm is used in which upcoming events have been predicted on the basis of ancient records. Training and testing are two stages of supervised learning.

Unsupervised Learning

There are no labels given to this unsupervised learning approach. The unsupervised deals in contrast to the data that has no ancient labels. This kind of learning approach works on unlabelled training data. Fig. (**1**) shows the various machine learning methods below:

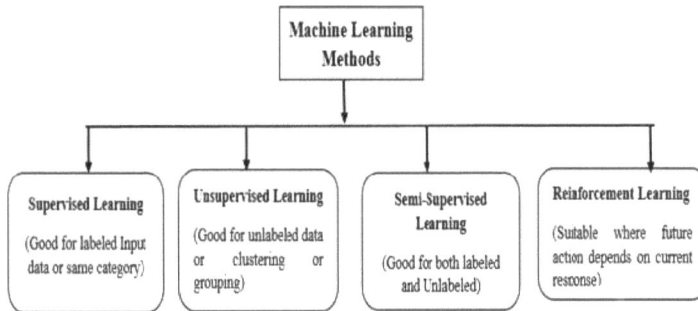

Fig. (1). Machine Learning Methods.

Semi-supervised Learning

For related employment, like supervised learning approaches, this approach of learning is vital. For training, it uses both labelled and unlabelled information. Semi-supervised learning approach is used for regression, classification, and prediction. Overall, it is a grouping of both unsupervised and supervised learning approaches.

Reinforcement Learning

The trial-and-error concepts have been used in these learning approaches. The output of the problem has been predicted on the set of tuning constraints. There are mainly three components that are agent, environment and actions.

Despite this, another classification of learning arises, which studies the output of a system. Hence, machine learning has also been categorized as follows:

- Classification: For the classification of ML, the learner has produced a model and divided all inputs into various classes. Typically, this classification is handled in a supervised way. A classification example is Spam filtering in the mail where the class is "spam or not spam" and input is mail or simple messages.
- Clustering: In clustering ML, a group of inputs is to be divided into clusters. Its work was dissimilar to classification.
- Regression: The regression of ML has based on discrete value rather than continuous value. It is also used for supervised problems.
- Density estimation: In Density estimation, the distribution of inputs has been found in some space.
- Dimensionality reduction: Dimensionality reduction makes simpler inputs

through mapping inputs into some lower-dimensional space.

ADVANCED MACHINE LEARNING ALGORITHMS

All manual work has changed totally due to the use of advanced and sustainable machine learning algorithms worldwide. It acts as a revolution for the world. Currently, machine learning approaches help to make advanced systems in all sectors such as a bank, healthcare, software, Automotive, Education, Finance, Retail, Government sectors *etc*.

Machine Learning approaches can allow computers to show chess, perform operations, and get smarter and more private. In this chapter, the various advanced machine learning algorithms have been discussed:

Linear Regression

In subfield machine learning of AI, we have determined an output variable (y) based on a group of input variables (x). An association happens between the group of inputs and the output variable.

In Linear Regression learning, the association or relationship of both variables, like input (x) and output (y), is represented as an equation form y = a + bx. The plot of linear regression is shown in Fig. (**2**):

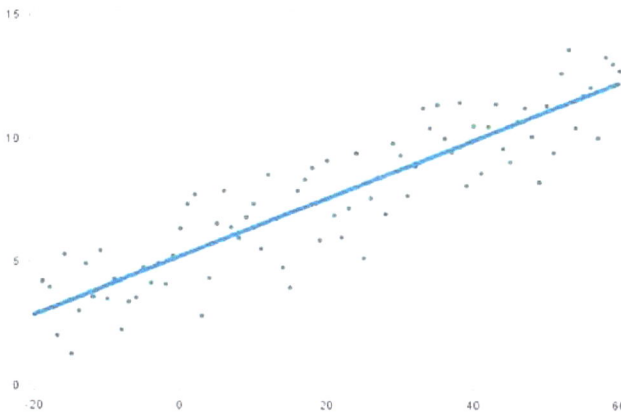

Fig. (2). Linear Regression for Y= a *X + b..

All the terms of the above linear equation are represented as:

- X is defined as an independent variable.
- Y is defined as a dependent variable.

- a is defined as Slope and b is as Intercept.

Logistic Regression

For estimating the discrete values, the Logistic Regression approach from a set of independent values was used. It is basically used to calculate the 0 or 1 binary values of variables.

Its assistance is to predict the event probability by appropriate data to a logit function. The logistic regression model is shown in Fig. (**3**):

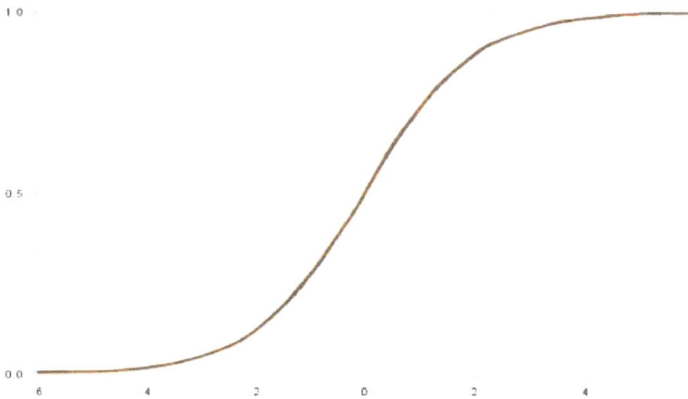

Fig. (3). Logistic Regression Approach Model..

The approaches itemized below are frequently used to assist to progress logistic regression models:

- Regularize techniques
- Use of non-linear model
- Contain interaction terms
- Eliminate features

KNN (K-nearest neighbor) algorithm

For both regression and classification problems, k-nearest neighbor algorithms can be applied. It is mostly used to resolve classification problems. KNN algorithm suppositions are compared between the new data with already available data points and laid into the most similar data classes. All the data is stored in a similar class through the KNN algorithm. The two properties which will well define the K-NN algorithm are:

- Lazy learning algorithm
- Non-parametric learning algorithm

KNN can be simply understood by performing a comparison with real life. Like, if anybody wants to know about a person, it makes sense to have a conversation with their friends, family members, colleagues *etc.*

A basic diagram of the K-nearest neighbour (KNN) algorithm is in Fig. (**4**) [11]. When the value of K is 3, the sample object ('blue star') is classified as the color 'black' because the star gets an extra 'vote' from the color 'black' class. Still, for the K value 5, the sample object (same star) is classified as color 'red' because now the star gets an extra 'vote' from the 'red' color class, which is shown more clearly in Fig. 4.

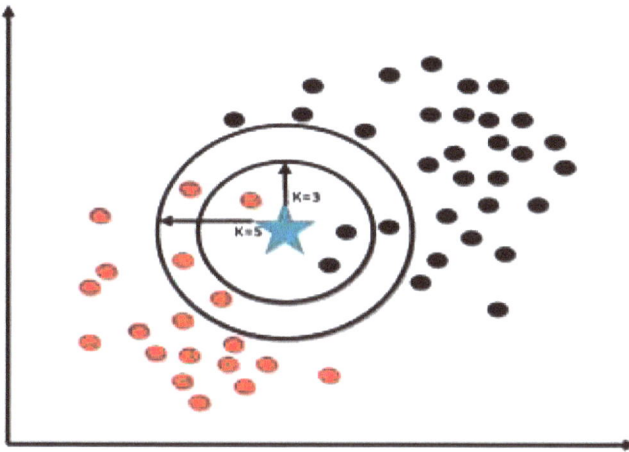

Fig. (4). K-nearest neighbour (KNN) algorithm.

SVM (Support vector machines) algorithm

SVM is a classification learning approach that plots raw data as data points in a set of n-dimensional space. The value of every data property is tied with a specific coordinate, creating it simple to categorize the data. In this approach, straight lines are called classifiers in this approach which split the data.

A basic diagram shown in Fig. (**5**) represents how the support vector machine (SVM) works. The SVM algorithm has recognized a hyperplane (which is actually a line) to maximise the parting between the various classes like the 'blue star' and 'circle' class.

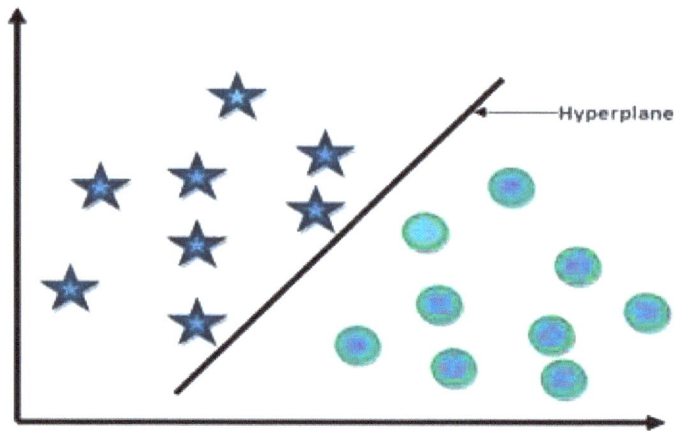

Fig. (5). SVM (Support vector machines) algorithm.

In 1960, the SVM approach was introduced for the first time, and it generated a plane which was called a hyperplane between two classes. Support vector machines are categorized into two types:

- Linear SVM learning
- Non-linear SVM learning
    Some major principles related to the SVM approach are –
- Support Vectors
- Hyperplane
- Margin

Naive Bayes algorithm

A Naive classifier takes up the occurrence of specific properties of a class dissimilar to the occurrence of other data properties. Suppose all properties are interrelated to each other, then this classifier would handle all of these characteristics autonomously during manipulating the probability of a specific outcome.

Decision tree

The most common supervised learning-based advance algorithm is the Decision Tree approach in learning that is used for classifying problems. For both continuous and categorical dependent variables, the decision tree learning approach is used for classification. In this learning algorithm, the population is divided into two or more similar sets based on the most substantial independent variables.

A diagram of a Decision tree approach is shown in Fig. (**6**). Each variable of the tree, like C1, C2, and C3, is denoted through a blue circle, and the decision outcomes are shown through the rectangular like Class A and Class B in the figure. In order to positively categorize an example to a class, each branch of the tree is labelled with either 'False' or 'True'. These labels are based on the outcome of its ancestor node of the decision tree.

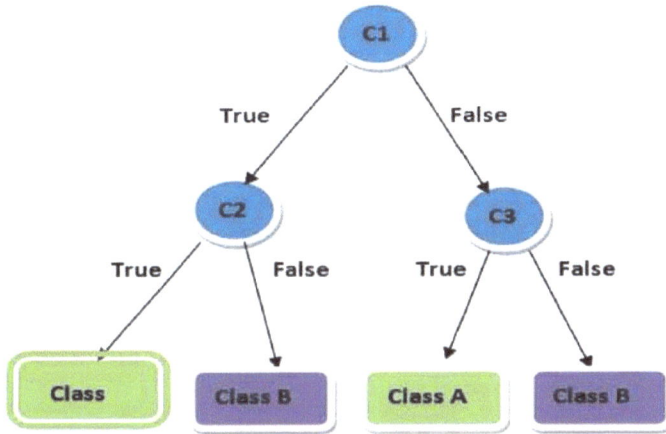

Fig. (6). Labelled Decision Tree Approach.

K-means

K-means learning is an approach based on unsupervised learning used to solve clustering issues. The sets are splatted into several clusters in a manner that all the inside cluster data points are similar and dissimilar with the other data in clusters.

For each cluster, the K-means learning chooses the number of points k, as centroids point of the cluster. The various clusters are created as k cluster through each point and the neighbouring centroids. This procedure is continuously performed till the found centroids point does not change in calculation. Fig. (**7**) shows the K-mean clustering approach.

Random Forest algorithm

For the decision concept, the cooperative or joint approach is called a Random Forest approach. To categorize any current object constructed on its parameters, each decision tree and the corresponding tree "normal votes" are categorized for that class. Then based on the maximum tree votes, overall trees are chosen. Each tree leaf of the forest is increased up to the most considerable level possible.

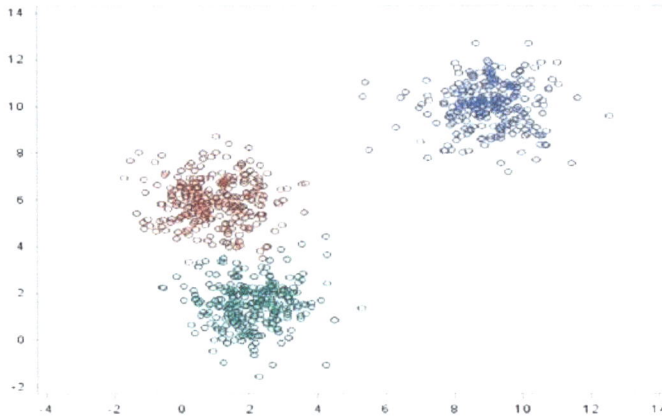

Fig. (7). K-Mean Learning Approach.

Classification and Regression Trees (CART)

The Regression and Classification Trees approach is one which is used for various application implementations related to Decision Trees.

The non-terminal types of nodes of this algorithm are the internal node and root node. The leaf nodes are terminal nodes. The input variable (x) is represented by non-terminal and output variable (y) through the leaf node.

Fig. (**8**) shows the part of the decision tree in which a person will purchase a mini van or a sports car depending on his marital status and age. If the person's age is more than 30 years and he is not married, then walk the tree in the sequence: 'more than 30 years?' -> yes -> 'married?' -> yes. Therefore, the output is the mini van of the model.

Apriori

The Apriori learning is used to produce an association rule to mine the frequent data item sets in a transactional database.

It is generally used for analysing market baskets, where one forms mixtures of goods which occur frequently in the transactional database. Generally, the association rule is written like 'if any person buying item X, then he buying item Y' as: X -> Y.

Similarly, if anybody buys sugar and milk, then he is likely to buying coffee powder. Then an association rule for these is: {sugar, milk} -> coffee powder. The formulas of association rules X-> Y are given below to calculate confidence, lift, and support.

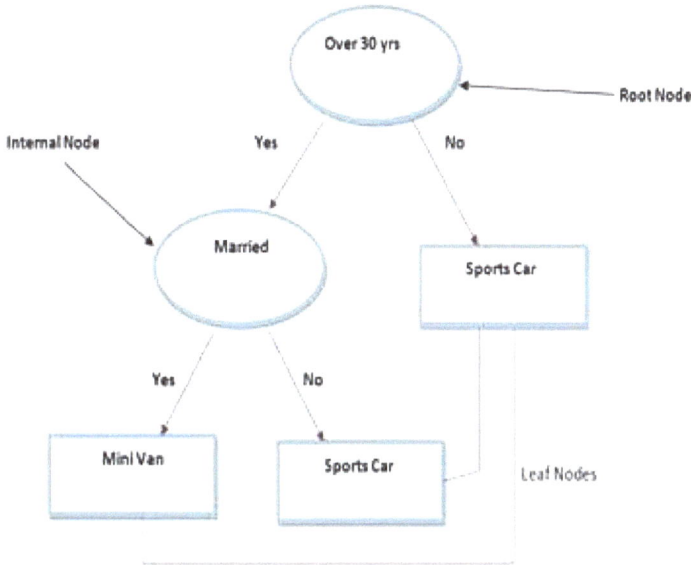

Fig. (8). CART implementation based on Decision Tree.

$$\text{Support} = (\text{frequency } (X, Y))/N$$

$$\text{Rule: } X \Rightarrow Y \rightarrow \text{Confidence} = (\text{frequency } (X, Y))/(\text{frequency } (X))$$

$$\text{Lift} = \text{Support}/(\text{Support } (X) \times \text{Support } (Y))$$

PCA (Principal Component Analysis)

PCA is the greatest appropriate algorithm for exploration and visualization by dropping several variables. This is finished by taking the extreme adjustment in the data point into a new system coordinate with x and y axes called as 'principal components.'

Every component of PC is a direct line mixture of the innovative variables and is rectangular or orthogonal to each other. Perpendicular between data components entitles the correlation between these data points, *i.e.*, zero. The primary element seizes the direction of the maximum inconsistency in the data. Another primary element seizes the remaining adjustment in the data point but has a variable quantity uncorrelated with the first element, as shown in Fig. (9). Correspondingly, all consecutive primary elements, PC3, PC4, *etc.*, capture the remaining adjustment although being uncorrelated with the prior element.

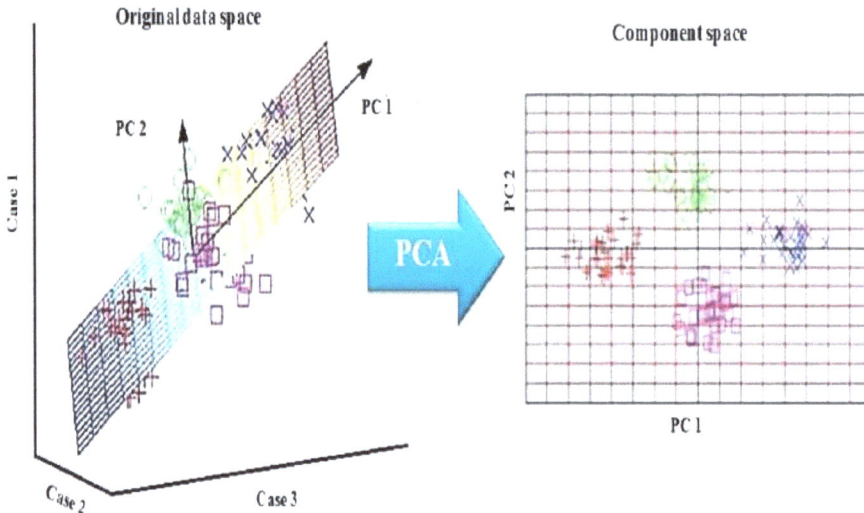

Fig. (9). CART implementation based on Decision Tree.

In this direction, the maximum inconsistency is captured *via* the first component of principal, and the other principal component is captured *via* the remaining alteration in the components, while these variables are not related to the first data or component. Correspondingly, all consecutive primary components (such as PC3, and PC4, *etc.*) seize the remaining variance although being not related to the preceding data or component.

Boosting with AdaBoost

AdaBoost acronym is Adaptive Boosting approach. Boosting is a consecutive collaborative approach in which every model is made to correct the misclassifications of already classified models. While, Bagging is a corresponding collaborative approach in which every model is constructed autonomously. Bagging is generally based on a 'modest voting' concept, where every classifier simply votes to get a concluding outcome.

Boosting includes 'weighted voting', in which every classifier votes to gain a concluding outcome that is calculated by the common– while the successive models were made by passing on better weights to that instance misclassified of the earlier models.

COMPARISON OF VARIOUS ADVANCED MACHINE LEARNING

Machine learning algorithms have been used in various applications based on their features and limitations as well. This section discusses the comparison Table **1** of various learning algorithms of several parameters.

Table 1. Comparison of Various Advanced Machine Learning.

Learning Method	Loss Function	Generative or Discriminative	Decision Boundary	Model Complexity Reduction	Parameter Estimation Algorithm
Logistic Regression	-log P (Y jX)	Discriminative	Linear	L2 regularization	No closed form estimate
Decision Trees	Either -log P (Y jX) or zero-one loss	Discriminative	Axis-aligned partition of feature space	Prune tree or limit tree depth	ID3, CART, C4.5
K-Nearest Neighbor	zero-one loss	Discriminative	Arbitrarily complicated	Increase K	Store all training data to classify new points
Support Vector Machines	hinge loss: |1-y (wT x) j+	Discriminative	linear (depends on kernel)	Reduce C	Solve quadratic program to find boundary
Linear Regression	square loss: (Y -Y)2	Linear	___	Y = X(Beta)	Solve _ Beta = (XTX)-1 X TY
K-means	Within-class squared distance from mean	Predetermined	-	Isotropic	K-mean

FUTRUE ROAD MAP

Machine learning is making a variance smart way to offer businesses. Through machine learning, the changing face of businesses is determined *via* preferences-based ads and Voice-based search. Machine Learning will be an essential term of all Artificial Intelligence advanced systems. Machine Learning approaches will be made by continuous training with the day-to-day updating data. A look into the future road map and evolution of machine learning algorithms over the reports of the PAML market demonstrates a 21% CAGR in 2021. All the advanced machine learning will be used for data science.

CONCLUSION

This chapter focused on the study of AI and ML applications, choosing the literature review to show various machine learning algorithms. The conception is that machine learning automation acts as threat to jobs, and the social workforce is dominant. It should be remembered that machine learning is only a technology that has evolved to comfort the human's lifestyle by dropping the requirement of manpower, and it also suggests improved effectiveness at lower costs. The most significant machine learning algorithms are Linear Regression, Apriori, K-means, PCA, Logistic Regression, CART, Naïve Bayes, KNN, *etc*. Besides that, various machine learning algorithms have been compared in this chapter.

CONSENT FOR PUBLICATION

Not applicable.

CONFLICT OF INTEREST

The authors declare no conflict of interest, financial or otherwise.

ACKNOWLEDGEMENT

Declared none.

REFERENCES

[1]   R. Cioffi, M. Travaglioni, G. Piscitelli, A. Petrillo, and F. De Felice, "Artificial intelligence and machine learning applications in smart production: Progress, trends, and directions", *Sustainability (Basel)*, vol. 12, no. 2, p. 492, 2020.
[http://dx.doi.org/10.3390/su12020492]

[2]   M. Alizamir, O. Kisi, A.N. Ahmed, C. Mert, C.M. Fai, S. Kim, N.W. Kim, and A. El-Shafie, "Advanced machine learning model for better prediction accuracy of soil temperature at different depths", *PLoS One*, vol. 15, no. 4, 2020.e0231055
[http://dx.doi.org/10.1371/journal.pone.0231055] [PMID: 32287272]

[3]   J. Qiu, Q. Wu, G. Ding, Y. Xu, and S. Feng, "A survey of machine learning for big data processing", *EURASIP J. Adv. Signal Process.*, vol. 2016, no. 1, p. 67, 2016.
[http://dx.doi.org/10.1186/s13634-016-0355-x]

[4]   C. Iwendi, S. Khan, J.H. Anajemba, A.K. Bashir, and F. Noor, "Realizing an Efficient IoMT-Assisted Patient Diet Recommendation System Through Machine Learning Model", *IEEE Access*, vol. 8, pp. 28462-28474, 2020.
[http://dx.doi.org/10.1109/ACCESS.2020.2968537]

[5]   F. Musumeci, C. Rottondi, A. Nag, I. Macaluso, D. Zibar, M. Ruffini, and M. Tornatore, "An Overview on Application of Machine Learning Techniques in Optical Networks", *IEEE Commun. Surv. Tutor.*, vol. 21, no. 2, pp. 1383-1408, 2019.
[http://dx.doi.org/10.1109/COMST.2018.2880039]

[6]   E. Adi, A. Anwar, Z. Baig, and S. Zeadally, "Machine learning and data analytics for the IoT", *Neural Comput. Appl.*, vol. 32, no. 20, pp. 16205-16233, 2020.
[http://dx.doi.org/10.1007/s00521-020-04874-y]

[7]   S.M. Tahsien, H. Karimipour, and P. Spachos, "Machine learning based solutions for security of Internet of Things (IoT): A survey", *J. Netw. Comput. Appl.*, vol. 161, no. April, 2020.102630
[http://dx.doi.org/10.1016/j.jnca.2020.102630]

[8]   S. Zeadally, and M. Tsikerdekis, "Securing Internet of Things (IoT) with machine learning", *Int. J.*

Commun. Syst., vol. 33, no. 1, pp. 1-16, 2020.
[http://dx.doi.org/10.1002/dac.4169]

[9] Y. Alsouda, S. Pana, and A. Kurti, *A machine learning driven iot solution for noise classification in smart cities,* .

[10] G.A. Tahir, and C.K. Loo, "An open-ended continual learning for food recognition using class incremental extreme learning machines", *IEEE Access,* vol. 8, pp. 82328-82346, 2020.
[http://dx.doi.org/10.1109/ACCESS.2020.2991810]

[11] S. Haque, D. Sonal, and K. Kumar, *Materials Today : Proceedings Security Enhancement for IoT enabled Agriculture ScienceDirect Security Enhancement for IoT enabled Agriculture..*

SUBJECT INDEX

A

Acute respiratory diseases 93
Adaptive 1,2, 16, 44, 59, 113
  computer systems 59
  immune reaction 44
  machine learning 1, 2, 16
  tutoring application 113
AI-based 105, 106, 199
  machine learning techniques 199
  system 106
  touch tracing applications 105
Algorithms 26, 27, 37, 113, 134
  decision-making 26, 27
  noisy 37
  population-based 134
  rules-based 113
Amazon alexa 27
Amino acids 92
Analysis, deep syntactic 187
Angiotensin-converting enzyme 93
Animation, final robotic 140
Antibodies 44, 47, 48, 100, 101
  deactivating 48
Antifungals 46
API, network-based 105
Applications 3, 53, 76, 80, 81, 92, 93, 94, 103, 104, 170, 171, 181, 192, 193, 199, 200, 209, 210
  aggregate computing 76
  engineering 3
  of Python 181
  real-time 199
Approach 148, 203, 205
  decision tree learning 205
  dynamic clustering 148
  logistic regression 203
Apriori learning 207
Arrhythmia 161
Artificial intelligence 19, 24, 27, 32, 54, 59, 92, 93, 96, 112, 128, 197, 198, 199, 200
  algorithms 112

methods 112
researchers 128
Artificial neural network (ANN) 19, 24, 25, 34, 38, 199
Astronomical measurements 182
Automatic 2, 4, 112
  E-learning personalization method 112
  image processing techniques 4
  Learning 2
Autonomous 128, 129
  mobile robots 129
  robots 128

B

Bayesian 21, 153
  analysis 21
  theorem 153
Bayes theorem 153
Betacorona virus 93
Big data analytics 199
Birds 25, 134, 135
  obligate brood parasitic 134
Body phrase method 185
Boosting algorithm 110, 120

C

Capability, in-memory processing 80
CART implementation 208, 209
CHD 31, 33, 34, 39
  detection 31, 34
  diagnosing 34
  on medical clinic-based information 33
Cheminformatics 198
Chest 46, 103
  discomfort 46
  X-rays 103
Classifier Naïve Bayes 160
Classifying DNA sequences 198
Clinical symptoms stretching 95